BABY
NAMES
2016

Ella Joynes and Mark Woods

white
L

Acknowledgements

I would like to extend my utmost gratitude to Michael Turner for his contribution; without him this book would have been much shorter. My thanks are also given to Beth Bishop and Hugh Brune at Crimson Publishing for their patience and guidance throughout this project, and to Mark Woods for his excellent introduction. Finally, the greatest thanks go to my children, Owen Henri, Jasper Hugh, and Josie May. I fall more in love with them, and their names, every day.

This seventh edition published in Great Britain 2015 by
White Ladder, an imprint of Crimson Publishing Ltd, 19–21c Charles Street
Bath BA1 1HX.

First, second, third, fourth, fifth and sixth editions published by
Crimson Publishing in 2009, 2010, 2011, 2012, 2013 and 2014.

Introduction © Mark Woods 2015

All other material © Crimson Publishing 2015

ISBN 978 1 91033 601 4

Typeset by IDSUK (DataConnection) Ltd

Printed and bound in Italy by L.E.G.O. S.p.A., Lavis TN

Contents

A note on how to use this book

While the author and publisher acknowledge that baby names vary widely in spelling and pronunciation, this book usually lists each name only once: under the most common initial and spelling. If a name has an alternative spelling with a different initial, it may be listed under that letter also.

Information relating to statistics and trends in baby names is based on the most recent data at the time of writing.

Introduction

Having very recently been through the baby name game myself I know the kind of thing you're thinking right now.

What if they hate it when they get older?

What if we hate it the second after we've chosen it?

What if we hate each other before we've actually managed to agree on one?

Take a breath and if you're the one carrying the baby, put your feet up. If you're the one supporting the one carrying the baby, take those feet and rub them – then dive into this book free from worry and stress.

Why? Because if the last 12 months of baby naming has shown us anything at all it's that no matter how much thought we might put in, the popularity and longevity of names is down to a whole host of variables, most of which are way beyond our control.

Firstly, like it or not, there's popular culture, often of the type emanating from across the Atlantic. You don't have to be a reader of celebrity magazines to be affected by what actors, musicians and the like choose to call their children. The trends they set filter down and you can move towards them or away from them – but you'll definitely be aware of them.

Unisex names, for instance, are without doubt the major celebrity-driven direction of travel as we move towards 2016. Hollywood heart-throb Ryan Reynolds and Blake Lively naming their daughter James is credited with bolstering the unisex push in the US that's now well on its way to the UK.

News events also play their part in shaping name couture. More than two dozen babies for instance have been named either 'Indy' or 'Indie' in Scotland since the referendum, and since new First Minister Nicola Sturgeon took over her name has also seen a spike – although you do wonder if there's been a typo when it comes to the one boy listed as 'Spurgeon'!

Then there's perhaps the biggest event of all in the baby-naming world – the arrival of Princess Charlotte Elizabeth Diana. It came as no surprise that Kate and William chose traditional family names, including his mother's name. Time will tell if she'll become a Lottie or a Charlie . . . What's for certain, though, is that the intense global interest in what that tiny little girl was called reinforces the fact that naming a child is more than just a lucky dip, it's a responsibility bestowed upon parents that has lifelong ramifications.

Armed with this book, you are very well placed to ditch the worry and angst and throw yourself into the process of naming your baby-to-be. You've the best possible collection of names and up-to-date trends in your hands – enjoy the name game.

Mark Woods

part one

Naming
your baby

1 Current baby-naming trends

No matter what your parenting philosophies are, there is one thing that binds all parents everywhere: naming our babies. We all have to do it, and there's no reason why it shouldn't be a time of excitement, humour, love . . . and strategy.

So, let's start our quest for the perfect baby name by looking at what's recently caught the nation's attention – including the royal princess! What names have skyrocketed up the charts this past year, and what trends can we see in baby-naming statistics?

Go with the flow

Currently, the biggest trend for naming babies is to maintain the status quo – which in the worst financial crisis in a century perhaps isn't surprising. Keep your head down, work hard and don't draw attention to yourself. The Top 10

Top 10 baby names

Boys	Girls
1. Oliver	1. Amelia
2. Jack	2. Olivia
3. Harry	3. Emily
4. Jacob	4. Ava
5. Charlie	5. Isla
6. Thomas	6. Jessica
7. Oscar	7. Poppy
8. William	8. Isabella
9. James	9. Sophie
10. George	10. Mia

names for both boys and girls stayed the same last year, with only one new name in each list. Amelia kept her spot at number one, and although Oliver has taken the lead for boys' names, it's not the first time it's been there in recent years. Right behind them are names that have stayed in the top ten pretty consistently: Jack, Harry, Olivia, and Emily.

For girls, the most popular names are all pretty similar-sounding. In the Top 10 alone there are seven names that sound strikingly similar: Amelia, Olivia, Ava, Isla, Jessica, Isabella, and Mia. Even the three remaining names sound the same as each other: Emily, Poppy, and Sophie.

So what does it all mean?

Parents, it seems, are choosing names that they hear circulating from other people, or from the media, and deciding that they like the sound of them – and that fitting in is, for now, better than standing out. This means that ANY name ending in -a or -ie/-y is immensely popular for little girls right now, and midwives up and down the country can pretty accurately predict what parents are likely to announce in the delivery room (and clean up at the hospital bookies, which is usually run by one of the blokes who transports all the gas canisters around).

I've made that last bit up, but you get the picture – there's a conservatism to the way we name our children that has prevailed for more than a decade now.

Although for boys the story is a little more complicated, one fact remains true year-on-year: there are fewer names chosen for boys than girls. For each name listed in the Top 10, there are greater numbers of boys with those names than there are girls in their respective list. For example, there were nearly 2,000 more babies called Jack than Olivia, even though both names occupy second place. In seventh place in both lists, Oscar had over 1,000 more babies with that name than Poppy did. Ultimately this means that while it might seem like parents aren't being that creative with girls' names, ending everything in -a or -ie/-y, the parents of little boys aren't branching out very much either. You now need far more boys to be given the same name to reach a spot in the Top 10 than you do for girls.

Elsewhere in the boys' list are names with a clear nod to royalty (at least in the UK, anyway): William, James, George . . . and of course Harry, although Prince Harry's given name is actually Henry. William, James, and George have all moved up the charts from last year, and Harry has stuck around for years in the Top 10 – probably as a result of the Harry Potter phenomenon as well as our favourite red-headed prince. Also, the names Victoria and Sofia have been big climbers for baby girls (see page 10), being directly affected not only by England's Queen Victoria, but also Disney's smallest princess Sofia the First. Apparently, even cartoon royalty has the capacity to rule over us all . . .

The arrival of Princess Charlotte

On 2 May 2015, Her Royal Highness Princess Charlotte of Cambridge was born at St Mary's Hospital, Paddington. Her full name is Charlotte Elizabeth Diana – a name steeped with royal history, with links to both sides of her family. She is the first princess to be born into the British monarchy in 25 years. The last was Prince Andrew's daughter Princess Eugenie in 1990.

Her first name, Charlotte, means 'little and feminine' and is Kate's sister Pippa's middle name, as well as the female equivalent of William's father, Charles. Although she will probably never become queen, being fourth in line to the throne behind her brother, the little princess follows the royal footsteps of Queen Charlotte, wife of King George III.

Elizabeth, the first of her middle names, means 'oath of God' and was chosen in tribute to the Queen (her great-grandmother). It was also the name of Charlotte's great-great-grandmother, the Queen Mother, who

William is said to have been very close to. Queen Elizabeth II was surely delighted by this acknowledgement, in the year she overtook Victoria as Britain's longest-reigning monarch. Elizabeth also has links to the Middletons – it is Kate's and her mother Carole's middle name.

No one was surprised that William's baby girl was given his mother's name as a middle name, and it is a thoughtful tribute to her. Soon after the announcement, Rosa Monckton, a friend of the late Princess of Wales, tweeted, 'Diana's spirit lives on in her sons, and now her name lives on in her granddaughter.' William also has a cousin called Charlotte Diana, daughter of Diana's brother, Earl Spencer. Diana is Roman, and means 'divine'.

Time will tell how the choice of the royals affects our baby-naming choices, but with such classic, traditional names, our guess is that we'll see at least two of them in next year's top 10.

Biggest winners and losers

In an interesting development this year, two of the biggest climbers up the Top 100 chart for boys are Teddy and Theodore, which are essentially the same name. In fact, using long and short versions of the same name has been an established trend for several years now. Ronnie, the fifth-biggest climber for baby boys last year, is leagues ahead of Ronald (hovering somewhere around 770th place), but Ronnie, Ron, Ronald, and the numerous spelling variations of them, have been more popular for a while now since Harry Potter's best friend started a cult following.

It's not all good news for nicknames though: last year this very book reported on the increasing popularity of the name Sonny, which followed the trend of shortened names and names ending in -ie/-y. However, you'll notice that Sonny's shelf life was short-lived: poor old Sonny has moved from the winners to the losers, and was the eighth-biggest loser of last year.

Watch this space to see if this is the beginning of the end for short names and nicknames, or just a small bump in the road to total domination.

Other trends for high-climbers include old-fashioned names that were popular around 100 years ago, such as Elsie, Ivy, Violet, and Beatrice in the girls' names list. We are definitely seeing a return to traditional names now, and a move away from names popular in the 1990s and 2000s – such as Paige, Madison, Callum, Liam, and Cameron. This may be due in part to the 100-year rule (see page 21), but may also be due to our fascination with nostalgia and tradition in a time of economic uncertainty. Whatever the cause, it's nice to see some old favourites back in the game.

By George!

What about Prince George Alexander Louis? Well, after his birth on 22 July 2013, the world went a little wild in anticipation of trying to guess his name, and it turns out it was all for good reason. All three of George's names ran up the charts the year he was born, although the name George itself actually dropped in favour during the months following the announcement. However, our future king needn't be concerned about his popularity waning: with the current trend of using royal baby names he's likely to see his influence continue for years to come.

Some other big losers for boys' names were Aiden, Tyler, Riley, and Aaron, which is quite surprising. Only a couple of years ago Aiden was a massive hit with parents, and Riley appeared in the Top 10 just the year before. Names that were also fashionable for girls within the last few years, such as Hollie, Amy, Katie, and Maisie, aren't nearly as common anymore and are rapidly sliding down the charts. It's not enough of a pattern yet to decide if we're getting fed up with the -ie/-y ending trend, but it's definitely interesting to watch.

Biggest winners

Boys	Girls
1. Teddy	1. Elsie
2. Felix	2. Ivy
3. Theodore	3. Violet
4. Ibrahim	4. Beatrice
5. Ronnie	5. Victoria
6. Reuben	6. Willow
7. Austin	7. Darcy
8. Hugo	8. Mollie
9. Elijah	9. Sofia
10. Elliott	10. Evelyn

Biggest losers

Boys	Girls
1. Callum	1. Hollie
2. Liam	2. Paige
3. Cameron	3. Madison
4. Tyler	4. Heidi
5. Riley	5. Amy
6. Aaron	6. Katie
7. Aiden	7. Maisie
8. Sonny	8. Gracie
9. Ryan	9. Isabel
10. Connor	10. Lola

In 2015, only six new names entered the Top 100 for boys' names: Albert, Austin, Felix, Ronnie, Ibrahim, and Teddy. These pushed Rhys, Ellis, Kayden, Bailey, Taylor, and Kyle out of place. There were only three new entries in the girls' Top 100 list, Beatrice, Darcy, and Victoria, and they forced Keira and Caitlin down the charts. Only two names left the Top 100 as Lydia and Sara share position 100 together.

The *Frozen* effect

You can't escape the impact of Disney's *Frozen* anywhere these days, even in the world of baby names. Since the release of the main title in late 2014 and the animated short *Frozen Fever* last year, the name Elsa has moved up to 183rd place, and remarkably Olaf now outranks Kristof and Hans combined. However, Anna hasn't been quite as fortunate, being one of those names that hasn't escaped its waning popularity since the 1990s. It's definitely time for a comeback, Anna.

Tis the season to be . . . Holly?

Another way to look at baby name trends is to assess them by season or month. In terms of popularity, Amelia was the name most chosen for little girls every single month, while Olivia came in second place every single time. Oliver was the most popular name for baby boys every month last year, which this book actually predicted the year before! In the previous year's data Harry was in the top spot every month until August, when Oliver took over. In *Baby Names 2015* we suggested this meant Oliver was primed for a complete takeover and apparently you can now believe we are omniscient beings with the power to predict the future . . . well, of baby name statistics, anyway, because of course Oliver is now in first place overall.

Incidentally, it's really not a myth that parents are more likely to choose seasonal-themed names during certain months. For example, Holly came in fifth during the month of December but was 33rd overall, and the name Summer hits a high of 23 in the summer months but after falling to 94th place in December ends up in 48th place over the span of the year.

Cracking Christmas names

A name search conducted by 192.com found that there are 23 people in the UK called Mary Christmas, seven people called Holly Berry, and eight called Carol Singer. They also discovered that over 200 people in the UK have the surname Stocking, 10 have the surname Cracker, 21 have the surname Turkey, and perhaps most tragically of all 42 people are called Sprout. Lets just take a moment to wish them well shall we? Thank you.

Helen Fairey of Derby changed her name by deed poll to Christmas Fairy in 2010. She now works for a large hotel chain, ensuring guests have plenty of Christmas cheer every year, and even has her own YouTube channel!

You'll also find that across the UK, each country favours different names. For example, parents in Wales are more likely to name their child Jacob than those in England, and the name Dylan also features in the Top 10 there – perhaps unsurprisingly. However, England's parents choose Thomas more frequently than the Welsh, and Welsh parents enjoyed Alfie and Noah more than the English.

When it comes to girls' names, parents from both England and Wales agree that Amelia is the favourite followed by Olivia, as they both appear in first and second place in both Top 10s. They also agree that Ava and Isla are excellent choices, as they appear in both lists, but disagree on some others. English parents overwhelmingly liked Sophie, while Welsh parents preferred Ella and Seren – which makes sense, given Seren's Welsh origins.

In Scotland and Northern Ireland, Jack is a runaway winner for boys' names – a name that has appeared all over the UK Top 10 for years. In fact, it reigned supreme for a whopping 16 years before being toppled by Oliver and Harry a few years ago. As its popularity continues to dominate in Scotland and Northern Ireland, it's possible it could return to glory in the rest of the UK too. For girls, Sophie stands at the top of the heap in Scotland – this name doesn't appear anywhere in the list for Wales, which is unusual for a name that's present in the other Top 10 lists around the UK – and in a staggering demonstration of just how important each registered baby name is for statistics, both Emily and Grace appear in first place in Northern Ireland. Amelia and Emily are the only names that parents of little girls in the four regions agree on, showing up in all four lists around the UK (see lists below). Parents of little boys, however, agree that Oliver, Jack, Harry, and Charlie are all great names for new babies wherever they're born.

Top 10 baby names in England

Boys

1. Oliver	6. Thomas
2. Jack	7. Oscar
3. Harry	8. James
4. Jacob	9. William
5. Charlie	10. George

Girls

1. Amelia	6. Isla
2. Olivia	7. Poppy
3. Emily	8. Isabella
4. Jessica	9. Sophie
5. Ava	10. Mia

Top 10 baby names in Wales

Boys

1. Oliver	7. Harry
2. Jacob	8. Riley (tied)
3. Jack	8.William (tied)
4. Charlie	10.Dylan (tied)
5. Alfie	10. Mason (tied)
6. Noah	

Girls

1. Amelia	7. Ella
2. Olivia	8. Mia
3. Ava	9. Isla
4. Ruby	10. Isabella (tied)
5. Emily	10. Seren (tied)
6. Poppy	

Top 10 baby names in Scotland

Boys

1. Jack	6. Logan
2. James	7. Alexander
3. Lewis	8. Lucas
4. Oliver	9. Harry
5. Daniel	10. Charlie

Girls

1. Sophie	6. Ava
2. Olivia	7. Jessica
3. Emily	8. Ella
4. Isla	9. Amelia
5. Lucy	10. Millie

Top 10 baby names in Northern Ireland

Boys		Girls	
1. Jack	6. Noah	1. Emily (tied)	6. Lucy
2. James	7. Matthew	1. Grace (tied)	7. Aoife
3. Charlie	8. Ethan (tied)	3. Sophie	8. Amelia
4. Harry	8. Jacob (tied)	4. Ella	9. Anna (tied)
5. Daniel	9. Oliver	5. Sophia	9. Jessica (tied)

Jessica Alba called her daughter Haven after the baby was born still in the 'caul', or the intact bag of waters. She said, 'She came into the world in her "safe haven" and her name just clicked.'

Being creative with tradition

Although it's true that parents are choosing similar names to each other, it seems we are still putting our personal slant on these traditional or popular names. The Top 10 names for both boys and girls account for only 13% of all registered names in the UK, down from 14% in previous years, which means that there is a greater diversity in the names, or spellings, parents are choosing. Compare this with 50 years ago, when nearly 50% of all names appeared in the Top 25, and you'll see why this is so surprising.

Essentially, there are fewer babies being given the same name, and a greater number of baby names registered. There were 27,000 different names registered for baby boys and 35,000 for baby girls; the Office for National Statistics counts each spelling as a separate entry, even if it's essentially the same name. For example, Lily is counted separately from Lilly, Lillie, and Lili, and the spelling with the most registrations reaches a higher place on the charts. Hyphenated names are also separated: Lily-Mae, Lily-May and Lily-Mai are all counted as individual names in the UK's official statistics (see page 18 for more on hyphenated names).

This is not how all countries create their baby name statistics: Australia tallies names by sound, not spelling, which means that in fifth place for boys is Jackson/Jaxon, and in eighth place for girls is Sophia/Sofia. In fact, this affects the overall position for names quite profoundly. By combining spellings, certain names appear to be more popular than they would be if counted separately: although Jackson/Jaxon appeared in the Australian Top 10 for boys for the first time two years ago, neither would have been anywhere near there if they had been tallied by themselves.

Some of Britain's quirky baby names during the last year have included:

Boys	Girls
Bow	Blousey
Gift	Disney
King-David	Euphemia
Lazer	La
Pious	Nimco
Royal	Pip
The	Qi
Winter	Yue

So, what do parents do if they really like a traditional or already-popular name but are afraid that everyone in their child's class will also be named that? Well, it looks like they are picking a name they like and then adding their own unique spin on it. While it's certainly true that traditional names still dominate the charts, and the Top 10 for both boys and girls has been made up of pretty much the same (or similar) names for the last decade, there is a move towards the unique as well. Take a fairly conservative name like Lucy, for example. It's definitely still popular, as last year it ranked 28th, but 10 years ago it was 7th. The alternative spelling of Lucie, though, has jumped 53 places in the same time, and Luci, which is even more unusual, has yet to fall out of favour as well. Other spellings include Lucia, Lucee, and Lwci. The births of Princess Charlotte in 2015 and Prince George in 2013 have also increased our use of traditional names.

All of which feels like parents don't want to move away from the norm – but total conformity doesn't sit well with them either, so they add a little twist. The naming equivalent of wearing 'snazzy' red socks with a straightforward suit perhaps?

Other old-fashioned names, such as Arthur, Ava, Florence, and Sebastian, have maintained their place in popularity ranks of the Top 100 lists, joining such stalwarts as Alexander, Alice, Grace, and Thomas. However, over the last year or so their more unusual counterparts have started to join them, including Arte, Avah, Florrie, and Sebastiaan, as well as Alexandr, Aliz, Graice, and Tomaz.

The traditional Muslim name Mohammed has now become so popular in the UK that if just the three spelling variations in the Top 100 were counted as the same name, it would be the most popular name for baby boys. The spelling 'Muhammad' is the most common (ranked 15th), followed by 'Mohammed' (23rd) and 'Mohammad' (57th). Other spelling variations include Mohamed, Mohamad, Mohammod, and Mohamud.

Spelling options for traditional names

Boys		**Girls**	
You like . . .	**You could try . . .**	**You like . . .**	**You could try . . .**
Benjamin	Bennie	Charlotte	Lottie
Daniel	Danial	Jessica	Jessika
Joseph	Josef	Lucy	Lucie
Thomas	Tomaz	Molly	Mollie
William	Willem	Robin	Robyn

Giving a baby boy a shortened version of a traditional name as his complete first name is becoming increasingly popular. Take the third most popular boy's name, Harry, as an example. This in itself is a short-ened version of Henry (18th) or Harold (1,617th), but it also lends itself – perhaps a little uneasily – to Harree or Arry (appearing on the charts for the third year in a row). The name James is also never far from the Top 10, and last year its nickname Jamie slotted in at position 68. This has also happened with William (ranked 8th): Billy is 112th, Will is 382nd, and Wil appears further down – which for all the world just looks like a typo, doesn't it. Surprisingly, though, the names 'Willy' and 'Willie' weren't given to a single child last year in the entire UK! I wonder why . . .

> How about a name without vowels? Last year the names Bryn, CJ, Kym, MD, and Vy were all given to at least three children apiece.

And how do you spell that?

A selection of last year's original spellings for girls include: Caitie (from Katy), Tiffanie (from Tiffany), Lejla (from Leila), and Zoi, Zoie, Zoey, and, Zoeya (from Zoe). The spelling of Emily as Emeli can also be attributed to the stonking success of songstress Emeli Sandé.

Boys' names variations include: Xzaviar (from Xavier), Juels (from Jules), Fynlee (from Finlay), and Rilee, Rileigh, Ryle, Rylea, and Rylei (from Riley).

Heavenly hyphenation

One of the most common ways parents add a twist to tradition is by hyphenating their children's names. There are over 1,000 names with a hyphen tacked onto the end of another name in this year's combined list of boys' and girls' names.

Popular hyphenations include: -Rose, -May/-Mae and -Leigh/-Lee, which make names such as Lily-Rose, Ella-Rose, Gracie-Mae, Demi-Leigh, and Lacey-May. In fact, if you add all the spelling variations together, names that end in -May or -Mae would be in the Top 20 and those that include Rose would be around position 50! The highest-ranking hyphenated girls' name is Amelia-Rose, in position 214, with almost 250 baby girls named that last year. Also popular are Lily-Rose, Lily-Mae, Ellie-Mae, and Lilly-May.

Boys are not exempt from this rule either, as it has become fashionable to add -James or -Lee to the end of a baby boy's name. The highest-ranking version is Tyler-James (in position 451), with nearly 100 birth certificates to show for it. Also becoming more commonly used are Tommy-Lee, Riley-James, Alfie-James, and Tyler-Jay.

Top 10 names in Australia

Boys	Girls
1. Oliver	1. Charlotte
2. William	2. Olivia
3. Jack	3. Ava
4. Noah	4. Emily
5. Jackson/ Jaxon	5. Mia
6. James	6. Amelia
7. Thomas	7. Ruby
8. Ethan	8. Sophia/ Sofia
9. Lucas	9. Chloe
10. Cooper	10. Sophie

A French court ruled in 2015 that Nutella was not an acceptable name for a baby girl, and ordered the parents to change it to Ella, saying it could cause 'mockery or disobliging remarks'.

2 This year's predictions

Looking ahead to 2016, the trend for choosing a traditional name and altering the spelling looks set to continue. There is a theory that names cycle through popularity every 100 years or so, meaning that names that were popular during World War I are likely to see another spike in popularity around now. We predicted last year that a deluge of Lloyds or Georges was coming to a nursery near you soon, and we weren't wrong! Better watch out for some Elsies and Winnies next year as well.

What's possible this time around is that parents will pick a name that was popular 100 years ago and add their own twist to make it modern. Certainly the past few years have shown this rule to be pretty spot-on, and 1916 names will undoubtedly be appearing in the 2016 charts – albeit with some more unusual spellings sprinkled in.

For girls, soft-ending names will continue to dominate the charts. Half of the names in the Top 20 end in -a at the moment (Amelia, Olivia, Ava, Isla, Jessica, Isabella, Mia, Sophia, Ella, and Freya), and names ending in -y or -ie sounds will also stick around for a few more years (think Emily, Poppy, Sophie, Ruby, Lily, Evie, and Chloe, all of which are also in the current Top 20). We should also see the rise in the use of Charlotte, Elizabeth and possibly also Diana, after our Princess was born in May 2015.

In the case of boys' names, trends are a little harder to pinpoint. There is also a great deal more shuffling in the ranks going on in the list of boys' names, with huge differences over the last 10 years. Therefore, it's probable that parents expecting baby boys in 2016 will be following trends such as nicknames and short names, instead of sound trends. This phenomenon can be seen emerging as Bobby becomes more popular than Robert (which dropped nearly 50 places recently) and Alfie more popular than Alfred (sitting in 11th place – miles ahead of Alfred's 136th position). However, as nicknames tend to have -y or -ie sounds anyway, it's entirely possible there will be greater numbers of names ending in those sounds as a result.

Predicted Top 10 baby names in 2016

Boys	Girls
1. Oliver	1. Amelia
2. Harry	2. Olivia
3. Jack	3. Isla
4. George	4. Ava
5. William	5. Emily
6. Oscar	6. Poppy
7. Jacob	7. Jessica
8. Charlie	8. Sophie
9. James	9. Isabella
10. Thomas	10. Grace

Other trends to hit in 2016 include a move towards 'statement' names for babies, such as Noble, Royal, Saint, or Titan. According to the naming website Nameberry.com, babies may also be given more unisex names, including Alex, Darryl, Jordan, Robin, and Tracy. The website also suggests that we will be seeing a spike in popularity for names that end in either -ella for girls or -ett for boys (such as Arabella and Mirabella, and Brett or Rhett), or names for either gender that end in -o sounds (like Juno, Margot, Milo, Theo, and Willow).

2016 events

As well as getting ideas from the names that other parents choose, some influences on baby names in 2016 may come from the worlds of sport, politics and celebrity.

In 2016 there are a number of major sporting events, and athletes who perform well at them will no doubt become inspirational for new parents. The Summer Olympics and Paralympics, football's UEFA Euro 2016, the European Figure Skating Championships, and other annual events such as Tour de France and Wimbledon are all taking place this year. The success of Great Britain's Olympic team in 2012 did lead to a small increase in babies being born with the names Victoria (after cyclist Victoria Pendleton), Bradley (after cyclist Bradley Wiggins), Charlotte (after dressage rider Charlotte Dujardin), and Alistair (after triathlete Alistair Brownlee), so it's very plausible the same could happen again.

A speedy name

The name Jenson is a great example of how the success of sporting figures can impact baby names. Jenson, one of the fastest climbers in boys' names over the last 20 years, only really took off in the year 2000, when Jenson Button became the UK's youngest Formula One driver. It jumped again in 2004 after Button had more success, and then screamed up the charts, tyres squealing, in 2009 when he won the World Drivers' Championship for the first time.

2016 anniversaries

So, what else might influence baby names this year? Well, there are a number of significant anniversaries that might alert new parents to some names they haven't come across before. See if the anniversaries listed below provide you with any inspiration:

5th wedding anniversary of Prince William, Duke of Cambridge, and Catherine, Duchess of Cambridge. William is currently 8th, and while Kate is hovering around the 300th mark, Catherine is actually on the rise again. Their children, George and Charlotte, will no doubt be mentioned in the press a lot during this time too.

50th anniversary of England beating West Germany to win the FIFA World Cup – players included Bobby Moore, Geoff Hurst and Bobby Charlton.

75th anniversary of the death of author Virginia Woolf. After a spike in popularity a few years ago Virginia is on somewhat of a wane. Could be time for another wave of interest though.

150th anniversary of the birthday of authors Beatrix Potter and H.G. Wells (author: real name Herbert George Wells). Beatrix is becoming incredibly popular right now, and has jumped 1,000 places in the last decade. Remarkably, the same is also true of Herbert (thanks to the 100-year rule), and George of course is in its heyday.

200th anniversary of the publication of *Emma*, by Jane Austen. Poor Jane looks a little plain to parents in 2016, but Austen is becoming very cool for both boys and girls.

500th anniversary of the publication of *Utopia* by Thomas More. Thomas is currently ranked 6th, and both Tom and Tommy are hugely popular in the nicknames-as-formal-names trend – one that shows no sign of stopping.

3 The world of celebrity babies

Celebrities are infamous for choosing obscure names for their babies, but sadly for our love of their weird and wonderful name concoctions, it seems as though there's a trend for the more mundane right now. This has been the case for the last few years, with only a few really bizarre choices sneaking through (see page 28 for a list of the weirder ones).

It came as no surprise when the Duke and Duchess of Cambridge chose traditional, family names for their daughter Charlotte. Unbeknownst to them, they were bang on trend, following the 100-year rule. And celebrities seem to be following the royal example . . .

In general, celebrities are picking names that most parents wouldn't be embarrassed to admit liking, such as Amanda Peet's son Henry, Vanessa Carlton's son Sidney, Hayden Panettiere's daughter Kaya, and Holly Branson's twins Etta and Artie. All in all, pretty traditional and commonly found among us lesser-known folk.

However, there is also a definite wave of celebrities choosing 'big' names, which suggest lofty aspirations or high achievements. Take Reign, Kourtney Kardashian's son, or Titan Jewell, Kelly Rowland's new baby boy. Even Genesis, Alicia Keys's little boy, and Delta Bell, Kristen Bell's new daughter, have names that make you think outside the box.

Other celebrities have gone with names for their newborns that, while they might not be very common these days, aren't *so* weird that you'd raise an eyebrow. Examples of this trend include Natalie Pinkham's son Wilfred Otto, Stanley Tucci's baby Matteo Oliver, and Martine McCutcheon's son Rafferty Jack.

In fact, the only kooky names on the list are Zoe Saldana's twins Cy Aridio and Bowie Ezio, and the fact that Mila Kunis and Ashton Kutcher named their daughter Wyatt Isabelle – because Wyatt's not normally found in the girls' names list . . . but hey, I'm all about equal opportunities, so why not? Anyway, the lack of really wacky celebrity names for the second year in a row makes you wonder if it's the celebs who are going all vanilla or if it's the rest of us who just don't bat an eyelid anymore? Eyelid – now there's a celeb baby name in waiting.

Recent Celebrity Babies

Art (Chris O'Dowd and Dawn O'Porter)
Beau (Rosie Marcel and Ben Stacy)
Charlotte Elizabeth Diana (Duke and Duchess of Cambridge)
Cy Aridio and Bowie Ezio (Zoe Saldana and Marco Perego)
Ella Rose (Charlotte Hawkins and Mark Herbert)
James (Blake Lively and Ryan Reynolds)
Liberty (Abbey Clancy and Peter Crouch)
Matteo Oliver (Stanley Tucci and Felicity Blunt)
Montgomery Moses Brian (Isla Fisher and Sacha Baron Cohen)
Rafferty Jack (Martine McCutcheon and Jack McManus)
Sailor (Liv Tyler and David Gardner)
Sasha (Shakira and Gerard Piqué)
Sidney Aoibheann (Vanessa Carlton and John McCauley)
Tadhg John (Una Foden and Ben Foden)
Wilfred Otto (Natalie Pinkham and Owain Walbyoff)

How's this for coming up with a name for your newborn? James Corden and his wife Julia had a baby girl in 2014, giving her the name Carey after Julia's maiden name, and during the press rounds it also came out that the couple's first son, Max, was given the middle name McCartney after Sir Paul McCartney. Corden told the story of grovelling to Sir Paul to appear on a charity sketch show, and said, 'I laid it on very thick, telling him, "People won't die if you do our sketch." It makes it very difficult for people to say no. He said, "Bloody hell, James, I've heard some grovelling in my time." I then said, "That's nothing – if you'd said no, I was going to say I would name my unborn child after you." To which he said, "If you promise to do that, I'll do the sketch." And that's why my son is called Max McCartney Kimberley Corden.'

There are two names on the recent celebrity babies list that might seem unusual to folks outside of Ireland, but are pretty common if you're from there. Una Foden welcomed her baby Tadhg last year, which is pronounced like 'tiger' without the 'r'. Una said of her decision, 'We were unsure of a name for a while but it was always [husband] Ben's decision that would win in the end. He asked me to list possible Irish boys' names and, as soon as he heard the name Tadhg, it really stood out to him. It's become a tradition to give our children classic Irish names', which is why their first daughter was named Aoife.

Surnames for celebrity babies can be pretty important too. Kate Winslet chose to pass on her own surname to her third child, Bear Winslet, instead of her husband's name. (Her husband, Ned Rocknroll, changed his name in 2008 from Abe Smith.) Kate was very vocal about this decision, stating before their son was born, 'Of course we're not going to call it Rocknroll. People might judge all they like, but I'm a f***ing grown-up.' Winslet also has two older children by her previous marriages, Mia and Joe, both of whom have their fathers' last names.

Upcoming arrivals

Celebrity couples expecting new arrivals include Kim Kardashian and Kanye West, Fearne Cotton and Jesse Wood, and Lily Cole and Kwame Ferreira. As is always the case, the names these couples pick this year will be highly scrutinised and influential on the rest of us, if previous years are anything to go by.

> Beyoncé and Jay-Z have applied to trademark their daughter's name – not once, but twice. Recently the couple asked for 'Blue Ivy Carter' to be trademarked exclusively to them, for use with baby products and music.

Also making waves is the progeny of Benedict Cumberbatch and Sophie Hunter. Hilariously, various websites sprang up after the couple announced the pregnancy, generating potential names for the baby of the man with possibly the most infamous name in Britain right now. Examples included Burlington Wafflesnack, Bakery Crackerjack, and Bedlington Cuckatoo. Try putting one of them down on your kid's birth certificate, and see what happens.

4 Big-screen inspiration

What's exciting or tragic about popular culture nowadays (depending on your point of view) is how everything, from films and TV to books and blogs, can shape the world of baby names.

The impact of characters in movies, books, and TV programmes has been huge on baby names in the last few years. There are some predictable trends, such as *Frozen*, *The Hunger Games* and *Fifty Shades of Grey* series, but also some unexpected ones. Who would have thought, for example, that the children's animation *Hotel Transylvania* would have had an impact a few years ago? The lead character Mavis, voiced by actor Selena Gomez, inspired many new parents to choose either Mavis or Maeve: Maeve moved up a few hundred places and Mavis is back in the charts after several long years away.

Disney's *Frozen* was about as massive as you can get: one of the highest-grossing animated films of all time, and an entire industry of merchandise to boot. Last year saw the launch of an animated short called *Frozen Fever*, and it served the desired purpose of reminding folks why they love Nordic princesses so much ... oh, and why they should pick Scandinavian names for their babies. Elsa has been the biggest hit with new parents, now appearing in 183rd place, and Olaf is more popular than Kristof and Hans combined. However, Anna is still patiently waiting for her turn in the spotlight, as the popularity of this name has been in decline since the 1990s. Still, with discussions afoot over a full-length *Frozen* sequel, it's really only a matter of time until Anna catches up with her peers.

The movie trilogy based on *The Hunger Games* novels provided parents with a whole host of alternative spellings for already popular names. Last year the fourth and final film, *Mockingjay – Part 2*, came out. Since the books and original movie were released, the names Peeta and Gale have entered the boys' names lists for the first time ever, and it's only a matter of time before Katniss herself becomes an influence on girls' names. Effie has had a huge jump in popularity – before the first *Hunger Games* book and film were released it languished somewhere at the bottom, but last year it ranked 509th (meaning it leapt a whopping 1,200 places in just a few short years). The name Primrose, or 'Prim', jumped a staggering 300 places last year, confirming the idea that parents are starting to choose old-fashioned names again.

Divergent and *Insurgent*, the first two instalments of another trilogy of films based on young adult fiction, were released recently. The protagonist goes by the name of Tris, after changing it from Beatrice. Both Tris and Beatrice are gaining ground in the baby names charts, although Beatrice is currently ranked 95th and much higher than Tris at the moment. Last year actually marked the first time Beatrice has been in the Top 100 for nearly 20 years, and it's due in part to these movies. The third instalment, called *Allegiant*, will be out in 2016 and further cement Beatrice and Tris's popularity in the baby names charts.

> Author Neil Gaiman, when asked about fellow author Eoin Colfer by a journalist, once replied: 'It's pronounced "Owen", so stop making that noise like a car whooshing past you at the Grand Prix.'

Other influential books and films include the runaway success of the *Fifty Shades of Grey* trilogy. The main characters, Anastasia (Ana) and

Christian, persuaded many parents to use their names for their babies. Anastasia has jumped 30 places, while Christian, which was in 239th place last year, is set to be in the Top 100 next year. Ana is also moving up the charts, albeit more slowly. All three names are also trending in online searches: last year Christian was searched for three times as often on baby name websites than the year before. The sequel to the first film, called *Fifty Shades Darker*, is due for release in 2016.

2012's *Pitch Perfect* didn't have commercial success until it went to DVD, but once it landed there, both the video and soundtrack became the biggest sellers of that year. Its influence extended to baby names too, surprisingly. The protagonist's name is spelled Beca, which hasn't had much of an impact yet, but the spelling of Becca saw a leap of nearly 1,000 places between the year the movie first came out, and again in 2015 when the sequel, *Pitch Perfect 2*, was released. Aubrey, the name of another character, had an even more impressive rise: its popularity has grown for both boys' and girls' names, and it's now in the Top 1,000 for both lists.

> Did you know that the Queen gets a say in what new princes and princesses are called? In 1988, Princess Beatrice was going to be called Annabel but the Queen dismissed it as 'too yuppie', according to the *Sun* newspaper. (Good work Your Maj.) She suggested the more traditional Beatrice and it stuck. Maybe she had the final say in Prince George's naming – George was her father's name, after all. But we think it was probably her grandson who chose to use Elizabeth as a middle name for Princess Charlotte, and we bet she was pleased!

Popular TV shows in 2015 included *Game of Thrones*, *Doctor Who*, *Call the Midwife*, *Sherlock*, *Mad Men*, and *Downton Abbey*. *Downton Abbey* has been directly responsible for the increase in popularity of the names Violet and Cora.

In the UK, the name Sherlock has seen a whopping 250% increase in popularity, while Arya, from *Game of Thrones*, has gone from 0 babies named that before *Game of Thrones* appeared on our screens, to the 257th most popular name for little girls. It also shows no sign of stopping, and its influence has even tipped over into boys' names – where it appeared on their charts for the first time a few years ago. The name Khaleesi, which is actually a royal title rather than a name in *Game of Thrones*, was given to 50 British babies last year. Popular American drama *Homeland* is definitely having an impact in the UK. Brody, the surname of the male lead, is up by 40% over here and entered the Top 100 on BabyCenter.com. Likewise, Carrie and Dana, the two female leads, rose by a whopping 200% and 66% respectively.

Foyle's War returned to our screens last year, starring Michael Kitchen and Honeysuckle Weeks. The name Honeysuckle (yes, it's her real name) has not been popular with the general public, although a shorter form, Honey, has risen considerably. Currently in 200th place, it has stormed up the charts and doesn't show signs of slowing down any time soon. Continuing the theme of period detective programmes, a third series of Australia's *Miss Fisher's Murder Mysteries* was also broadcast. Actress Essie Davis plays the lead role of Phryne Fisher, and the name Phryne has become far more popular across the globe since the show first appeared. In its home territory, for example, it increased 2,000% in popularity in the last two years alone; will the same be true in the UK soon?

Banned names around the world

@ – China
Chow Tow (meaning 'smelly head') – Malaysia
Mona Lisa – Portugal
Monkey – Denmark
0 – Sweden
Osama Bin Laden – Germany
Stompy – Germany

So what's next?

The year 2016 looks set to continue a recent pattern of remakes, reboots and sequels. Upcoming movies in 2016 include *Finding Dory*, a sequel to Disney/Pixar's *Finding Nemo*; a new *Tarzan* film; a sequel to *Alice in Wonderland*; *Ghostbusters III*; and yet another *Resident Evil* movie. There will also be the usual sprinkling of superhero films to wade through, such as *Batman v. Superman: Dawn of Justice*, and *X-Men: Apocalypse*.

Names that are featured in these films stand a good shot of influencing baby names if past years are anything to go by. *Finding Dory*, for example, could spike an interest in the name Dory – which is currently fairly popular in the USA but has yet to find traction in the UK. *Tarzan* has the potential to influence the name Jane – which hasn't been that popular in recent memory and is due a comeback. Also, *Alice in Wonderland* and *Resident Evil*'s sequels could help launch Alice into the UK's Top 20, as it's been making a slow but steady climb in recent years to position 27.

Bruce Wayne, the brooding star of the Batman franchise, is an unlikely influence on baby names in 2016, just like his counterpart Clark Kent – aka Superman – although it's interesting that both characters each have two names that could work as either forenames or surnames – the sneaky masked crime fighters. Both Bruce and Clark have had a small surge in popularity over the last few years, but unfortunately none of the four names listed are anywhere near the top of the charts at the moment. Seeing as there has been a run of Batman and Superman-themed flicks in recent years, it's unlikely that this particular sequel will make much of a difference . . . but you never know.

> An Israeli couple called their baby girl 'Like' after the Facebook button. Their other children are called 'Pie' and 'Vash', which means honey.

TV programmes set to air in 2016 include a new series of *The Walking Dead*, the popular American drama all about a zombie apocalypse. The series stars Brit actor Andrew Lincoln, and his last name's appearance in the charts has been significantly impacted by the original programme. Lincoln has risen about 1,000 places in the last ten years, and Maggie, the name of another character, has jumped 500. Any new series of this programme could have the same, or similar, impact from the names of its characters or actors.

The Hollow Crown, a fairly recent BBC production based on the plays of William Shakespeare, will conclude its run in 2016 with the name *The Wars of the Roses*. Covering Shakespeare's *Henry VI* plays and *Richard III*, it was announced that Benedict Cumberbatch and Judi Dench will be starring. Maybe there will be a flurry of Henrys, Richards, Benedicts, and Judis in 2016 too?

Continuing with a royal theme, *The Crown*, a new series about our current Queen and her relationships with various Prime Ministers over the years, will be shown on Netflix in 2016. Given our feverish obsession with the Royal Family, this is likely to not only be a popular series, but may also pave the way for new trends in baby names. Look forward to dozens of little Elizabeths, Winstons, Harolds, and Margarets, coming to a nursery near you soon.

2016 rising stars

Boys	Girls
Andrew	Alice
Benedict	Betty
Bruce	Dory
Clark	Elizabeth
Harold	Elsa
Henry	Jane
Lincoln	Judi
Olaf	Maggie
Richard	Margaret
Winston	Rose

5 How to choose a name

Top tips

- **Fall in love with the name(s) you've chosen.** If you plough through the thousands of names in this book and none of them jump off the page at you, then you probably haven't found the right one yet. Pick a name that makes you smile because if you love it, hopefully your child will too – and won't grow up resenting and hating you with all of their being. That was a little joke. Relax and get picking.

- **Try it out.** While you're pregnant, talk to your baby and address it by using a variety of your favourite names to see if it responds. There is plenty of anecdotal evidence, by which we mean second-hand nonsense, of names being chosen because the baby kicked when it was called Charlie or Aisha but was suspiciously silent when addressed as Dexter or Mildred, so see if yours has a preference! You can also try writing names down, practising a few signatures, or saying one out loud enough times to see if you ever get sick of it. Don't forget to say it out loud with the last name attached to make sure it feels right. What have you got to lose?

- **Don't listen to other people** (which actually isn't bad advice on the entire parenting front at times). Sometimes, grandparents and friends offer baby-naming 'advice', which may not always be welcome. If you've got your heart set on a name, keep it a secret until after the birth to avoid any unnecessary criticism. Trust your own instincts and remember: no one will really care once they see your baby. Its name will simply be its name.

> A mother in Norway was jailed in 2007 for refusing to pay a fine ordered by the courts after she tried to name her baby 'Gesher', which means 'bridge'. Norwegians are only allowed to use names that appear on an approved list – and Gesher was not on it.

- **Find a name with meaning.** Choosing a name that has a back story will help your child to understand their significance in the world so – whether you name them after a saint or prophet, an important political figure or a hero in a Greek tragedy – ensure that they know where their name came from. They may just be inspired to be as great as their namesake. There's research to suggest this inspirational rub-off effect has real legs, so even if you pick a name out of the air, consider making something up to tell them later!

- **Have fun.** Picking out names should be fun. Laughing at the ones you'd never dream of choosing can really help you to narrow it down to the ones you would. You can also experiment with different spellings, pronunciations or variations of names you like. There's time later for thinking through whether the bizarre name will actually give your little one a headache when they have to spell it every time they say it! See page 50 for more on this.

- **Expand your mind.** Don't rule out the weird ones just yet! As a teenager, I went to school with a girl named Siam. Her parents had conceived her on a honeymoon trip to Thailand and gave her the country's old name in honour of their visit. She loved growing up and having an unusual name. So be brave and bold if that's what you want. But just in case you get it massively wrong you might want to give them a straightforward second name so they can jump ship to that instead!

- **Do NOT pick the name of an ex.** No matter how lovely Brad Pitt might have thought the name 'Jennifer' was, it's doubtful that Angelina Jolie would have allowed him to use it for one of their daughters. The same is probably true of picking the names of your friends' exes. They are unlikely to thank you if they have to say a name they loathe repeatedly. Just steer clear of any names you know will cause problems to other people, paying particular attention to your partner and loved ones.

    How's this for a tip? Awesomebabyname.com will let you pick a name based on what domain names are available, in case you want to get ahead of your child's celebrity status and start their online visibility early.

- **What if you can't agree?** This is probably the trickiest problem to solve in the entire baby-naming process. It's wise to research a number of names in which you and your partner are both interested, and make a point of discussing your reasons for liking or disliking them long before the baby is due to be born. Arguing about it in the delivery room isn't a great first impression to give to junior.

- Avoid sticking to your guns on a name that one of you really doesn't like because it might lead to resentment down the road and you'll have so much more to argue about when your new baby actually arrives and plunges you both into a sleep-deprived stupor that you don't want this debate hanging around.

- Try the C-word. No, not that one – 'compromise'. Pick two middle names so that you each have one in there that you love, or you could each have five names that you're allowed to 'veto' – but no more. You could also try considering contractions made from names you both like, such as Anna and Lisa (Annalisa) or James and Hayden (Jayden). Whichever way you go about it, it's important that you eventually agree on the name you are giving your baby, even if it means losing out on the one you've had your heart set on for a while.

> If you are really really stuck and just can't agree, have a game of Connect 4 to decide the winner. It never fails and in seven years' time when you retell the tale to your child they will think you are both cool, rather than the ball of disagreement you actually were at the time.

Finally – keep reading and re-reading this book – the answer is in here.

Think to the future

One important aspect of naming your child is thinking ahead to their future. Will the name you've chosen stand the test of time? Will names popular in 2016 remain popular in 2050? Will the name get misspelled by everybody? Will they be able to enter a room and give a crucial business presentation confidently with an awkward or unpronounceable name? Even sooner, can they survive the potential minefields of primary and secondary school with a name that could be easily shortened to something embarrassing?

Buzzfeed.com recently ran an article on funny names of real people whose names were also reflective of their professions. Examples included Brad Slaughter, who was a meat manager at a supermarket; Les MacBurney, a firefighter; and Sue Yoo, a lawyer. At the same time another article appeared, listing all the reasons why having an unusual name was a pain – examples given were not ever being able to find your name on novelty souvenirs, coffee shop baristas not knowing how to spell or pronounce your name for your order, and other people giving you 'fun, new' nicknames because they can't be bothered with your normal one. Obviously these are just funny articles and not meant to be taken seriously, but they are things to consider when thinking long-term about your baby's name.

Although Sue Yoo is fantastic and very tempting just for the lifetime of laughs and free legal advice.

Stereotypes: true or false?

Will the name you choose actually affect your child's life? Will names that seem clever mean that your child will be brainier? Will names with positive meanings make your child into a happier person? The answer is . . . possibly.

Some experts believe that parents who choose inspirational names for their offspring (e.g. Destiny, Serenity, Unique) or names of products they would like to own (e.g. Armani, Jaguar, Mercedes) are projecting a future onto their child for them to aspire to, thus helping to shape their life. However, there's absolutely no evidence that this actually works!

Inspirational names		Aspirational names	
Destiny	Joy	Armani	Ferrari
Happy	Peace	Aston	Jaguar
Heaven	Serenity	Bugatti	Mercedes
Hope	Unique	Chanel	Porsche
Innocence	Unity	Dolce	Prada

One thing you should consider is how your child's name will be perceived by the outside world. Typically, judgements are passed on names, even before meeting a person, in situations such as job interviews or at school.

Recently, teachers across the country were asked to decide from a list of names which children were more likely to be badly behaved than others. Topping the 'naughty' charts were Callum, Connor, and Jack for boys, and Chelsea, Courtney, and Chardonnay for girls. On the other hand, the names in the 'clever' category were Alexander, Adam, and Christopher for boys, and Elizabeth, Charlotte, and Emma for girls.

Teachers were also asked to pick names that they felt were likely to be given to 'popular' children and these included Jack, Daniel, Charlie, Emma, Charlotte, and Hannah – meaning that little boys named Jack are naughty but popular!

Williams play the clarinet?

In 2015 Buzzfeed.com published a survey of British adults and their thoughts on British names. Responses included, 'Jennifers always have ponytails and exceptionally clear skin', 'Maxes get in one fight in university and nearly get kicked out, but you still fancy them', and 'Williams get good GCSE results, and they play the clarinet better than most'. You know . . . a highly scientific analysis of names. Thanks Buzzfeed.

In a different survey, teachers were asked to pick names that they felt were particularly 'chavvy'. Chantelle, Jordan, Kylie, and Paige came out on top for the girls, while Connor, Dwayne, Liam, and Rhys were ranked first for the boys. Around the same time, it was discovered that teenagers named Katherine and Duncan (or a variation of the two, such as Kate) were up to eight times more likely to achieve high GCSE results than those named Wayne or Jermaine. Another study in 2015 analysed the number of stickers given to children as rewards for good behaviour. Those named Amy and Jacob are more likely to be praised for being well behaved than children named Ella and Joseph; moreover, kids who do not shorten their name or go by nicknames are more likely to be better behaved, too.

Names which mean 'clever'

Abner	Shanahan
Cassidy	Todd
Haley	Ulysses
Penelope	Washington
Portia	Wylie

Names which *sound* clever

Alastair	Gabriel
Charles	Harriet
Christian	Sophia
Elizabeth	Spencer
Frances	William

Children who are told that they have inherited an ancestor's name or that of an influential character from history seem to be more driven and focused than children who are told disappointingly, 'We just liked the sound of it.' As a parent, it seems it's okay to pick an unusual name if you have a story or some interesting facts to support your choice. Naming your child Atticus (after Atticus Finch from Harper Lee's *To Kill A Mockingbird*, known for being a strong and moral character) may therefore not be a bad idea.

Top 10 names in New Zealand

Boys	Girls
1. Oliver	1. Charlotte
2. Jack	2. Olivia
3. James	3. Isla
4. Mason	4. Emily
5. Liam	5. Sophie
6. William	6. Amelia
7. Noah	7. Ella
8. Lucas	8. Harper
9. Benjamin	9. Sophia
10. Jacob	10. Ruby

Personality and character have a far greater influence than name alone and, after a while, a name becomes just a name.

Quirky names

Quirky. Such an ugly word. Like 'zany', it sounds forced and try-hard doesn't it? But while there are drawbacks to having an obviously out-there name, being different has advantages too. For one thing, your child's name will never be forgotten by other people, which means they won't be easily forgotten or homogenised, and if they do something influential with their life then their name could become an inspiration for other parents. On the other hand, a quirky name often requires a quirky personality – or does it actually create one? If you don't think your genes could stand up to a name like Satchel or Kerensa, perhaps it's time to think of one a little more run-of-the-mill.

What not to call your child

In Pennsylvania a few years ago there was a case of a supermarket bakery refusing to ice the words 'Happy Birthday, Adolf Hitler' onto a three-year-old's birthday cake. The parents were able to eventually fulfil the order at another shop but, as a result of the publicity surrounding the event, Social Services were called in to assess the child's home and Adolf was taken into care – along with his siblings Joycelynn Aryan Nation and Honszlynn Hinler Jeannie.

Melanie Ann Convery and Neal James Coughli legally changed their names to Melanie Seamonster Convery and Neal Seamonster Coughli in 2014.

> ## Controversial names adopted by real people
>
> | | |
> |---|---|
> | Adolf Hitler | Jezebel |
> | Beelzebub | Lucifer |
> | Desdemona | Mussolini |
> | Hannibal Lecter | Stalin |
> | Himmler | Voldemort |

A survey carried out recently by the National Centre for Social Research found that the more unusual the name, the less likely a candidate is to be called for a job interview after submitting a CV. Whether or not this fact would affect a child's development and future career is yet to be determined, but it is something to consider.

There is also new research from baby website Bounty, which says that as many as one in five parents regrets their choice of baby name. Of the 3,000 parents interviewed, 20% said they no longer thought the unusual choice of spelling or pronunciation was appropriate. Around 8% said they were tired of people mispronouncing their child's name and 10% thought the novelty of the original pick had worn off. They also said they would now pick a new name which had not occurred to them or been an option before.

Although parents are often discouraged from picking wild and crazy names for their babies (think about little Blue Ivy, Beyoncé's daughter, or Zuma Nesta Rock, Gwen Stefani's second son), there isn't actually any evidence to suggest that children are hindered in any way by them, unless they're really, really extreme.

Sex and gender

How do we define what makes a name masculine or feminine? Well, it may be connected to the sounds that the letters create when spoken. Harder-sounding combinations (-ter, -it, -ld, -id) tend to be found in masculine names, whereas softer-sounding combinations (-ie, -ay, -la) are generally associated with feminine names. Therefore, you end up with Sophie, Joanie, and Bella, and Harold, Walter, and David.

If you're planning on choosing a feminine-sounding name, approach with caution: recent research suggests that girls who are given particularly 'girly' names – think Tiana, Kayla, and Isabella – are much more likely to misbehave when they reach school age. These 'feminine' girls were also far less likely to choose subjects at school such as maths and science, while their sisters with more masculine names – for example, Morgan, Alexis, and Ashley – were encouraged to excel in these courses. Which is fascinating and scary in equal measure.

> An Icelandic girl won a 15-year battle in 2013 to keep her birth name after authorities originally deemed 'Blaer' too masculine for a girl. She is now free at last to use her real name, which means 'light breeze', on her passport and at school.

Nowadays, names are becoming more androgynous and many appear in both boys' and girls' lists, including Hayden, Riley, Madison and, of course, Alex – some form of which appears in the Top 100 for both boys and girls every year. Therefore, if you want a more gender-neutral name for your new arrival, you won't be alone.

But what about your own gender? Does the fact you're a man or woman mean you are more likely to pick certain names for your child? Well, in general, that's probably not the case, but there might be an element of truth to it. Apparently, mothers are prone to picking names that are similar to, or exactly the same as, their maiden name, if they got rid of it when they got married. This system allows a mother to pass on a part of their own lineage, as well as the father's. A famous example is comedian James Corden and his wife Julia, who named their daughter Carey, using Julia's maiden name.

A recent study by Bounty found that mothers tend to win the argument over who gets to pick the final name of a newborn, with four in ten mums ignoring the choices selected by dads, and one in ten dads simply backing down. However, four in ten couples don't make the final decision until after the baby is born, and a third will argue about it before settling.

Nicknames

Nicknames are unavoidable. They can range from the common – such as Mike from Michael or Sam from Samantha – to the trendy, funny or downright insulting. As we saw earlier, there's a growing trend of parents using nicknames as their baby's full name and getting rid of the longer name altogether. If you're going to stick with the longer name, however, make sure that you're going to be happy with any nicknames that emerge.

The first time your child encounters a nickname will probably be before they are even born – or at least within the first few months. Many older siblings find new names hard to remember or pronounce and your baby could end up with a nickname before you know it. If your baby has an older sibling, try talking to them about their new brother or sister using the name you've picked so you can discover how their imagination might choose to interpret it. If they are an older child you might even want to include them in the naming process from the start, if for no other reason than they might mention a friend at school who gets teased for having an unfortunate nickname derived from the name you've chosen.

You can pre-empt problem nicknames to some extent by saying the name you've chosen out loud and trying to find rhymes for it. This is a clever way to avoid playground chants and nursery rhyme-type insults, such as Andy Pandy or Looby Lou. It's a sad truth, though, that children will rhyme anything with anything else if they can, so while you might wish to take playground chants into account during your naming process, don't be too concerned about them. Most children are subjected to them at some point and emerge unscathed.

> French law prohibits all names other than those on an approved list. However, in 2012 French courts allowed one couple to call their child 'Daemon' after a vampire character in the TV show *The Vampire Diaries* called Damon – the first such deviation from the approved list in a decade.

Using family names

This is a huge trend at the moment, particularly among celebrities. It is very en vogue right now to choose a name from a grandparent or parent, and then to make sure everyone else knows the reason you chose it! See page 27 for more on celebrity baby names, and who chose family names to earn brownie points from their in-laws.

Some families have a strong tradition of using names that come from the family tree and therefore there are instances where naming your baby boy Augustine VIII is simply not just an option: it's a rule. Another way families do this is by giving children the name of their parent of the same sex and adding 'Junior' (Jr) to the end. This could only potentially create a problem if that child then decides to carry on the tradition and name their child after themselves – after all, who wants to be known as Frederick Jr Jr? Admittedly, this doesn't seem to happen very often in the UK but it is something to consider if it is one of your family's traditions. There are pros and cons with using family names.

- **Pro**: your child will feel part of a strong tradition, which will create a sense of security for them and help to make them feel a complete member of the family.

- **Pro**: if you're struggling to select a name that you and your partner both agree on, this is a very simple solution and will make your new child's family very happy.

- **Con:** you might not actually like the name that's being passed down. Naming your child the 12th Thumbelina in a row might not actually hold the same attraction for you as for the generation before.

- **Con:** another drawback could be if the cultural associations with that name have changed in your lifetime and it is no longer appropriate.

One way to navigate your way around choosing a family name is to compromise. You could use the name as a middle name or refer to your baby by a nickname instead. You could also suggest using a name from the other parent's family: if the name comes from your side, try finding one you like from the other side. If their argument is for tradition then this is an astonishingly effective counter-argument.

> Spend a lot of time on social media? How about doing what one British family did in 2012 and naming your baby 'Hashtag'? Or you could just copy the Egyptian baby called 'Facebook'. Steer clear of Pinterest though, as that would sound awful being shouted out in the supermarket.

Whatever you decide to do with regard to using family names, just remember that this is your baby. Just as your parents got to decide what they named you, you get to decide this. If family and friends are disappointed, don't be alarmed. Once the baby is here, all they will see is how much she has her grandmother's nose or he has his grandfather's ears, and the name will become far less important.

Top 10 boys' names in 1916 and 1996

1916	1996
I. John	1. Jack
2. William	2. Daniel
3. James	3. Thomas
4. Robert	4. James
5. Joseph	5. Joshua
6. Charles	6. Matthew
7. George	7. Ryan
8. Edward	8. Joseph
9. Frank	9. Samuel
10. Thomas	10. Liam

Top 10 girls' names in 1916 and 1996

1916	1996
1. Mary	1. Sophie
2. Helen	2. Chloe
3. Dorothy	3. Jessica
4. Margaret	4. Emily
5. Ruth	5. Lauren
6. Mildred	6. Hannah
7. Anna	7. Charlotte
8. Elizabeth	8. Rebecca
9. Frances	9. Amy
10. Virginia	10. Megan

Spellings and pronunciation

Once you've finally agreed upon a name, it's time to think about how you wish it to be spelt and pronounced. Some parents love experimenting with unusual variations of traditional names, while others prefer names to be instantly recognisable. The only advice here is to use caution in your experiments. There are many hilarious tales of parents seeing or hearing what they think are pretty names in the hospital during delivery and choosing them for their children, only to find out later that they are medical terms and therefore completely inappropriate.

Medical terms used as names

The following list was provided by a practising midwife who has vivid recollections of parents thinking they were naming their children something unique and original, only to be told that the name they'd chosen was in fact a medical term.

Chlamydia (pronounced cler-mid-EE-ya)
Eczema (pronounced ex-SEE-mah)
Female (pronounced fuh-MAH-lee)
Latrine (pronounced lah-TREE-nee)
Meconium (pronounced meh-COH-nee-um)
Syphilis (pronounced see-PHIL-iss)
Testicles (pronounced TESS-tee-clees)
Urine (pronounced yer-REE-nee)
Vagina (pronounced vaj-EE-nah)

Obviously, the examples above are a little extreme, but the choices you make regarding spelling and pronunciation are really important. And, as we have seen a growing trend in parents coming up with their own spellings, it's even more important that you take note if you are thinking of doing that too!

Try to avoid making a common name too long or too unusual in its spelling, as this will be the first thing your child learns how to write. They will also be subjected to constant corrections during their lifetime, as other people misspell or mispronounce their name in ever more frustrating patterns. Also, make sure that the name isn't so long that it won't fit on forms or name badges, as they'll simply stop using it

Britain has seen an increase in 'text' language spellings

An	Jaicub
Camron	Jayk
Conna	Lora
Ema	Patryk
Esta	Samiul
Flicity	Summa
Helin	Wilym

and take on a nickname instead. Substituting the odd 'i' for a 'y' isn't too bad, but turning the name Jonathan into Jonnaythanne doesn't do anyone any favours.

> Pronunciation matters: a Swedish couple were once banned from naming their child 'Brfxxccxxmnpcccclllmmnprxvclmnckssqlbbllll6', which they claimed was pronounced 'Albin'.

Middle names

Giving your child a middle name is pretty standard practice these days. In fact, it has become fairly uncommon not to do so, although the use of second and third names only became popular around the turn of the twentieth century. Before then, giving a child a middle name was seen as a status symbol; it was only really used when a man married a higher-class woman and they wanted to keep the woman's maiden name as a reminder of that child's heritage. Once the fashion caught on, it became very popular to give more than one middle name to children of status, but it's only been since the 1900s that it became standard for everyone.

Regardless of your status, a middle name can have just as much of an impact as a forename so your choice for your baby should be made as carefully as the one for their first name. After all, a recent study by the website Netmums.com found that three quarters of parents chose a single middle name for the baby, and one in six parents chose two or more.

> Sweden has a pretty strict naming law, enacted in 1982, which says: 'First names shall not be approved if they can cause offence or can be supposed to cause discomfort for the one using it, or names which for some obvious reason are not suitable as a first name.' However, they did recently approve the use of 'Google' as a middle name.

You may have already decided what middle name to give your child due to tradition or culture, in which case the following advice may be moot.

In Spanish cultures, for example, middle names are often the mother's surname or other name to promote the matriarchal lineage. Similarly, parents who have not taken each other's surnames or are not married may choose to give their child one surname as a middle name and one as a last name so that both parents are represented. However, be aware that doing either of these things can create some strange name combinations, as Richard Tiffany Gere, Billie Paul Piper and Courtney Bass Cox can testify. Other traditions may use an old family name, passed down to each first-born son or daughter, to encourage a sense of family pride and history. A decision about what middle name to pass on may have therefore already been made for you, even before your own birth.

Unique middle names are very much in vogue right now with celebrities, who are also using both the first and middle names all the time. Little Sienna-Rae (Lucy-Jo Hudson and Alan Halsall's daughter) has a hyphenated first and middle name, and Mason Mac (Ashley Taylor Dawson and Karen McKay's son) is also known by his full first and middle name combination.

Of course, there are always the stars who take trends and just run with them, using not only something wacky but also multiple names when one will do; ex-glamour model Holly Madison did that with her daughter: Rainbow Aurora. Holly defended her choice at the time, publicly saying:

> There are a lot of smug haters out there who bag on my choice of a name, but I don't care about what they think. I want my daughter to be proud of who she is and learn to speak up and stand up for herself at a young age.

If you are choosing a middle name, there are some common trends for 2016 to help you narrow it down.

- **Names from the family tree.** Honouring your ancestors is a very popular trend for 2016. Parents are frequently looking back to their own lineage for interesting, unusual or influential names.

- **Opposite-length names.** It has become pretty standard to give a child either a long forename and short middle name or a short forename and long middle name. If this idea attracts you, consider using syllables to give you an idea of length and combinations. Generally, if the forename has only one or two syllables (Owen, Steven, Yasmin, Zoe) then the middle name should have two, three or even four syllables (Owen Jonathan, Steven Michael, Yasmin Samantha, Zoe Jessica). If the opposite is true and the forename is three or four syllables long (Anthony, Jennifer, Nicholas, Rosemary) then the middle name may be better kept to only one or two syllables (Anthony Kevin, Jennifer Ruth, Nicholas John, Rosemary Dawn).

  The shortest baby names are only two letters long (Al, Ed, Jo, and Ty) but the longest could be any length imaginable. Popular 11-letter long names include Bartholomew, Christopher, Constantine and Maximillian.

- **Unusual names.** Along with a wider variety of first names recently, (Ruby, Lexie and Mia have all climbed the Top 20 charts over the last few years) parents are choosing more unusual middle names too. This makes sense, as a child named Bronte or Keilyn probably needs a fairly uncommon middle name to balance it out. Alternatively, as middle names are far less frequently used, this is an opportunity for parents to have an unusual name included which they wouldn't perhaps have used otherwise. If their child grows up not to like it then they have the option of only using their initial, or simply dropping it from daily use altogether.

  It is becoming increasingly common to use a parent's first name as a middle name.

As with first names, middle names can have hilarious consequences if not considered carefully. It's worth writing down your favourite combinations and saying them out loud to make sure you're not making one of these mistakes . . .

Of course, you don't have to narrow down middle name choices to just one. It is becoming increasingly common to have several middle names, particularly if parents like more than one or want to include a family name as well.

Be careful not to have too many, though, as this makes life very difficult when filling out official forms or enrolling your child in school. Most institutions only recognise one middle name and some only recognise a middle initial.

Predicted popular middle names for 2016

Boys	Girls
Adam	Anne
Christopher	Elise
David	Elizabeth
Jackson	Grace
James	Leigh
Joseph	Mae
Lee	Marie
Michael	May
Steven	Rose
Thomas	Ruth

Some famous examples of multiple middle names include British musician Brian Eno, whose full name is actually Brian Peter George St. John le Baptiste de la Salle Eno, and Canadian actor Kiefer Sutherland, who has shortened his name considerably from Kiefer William Frederick Dempsey George Rufus Sutherland. Even the Royal Family likes to give many middle names: Prince Charles's full name is Charles Philip Arthur George Mountbatten-Windsor and Prince William is William Arthur Philip Louis Mountbatten-Windsor. The newest heir to the throne, born in 2013, is of course Prince George Alexander Louis, named after King George VI and Lord Louis Mountbatten.

Many people actually choose to go by their middle name instead of their forename, so it could be seen as a safety net if you're worried that your child won't like their name. For example, Alyson Hannigan and Alexis Denisof have given their daughters, Satyana Marie and Keeva Jane, more traditional middle names as a way of counter-balancing their unusual first names, thus providing them with the option of switching to the more conventional option when they grow up.

Bizarre baby names from the US

Boys	Girls
Aero	Ace
Burger	Kaixin
Donathan	Leeloo
Espn	Monalisa
Haven'T	Rogue
Kix	Sesame
Pawk	Thinn
Rysk	Yoga
Zaniel	Zealand

Celebrities who go by middle names

Antonio Banderas (José Antonio Dominguez Banderas)
Ashton Kutcher (Christopher Ashton Kutcher)
Bob Marley (Nesta Robert Marley)
Brad Pitt (William Bradley Pitt)
Brooke Shields (Christa Brooke Camille Shields)
Dakota Fanning (Hannah Dakota Fanning)
Evangeline Lilly (Nicole Evangeline Lilly)
Hugh Laurie (James Hugh Calum Laurie)
Kelsey Grammer (Allen Kelsey Grammer)
Reese Witherspoon (Laura Jean Reese Witherspoon)
Rihanna (Robyn Rihanna Fenty)
Will Ferrell (John William Ferrell)

Long, longer and longest

How about trying to beat the record for the world's longest name? The Glastonbury teenager named Captain Fantastic Faster Than Superman Spiderman Batman Wolverine Hulk And The Flash Combined changed his name from George Garratt in 2008. At the time, he claimed to have the longest name in the world, replacing Texan woman Rhoshandiatellyneshiaunneveshenk Koyaanisquatsiuth Williams, whose 57-letter-long name paled in comparison to Captain's 81 letters. However, a woman from Hartlepool beat both these records in 2012, when she changed her name by Legal Deed Poll from Dawn McManus to Red Dreams (to raise money for her charity of the same name, set up after the death of her son) with no fewer than 159 middle names including Wacky, Strange, Lunar, Sheep and Coalition!

Perhaps the longest celeb baby name for a while: Uma Thurman's daughter, Rosalind Arusha Arkadina Altalune Florence Thurman-Busson, was born in July 2012.

Initials

What surname will your baby have? Does its first letter lend itself easily to amusing acronyms already? And would choosing certain forenames only exacerbate the problem?

If your child will inherit a double-barrelled surname this becomes a bigger consideration still, as there are more amusing four-letter words than there are three-letter ones. My brother-in-law was going to be called Andrew Steven Schmitt before he was born, until his parents realised at the last minute what his initials would spell. . .

The website Name of The Year pronounced a Chesterfield footballer as the winner of its annual competition last year: Shamus Beaglehole. He beat Chillie Poon, Loki Skylizard and Wubbo Ockels to win the top spot.

It's worth taking the time to think about the acronyms formed by initials in the real world too, such as how names are displayed on credit cards or imagining your child's name written out on a form. Nobody should have to go through life known as S. Lugg because their parents didn't think that far ahead.

Amusing acronyms of real people

David Vernon Durante – DVD
George Barry Holmes – GBH
Jake Clive Baxter – JCB
Neil Christopher Parker – NCP (the car park)
Patricia Mary Simpson – PMS
Sally Theresa Donaghue – STD
Samuel Alan Spencer – SAS
Victoria Helen Smith – VHS

Across the UK, there are people whose initials spell out three-letter words – from RAT and FAG to FAB or POP – and some are better than others, so do check!

Your surname

Tied to your child's potential new initials is their new surname. Whether they are receiving their name from their mother, father or a hyphenated combination of both, matching an appropriate first name to their surname is an important undertaking. In order to prevent a lifetime of embarrassment for your baby, try to avoid forenames that might lead to unfortunate outcomes when combined with certain surnames. The best way to work out whether this might happen is to write down all the names you like alongside your child's last name and have someone else read them out loud. This second pair of eyes and ears might just spot something that you didn't.

The age of the internet has given parents a wonderful new weapon in their baby-naming arsenal: the search engine. Before you settle on anything final, try searching for any examples of the complete first name, middle name and surname of your new baby. You may find out that your baby has an axe-murderer namesake or, like one of my colleagues, the same name as a well-known porn star.

There is also the danger of your child being subjected to having a spoonerism made out of their name, where the first letters or syllables get swapped around to form new words. Named after the Reverend Dr William Archibald Spooner (1844–1930), a spoon-erism can be created out of almost anything to make clever, amusing or downright inappropriate phrases instead. An unfortunate and recent example of this would be Angelina Jolie and Brad Pitt's daughter Shiloh, whom they named Shiloh Jolie-Pitt to avoid the inevitable Shiloh Pitt spoonerism. Try to avoid making the same mistake!

Unfortunate first name/surname combinations

Anna Sasin	Jenny Taylor
Barb Dwyer	Justin Time
Barry Code	Mary Christmas
Ben Dover	Oliver Sutton
Duane Pipe	Paige Turner
Grace Land	Russell Sprout
Harry Rump	Stan Still
Hazel Nutt	Teresa Green

Popular names in South Africa

Boys	Girls
Abrahem	Abri
Baruti	Dikeledi
Dingane	Jacoline
Fenyang	Kagiso
Lefu	Limpho
Letsego	Mosa
Moswen	Nobanzi
Nku	Nomuula
Tau	Siphiwe
Uuka	Tale

German law prohibits invented and androgynous names but the UK has some of the most liberal rules on naming a baby in the world, with only names which are deemed to be offensive making it onto the banned list.

Naming twins, triplets, and more

If you have discovered you are expecting multiples, congratulations! Naming multiples needn't be any different to naming a single child . . . unless you want it to be. You could stick to the same process as everyone else by picking a unique name for each child. 'Octomom' Nadya Suleman chose eight different names for her octuplets, although they do all sound reasonably similar: Isaiah, Jeremiah, Jonah, Josiah, Maliah, McCai, Nariah, and Noah.

The UK's first surviving sextuplets were the Walton family. Born in 1983, they were also the world's first all-female set. Their parents chose the names Hannah, Luci, Ruth, Sarah, Kate, and Jennie.

In 2014 the Fugate family had a surprise arrival: during a c-section for premature triplets, Kimberly Fugate was told 'more feet' by her doctor, and out popped a fourth baby! Kimberly and husband Craig are now the proud parents of identical quadruplet girls, called Kenleigh Rosa, Kristen Sue, Kayleigh Pearl, and Kelsey Roxanne, who join big sister Katelyn.

Some parents do like to use a theme, such as going down the alphabet (think Alastair, Benjamin, Christopher and David) or doing what the famous Phoenix acting clan did and giving each child a name to do with nature: River, Rain, Joaquin (Leaf), Liberty, and Summer. X-Men actress Rebecca Romijn did a similar theme with her twin daughters, giving them individual first names but flower-themed middles names: Dolly Rebecca Rose and Charlie Tamara Tulip.

A Texan woman gave birth to two sets of identical twin boys on the same day in 2013. Conceived naturally, the chance of which is one in 70 million, Tress and Manuel Montalvo's miracles were named Ace, Blaine, Cash and Dylan (ABCD).

The UK's biggest family title is currently held by the Radfords, though Sue and Noel Radford have not chosen to follow a theme when naming their 18 children: from oldest to youngest they are: Chris, Sophie, Chloe, Jack, Daniel, Luke, Millie, Katie, James, Ellie, Aimee, Josh, Max, Tilly May, Oscar, and Caspar. They even have their first grandchildren, Daisy and April, and another one on the way themselves after they lost baby Alfie, born at 21 weeks, in 2014.

Mariah Carey and Nick Cannon chose to use names starting with the same letter for their twins: Monroe and Moroccan Scott, girl and boy twins. 'Scott' is the same middle name as Nick Cannon's and his grandmother's maiden name, and as Mariah Carey doesn't have a middle name, they skipped one for Monroe.

Other multiple mums and dads, however, strongly prefer to give their twins unrelated names, like the Jolie-Pitts, who went for Vivienne and Knox, giving their little ones more chance of being seen as individuals.

Naming twins can be an opportunity for parental compromise. When Spanish model Elsa Pataky and Australian actor Chris Hemsworth announced their twins' names as Tristan and Sasha, it was suggested that they had plumped for one name from each of their backgrounds.

A palindrome name is a name that is spelt the same backwards and forwards, as with Bob, Elle, Eve and Hannah.

Twin names with the same meaning

Bernard and Brian (strong)
Daphne and Laura (laurel)
Deborah and Melissa (bee)
Dorcas and Tabitha (gazelle)
Elijah and Joel (God)
Eve and Zoe (life)
Irene and Salome (peace)
Lucius and Uri (light)
Lucy and Helen (light)
Sarah and Almira (princess)

Things to avoid

There are a few things to keep in mind when naming twins or multiples, but they are at least pretty simple ones:

- Don't use very long names. You will often find yourself needing to write both names down, or calling both children down for dinner, and very long names might get so bothersome you end up not using them. Instead, use shorter versions of the names you like (such as Max for Maximilian, or Eve for Evangeline) as either their registered first name or just as a common nickname you like.

- Don't get too complicated. Again, having to remember the spellings of all the names and middle names you've given your multiples can be made a lot easier if you keep things simple. Use traditional spellings if possible, like Cameron instead of Kammeryn and Elizabeth instead of Alyzybeth.

- Don't forget that your babies are still individuals. If you use names that sound so similar you often mix them up, your children may get frustrated as they get older and other people confuse them. Instead, keep those nearly identical names you love as middle names, and use this opportunity to explore more individual forenames to match your babies' unique personalities.

Of course, when all is said and done, you can just stick to giving each child an entirely new name unique to them. For triplets, quads and more, this is probably an easier choice than twisting your head around three names with the same meaning or trying to create four anagrams you like for all of your babies.

Names for triplets

Aidan, Diana, and Nadia (anagrams)
Amber, Jade, and Ruby (jewels)
Amy, May, and Mya (anagrams)
Ava, Eva, and Iva (similar)
Daisy, Lily, and Rose (flowers)
Jay, Raven, and Robin (birds)
Olive, Violet, and Sage (colours)
River, Rain, and Summer (nature)

Celebrity twin names of the past few years

Dolly Rebecca Rose and Charlie Tamara Tulip (Rebecca Romijn and Jerry O'Connell)
Jett and Jax (Caprice and Ty Comfort)
John and Gus (Julie Bowen and Scott Phillips)
Matteo and Valentino (Ricky Martin and unnamed surrogate)
Monroe and Moroccan Scott (Mariah Carey and Nick Cannon)
Vivienne Marcheline and Knox Leon (Angelina Jolie and Brad Pitt)
Tristan and Sasha (Chris Hemsworth and Elsa Pataky)

Registering a baby's name

There are slightly different guidelines for registering births and names depending on where you live in the UK.

In England, Wales, and Northern Ireland a birth must be recorded within 42 days of delivery and if not done at the hospital it requires a visit to a register office.

The birth certificate will be written in English if a child is born in England or Northern Ireland, and can be in both English and Welsh if they are born in Wales.

If the birth is recorded at the hospital or registered in the same district then birth certificates are usually issued straight away but if you end up going to a different office, the certificate may be sent to you after a few days. This is important when applying for Child Benefit or registering your baby with a doctor, as you will need a copy of the short birth certificate to apply.

If the parents of a newborn are married, either parent can register a birth. However, if the parents are not married there are several ways to ensure that both names are put on the birth certificate, including both parents being physically present at the registration or one parent submitting a declaration form in lieu of their presence. If neither parent can be present then someone who was present at the birth or someone who is now responsible for the child can also carry out the duty.

After the registration, the parents or those with parental responsibility also have the option of requesting a naming ceremony. These non-religious ceremonies are conducted by local authorities and can be a nice replacement for a baptism or christening, as adults outside of the family can be nominated to act in secular roles similar to godparents. A birth certificate is also needed for this event to take place.

In Scotland, births need to be registered within 21 days and can take place in any district. As well as either married parent being allowed to register the birth, their relatives may also do this duty. The exception here is if the parents are not married. In this case the father may register the birth only if the mother is also present, a declaration form is submitted or a court agrees that he has parental responsibility just like any other adult. Parents of newborns in Scotland should take a card given to them at the hospital and a copy of their marriage certificate to the birth registration.

If you are a British national and your baby is born abroad, you will have to register the birth in that country, following the appropriate rules and regulations. You should also register it at the local British Embassy or Consulate, or with UK authorities when you are back home, in order to obtain a British birth certificate, proof that the baby is a British citizen by birth, and to have the birth registered with the UK General Register Office. Unfortunately the name you choose won't be included in the official UK statistics, but it will be part of the statistics for the country where your baby was born instead . . . which is kind of cool!

If you decide at a later stage that you want to change details on the birth certificate then there are procedures in place to help, although it is often a time-consuming process.

Useful websites for registering a birth

In England and Wales: www.gov.uk
In Northern Ireland: www.nidirect.gov.uk
In Scotland: www.gro-scotland.gov.uk

It is worth remembering that if the father's details were not recorded on the original certificate or if the natural parents have married since the registration, a new birth certificate will have to be generated. Same-sex couples can have both mothers' names on the birth certificate, but a parental order must be obtained from the courts to have both fathers' names entered.

If you are unhappy with the forename you've chosen or it has been spelt incorrectly, you can change the birth record providing you have other documentation to prove this is the case. A passport or baptismal certificate is sufficient, as they will show the correct spelling or commonly used forename and should be presented to the register office where the initial application was made.

Changing the surname of your baby is only possible in two cases: either when the spelling is incorrect or if the details of the parents are being changed (such as the inclusion of the father or the parents now being married). A fee is usually incurred if a new certificate is required.

Keep in mind how difficult it may be for you to change your child's birth certificate at a later stage if you are in any way unsure about the choice you're about to make. However, also remember that if something unexpected happens and you need to make the change, it is possible.

part two

Boys' Names

Boys' names

Aaron

Hebrew, meaning 'mountain of strength'. In the Bible, Aaron was the older brother of Moses and the first high priest of Israel.

Abasi

Egyptian Arabic, meaning 'male'; Swahili, meaning 'stern'.

Abdiel

Hebrew, meaning 'servant of God'. Also the name of an important seraph in Milton's *Paradise Lost*.

Abdul

Arabic, meaning 'servant'. Often followed by a suffix indicating who Abdul is the servant of (e.g. Abdul-Basit, 'servant of the creator').

Abdullah

Arabic, meaning 'servant of God'.

Abel

Hebrew, meaning 'breath' or 'breathing spirit'. Associated with the biblical son of Adam and Eve, who was killed by his brother Cain.

Abelard

German, meaning 'resolute'.

Aberforth

Gaelic, meaning 'mouth of the river Forth'. The name of Dumbledore's younger brother in J.K. Rowling's 'Harry Potter' series.

Abhik
(alt. Abheek)

Sanskrit, meaning 'fearless'. Popular name for boys in India.

Abhishek

Sanskrit, meaning 'bath for a deity' or 'anointing'. Abhishek Bachchan is currently one of Bollywood's highest-paid and most popular actors.

Abner

Hebrew, meaning 'father of light'. Abner was the commander of Saul's army in the Bible.

Abraham

(alt. Abram; abbrev. Abe)

Hebrew, meaning 'father of the multitude'. Famous Abrahams include President Abraham Lincoln and Abraham Van Helsing – the vampire hunter and doctor in Bram Stoker's *Dracula*.

Absalom

(alt. Absalon)

Hebrew, meaning 'father/leader of peace'. The name of King David's favourite son in the Bible, and one of Chaucer's curly-haired characters in *The Canterbury Tales*.

Acacio

Greek, meaning 'thorny tree' or 'honourable'. Now widely used in Spain.

Ace

Latin, meaning 'unit'. Also used in English to mean 'number one' or 'the best'.

Achilles

Greek, mythological hero of the Trojan war, whose heel was his only weak spot.

Achim

Hebrew, meaning 'God will establish' or Polish, meaning 'the Lord exalts'. Also a shortened version of the name 'Joachim' in Germany.

Ackerley

Old English, meaning 'oak meadow'.

Adam

Hebrew, meaning 'man' or 'earth'. Found in the Bible, where the creation story names Adam as the first man on earth.

Adão

Portuguese variant of Adam, meaning 'earth'.

Addison

Old English, meaning 'son of Adam'. Also used as a female name in the USA.

Ade

Yoruba, meaning 'peak' or 'royal'. Ade is a common name in Nigeria.

Adelard

French or German, meaning 'brave' or 'noble'. A popular name in the nineteenth century for Canadian boys.

Adelbert

(alt. Adalberto)

Old German form of Albert. Popularity decreased in the nineteenth century, when Albert became more commonly used.

Adetokunbo

Yoruba, meaning 'the crown came from over the sea'.

Adin

Hebrew, meaning 'slender' or 'voluptuous'. Also Swahili, meaning 'ornamental'.

Aditya

Sanskrit, meaning 'belonging to the sun'. In Hindi, Aditya means 'sun god'. Aditya refers to the offspring of Aditi, the mother of the Gods.

Adlai

Hebrew, meaning 'God is just', or sometimes 'ornamental'.

Adler

Old German, meaning 'eagle'.

Adley

English, meaning 'son of Adam'.

Admon

Hebrew, variant of Adam meaning 'earth'. Also the name of a red peony.

Adolph
(alt. Adolf)

Old German, meaning 'noble majestic wolf'. Once popular, before World War II, this name has now become deeply unpopular due to its association with Adolf Hitler, and several European nations have actually banned its use.

Adonis

Phoenician, meaning 'Lord'. Adonis was the god of beauty and desire in Greek mythology.

Adrian

Latin, meaning 'from Hadria', a town in northern Italy.

Adriel

Hebrew, meaning 'of God's flock'. Adriel was one of Saul's sons-in-law in the Bible.

Adyn
(alt. Ade)

Irish, meaning 'manly'. Also the name of a UK men's streetwear company (presumably because of its meaning)

Aeneas

Greek/Latin, meaning 'to praise'. Name of the hero who founded Rome in Virgil's *Aeneid*.

Aero

Greek, meaning 'air'.

Aeson
(alt. Aesion)

Greek, father of Jason in ancient Greek mythology.

Afonso

Portuguese, meaning 'eager noble warrior'.

Agamemnon

Greek, meaning 'leader of the assembly'. Figure in mythology, commanded the Greeks at the siege of Troy.

Agathon

Greek, meaning 'good' or 'superior'. The name of a tragic poet in ancient Greece.

Agustin

Latin/Spanish, meaning 'venerated'.

Ahab

Hebrew, meaning 'father's brother'. Name of the obsessed captain in *Moby-Dick*.

Ahijah

Hebrew, meaning 'brother of God' or 'friend of God'.

Ahmad

(alt. Ahmed)

Arabic/Turkish, meaning 'worthy of praise'. Ahmad is also one of the prophet Muhammad's many given names.

Aidan

(alt. Aiden, Aodhán)

Gaelic, meaning 'little fire'. Derives from Aodh, which is the name of a Celtic sun god.

Aidric

Old English, meaning 'oaken'. St Aidric was a bishop and court diplomat in the ninth century.

Ainsley

Old English, meaning 'meadow' or 'clearing'. Also a girls' name. Ainsley Harriott is a well-known TV chef.

Airyck

Old Norse, from Eric, meaning 'eternal ruler'.

Ajani

Nigerian, meaning 'he fights for what he is'. Also Sanskrit, meaning 'of noble birth'.

Ajax

Greek, meaning 'mourner of the Earth'. A Greek hero from the siege of Troy.

Ajay

Hindi, meaning 'unconquerable'. One of the most popular names in India.

Ajit

Sanskrit, meaning 'invincible'. Alternative name for both Shiva and Vishnu in Hindu mythology.

Akeem

Arabic, meaning 'wise or insightful'. Popular name throughout Africa, particularly in Nigeria.

Akio

Japanese, meaning 'bright man'. Akio Morita was one of the co-founders of the electronics company Sony.

Akira

Japanese, meaning 'intelligent'. Name of a hugely influential animated Japanese film.

Akiva

Hebrew, meaning 'to protect' or 'to shelter'.

Akon

American, meaning 'flower'. Made popular by the rapper.

Aksel

Danish, meaning 'father of peace'. Its name day is 23 March, and babies with this name are sometimes celebrated in Nordic countries on this day.

Aladdin

Arabic, meaning 'servant of Allah'. From the medieval story in the *Arabian Nights*.

Alan

(alt. Allan, Allen, Allyn, Alun)

Gaelic or old French, meaning 'rock'. Alan is one of the oldest names still in popular use in the UK, and its roots can be traced back to the Norman invasion in the eleventh century.

Alaric

(alt. Aleric)

Old German, meaning 'noble regal ruler'. King Alaric I of the Visigoths played a key role in the downfall of the Roman Empire.

Alastair

(alt. Alasdair, Alastor, Alistair, Allister; abbrev. Ali, Allie)

Greek/Gaelic, meaning 'defending men'. Famous Alastairs include comedian and TV presenter Alistair McGowan, English cricketer Alastair Cook and Ali G, whose 'real name' is Alistair.

Alban

Latin, meaning 'from Alba'. Also the name of St Alban, the first British Christian martyr.

Alberic

Germanic, meaning 'Elfin king'.

Albert

(abbrev. Bert, Bertie))

Old German, meaning 'noble, bright, famous'. Probably most commonly associated with Prince Albert, Queen Victoria's husband, who died in 1861.

Albin

Latin, variant of Albus, meaning 'white'. Popular in some areas including Scandinavia, Slovenia, Germany and Poland.

Albus

Latin, meaning 'white'. Made famous by Albus Dumbledore, the headmaster of Hogwarts in J.K. Rowling's 'Harry Potter' series.

Alcaeus

Greek, meaning 'strength'. Alcaeus of Mytilene was an influential ancient Greek poet.

Alden

Old English, meaning 'old friend'. More commonly used as a given name in the USA.

Aldis

English, meaning 'battle-seasoned'.

Aldo
(alt. Aldous)
Latin, meaning 'the tall one'. Aldo is the main gorilla character in the *Planet of the Apes* movie series.

Aldric
English, meaning 'old king'.

Aled
Welsh, meaning 'child' or 'offspring'. Aled Jones is a Welsh singer and TV presenter, who shot to fame as a choirboy for *Walking in the Air*.

Aleph
(alt. Alef)
Hebrew, meaning 'first letter of the alphabet', or 'leader'.

Aleron
(alt. Aileron, Alerun, Ailerun, Alejandro)
Latin, meaning 'child with wings'.

Alessio
(alt. Alejo)
Italian, meaning 'defender'.

Alexander
(alt. Alexandro, Alessandro, Alejandro; abbrev. Alec, Alex, Alexei, Sandy, Xander)
Greek, meaning 'defender of mankind'. Alexander the Great was an undefeated fourth-century king whose empire stretched from Greece to modern Pakistan. Alec Baldwin is an Oscar and Emmy-nominated actor. Sir Alec Guiness is the renowned actor whose illustrious career took him from Shakespeare on stage to Hollywood blockbusters.

Alfonso
Germanic/Spanish, meaning 'noble and prompt, ready to struggle'. Associated with *Gravity* director Alfonso Cuarón Orozco, and actor Alfonso Ribeiro.

Alford
Old English, meaning 'old river/ford'.

Alfred
(abbrev. Alf, Alfie)
English, meaning 'elf' or 'magical counsel'. Alfred the Great was a ninth-century king of England who defended the Anglo-Saxons against Viking invasion. *Alfie* is the name of a successful 1966 British film starring actor Michael Caine.

Algernon
French, meaning 'with a moustache'. A popular name among the nobility in eighteenth- and nineteenth-century England.

Alois
German, meaning 'famous warrior'.

Alok
Sanskrit, meaning 'cry of triumph'. Also the name of a style of singing in Javanese gamelan.

Alon
Hebrew, meaning 'oak tree'.

Alonso
(alt. Alonzo)
Germanic, meaning 'noble and ready'.

Aloysius

Old German, meaning 'fame and war'. Also the name of an Italian saint.

Alpha

First letter of the Greek alphabet.

Alphaeus

Hebrew, meaning 'changing'. Alphaeus is mentioned in the Bible as being the father of two of the twelve Apostles, Matthew and James.

Alpin

Gaelic, meaning 'related to the Alps'. The House of Alpin refers to a dynasty of Scottish kings.

Altair

Arabic, meaning 'flying' or 'bird'. Altair is one of the brightest stars seen in the night sky from Earth.

Alter
(alt. Altar)

Yiddish, meaning 'old man'.

Alton

Old English, meaning 'old town'.

Alva

Latin, meaning 'white'. Used more commonly for girls than boys.

Alvin
(alt. Alvie)

English, meaning 'friend of elves'. Alvin and the Chipmunks are a cartoon singing group, first created in 1958 and still making films today.

Alwyn

Welsh, meaning 'wise friend'. May also come from the River Alwen in Wales.

Amachi

African, meaning 'who knows what God has brought us through this child'. Used for both boys and girls.

Amadeus

Latin, meaning 'God's love'. One of the given names of the composer Wolfgang Amadeus Mozart.

Amadi

Igbo, meaning 'appeared destined to die at birth'. Often given to babies who unexpectedly survive against the odds.

Amado

Spanish, meaning 'God's love'.

Amador

Spanish, meaning 'one who loves'.

Amari

Hebrew, meaning 'given by God'. Can be a boys' or girls' name.

Amarion

Arabic, meaning 'populous, flushing'. Made popular by the R&B singer Omarion.

Amasa

Hebrew, meaning 'burden'.

Ambrose

Greek, meaning 'undying, immortal'.

Americo

Germanic, meaning 'ever powerful in battle'. Popular in the nineteenth century, now this is an infrequently used baby name.

Amias
(alt. Amyas)
Latin, meaning 'loved'.

Amil

Sanskrit, meaning 'unavailable'. Popular name for boys in India.

Amir
(alt. Emir)

Arabic, meaning 'chieftain' or 'commander'. Emir or Amir is a title for a high-ranking Sheikh, used in many Muslim communities.

Amit

Hindi, meaning 'infinite'. One of the 108 names for the Hindu God Shri Ganesha.

Ammon

Hebrew, meaning 'the hidden one'. The Ammonites were an ancient tribe of people mentioned in the Bible.

Amory

German/English, meaning 'work' and 'power'. Its popularity has waned since the nineteenth century, when it was a common name.

Amos

Hebrew, meaning 'encumbered' or 'burdened'. St Amos wrote the Book of Amos in the eighth century, which is part of the Hebrew Bible.

Anacletus

Latin, meaning 'called back' or 'invoked'. Pope Anacletus was the third pope in history, and served during the first century.

Anakin

American, meaning 'warrior'. Made famous by Anakin Skywalker in the *Star Wars* films.

Ananias

Greek/Italian, meaning 'answered by the Lord'. Ananias Dare was the first baby born to English parents in North America, making him the first-ever 'modern' American.

Anastasius
(alt. Anastasios)

Greek, meaning 'resurrection'. Popular name for popes, emperors, and saints – there are nearly 20 St Anastasiuses on record.

Anatole
(alt. Anatolius)

French, meaning 'sunrise'. Monsieur Anatole was an influential nineteenth-century French composer, master, and ballet dancer.

Anders

Scandinavian, meaning 'lion man'. Currently the fourth most popular name for boys in Sweden.

Anderson

English, meaning 'male'.

Andrew
(alt. Andreas)

Greek, meaning 'man' or 'warrior'. One of the Top 10 names for baby boys during the 1980s and 1990s.

Androcles

Greek, meaning 'glory of a warrior'. *Androcles and the Lion* was a well-known folktale of the second century, made famous in the twentieth century by George Bernard Shaw's play of the same title.

Angel
(alt. Angelo)

Greek, meaning 'messenger'. Angels appear throughout the Bible and modern culture, and the name Angel is often used in Spanish-speaking cultures as a name for both boys and girls.

Angus

Gaelic, meaning 'one choice'. An ancient name used especially in Scotland. The name of Merida's trusty Clydesdale horse in Disney Pixar's *Brave*.

Anil

Sanskrit, meaning 'air' or 'wind'. Anil Gupta is the producer (and for some the creator) of many leading television comedies, including *Goodness Gracious Me*, *The Kumars at No. 42* and *The Office*.

Anselm

German, meaning 'helmet of God'. St Anselm was an archbishop of Canterbury and influential figure in the Christian religion.

Anson

English, meaning 'son of Agnes'. Most commonly used in the USA.

Anthony
(alt. Antony; abbrev. Ant, Tony)

English, meaning 'invaluable grace'. *Antony and Cleopatra* is a Shakespearean play depicting the romance between the Roman general Mark Antony and Queen Cleopatra of Eygpt.

Antipas

Israeli, meaning 'for all or against all'. Herod Antipas was the leader mentioned in the Bible as being responsible for the executions of John the Baptist and Jesus.

Antwan
(alt. Antoine)

Old English, meaning 'flower'. Older and more unusual spelling of Antoine.

Apollo

Greek, meaning 'to destroy'. Greek god of poetry, music and the sun.

Apostolos

Greek, meaning 'apostle'. The Apostolos book is a text believed to have been written by one of the twelve disciples of Jesus.

Ara

Arabic, meaning 'brings rain'.

Aragorn

Literary, a character in J.R.R. Tolkien's *The Lord of the Rings* trilogy.

Aram

Hebrew, meaning 'royal highness'. Aram is an ancient region in modern-day Syria, mentioned in the Bible.

Aramis

Latin, meaning 'swordsman'. Aramis is one of the three musketeers in Alexandre Dumas's eponymous novel.

Arcadio

Greek/Spanish, from a place in ancient Greece. The word 'Arcadia' (meaning paradise) comes from this.

Archibald
(abbrev. Archie)

Old German, meaning 'genuine, bold, brave'. A popular name in Scotland.

Ardell

Latin, meaning 'eager, burning with enthusiasm'.

Arden

Celtic, meaning 'high'. A very early English motor car.

Ares

Greek, meaning 'ruin'. Son of Zeus and Hera, and the Greek god of war.

Ari

Hebrew, meaning 'lion' or 'eagle'. Can also be used in Hebrew to refer to an important or honourable man.

Arias

Germanic, meaning 'lion'.

Aric

English, meaning 'merciful ruler'. Alternative spelling of Eric.

Ariel

Hebrew, meaning 'lion of God'. One of the archangels, the angel of healing and new beginnings.

Arild

Old Norse, meaning 'battle commander'. Arild Andersen is an internationally popular Norwegian jazz musician.

Aris

Greek, meaning 'best figure'. Popular name in both ancient and modern Greece.

Ariston

Greek, meaning 'the best'. Ariston of Athens was the philosopher Plato's father.

Aristotle

Greek, meaning 'best'. Also an ancient Greek philosopher.

Arjun

Sanskrit, meaning 'bright and shining'. Name is derived from Arjuna, an ancient and legendary archer.

Arkady

Greek, a region of central Greece. Popular name for boys throughout Eastern Europe.

Arlan

Gaelic, meaning 'pledge' or 'oath'.

Arlie

Old English place name, meaning 'eagle wood'. Sometimes used as a shortened form of Arlan.

Arliss
(alt. Arlis)

Hebrew, meaning 'pledge'.

Arlo

Spanish, meaning 'barberry tree'. Can also be linked back to the Old Norse world for 'army of troops'.

Armand

Old German, meaning 'soldier'. Armand van Helden is a top American DJ and producer of electronic house music.

Armani

Same origin as Armand, meaning 'soldier'. Also the name of an Italian fashion house after designer Georgio Armani.

Arnaldo

Spanish, meaning 'eagle power'.

Arnav

Hindi, meaning 'the sea'. Can be pronounced as 'Arnav' or 'Arnaf'.

Arnold
(abbrev. Arnie)

Old German, meaning 'eagle ruler'. Also the name of actor, former bodybuilder and US politician Arnold Schwarzenegger.

Arrow

English, from the common word denoting weaponry.

Art

Irish, name of a warrior in Irish mythology, Art Oenfer (Art the Lonely). Also a shortened form of Arthur.

Arthur
(alt. Art, Artie, Artis)

Celtic, probably from 'artos', meaning 'bear'. Made famous by the tales of King Arthur and the Knights of the Round Table.

Arvel

From the Welsh 'Arwel', meaning 'wept over'. Used frequently as a name for mythical characters – for example, Arvel Crynyd in *Star Wars*, and Arvel the Swift in *The Elder Scrolls V: Skyrim*.

Arvid

Old Norse, meaning 'eagle in the woods'. Commonly used in Scandinavia.

Arvind
(alt. Aravind)

Sanskrit, meaning 'red lotus'. May also be derived from the word for 'white lotus', upon which the Hindu goddess Lakshmi sits.

Arvo

Finnish, meaning 'value' or 'worth'. Also used as slang term for 'afternoon' in Australia.

Asa

Hebrew, meaning 'doctor' or 'healer'.

Asante

Asante, meaning 'thank you'. Also refers to the language of the Ashanti people.

Asher

Hebrew, meaning 'fortunate' or 'lucky'. One of the twelve sons of Jacob in the Bible, and one of the brothers who sells Joseph into slavery in the story of Joseph and his multi-coloured coat.

Ashley

Old English, meaning 'ash meadow'. The name of several football players, including Ashley Cole and Ashley Young.

Ashok

Sanskrit, meaning 'not causing sorrow'. Popular in India and Sri Lanka.

Ashton

English, meaning 'settlement in the ash-tree grove'. Name has been popularised due to the American actor Ashton Kutcher – although his first name is actually Christopher.

Aslan

Turkish, meaning 'lion'. Strongly associated with the lion Aslan in C.S. Lewis's *The Lion, the Witch and the Wardrobe*.

Asriel

Hebrew, meaning 'help of God'. Lord Asriel is an important character in Philip Pullman's *His Dark Materials* trilogy.

Astrophel

Latin, meaning 'star lover'. *Astrophel and Stella* is the name of a group of sonnets by Philip Sidney, written in the 1590s, and the first time the name is recorded as being used.

Athanasios

(abbrev. Thanasis, Thanos)
Greek, meaning 'eternal life'.

Atílio

Portuguese, meaning 'father'. Can also be lengthened to Attilius.

Atlas

Greek, meaning 'to carry'. In Greek mythology Atlas was a Titan forced to carry the weight of the heavens.

Atlee

Hebrew, meaning 'God is just'.

Atticus

Latin, meaning 'from Athens'. Atticus Finch is one of the main characters in Harper Lee's groundbreaking novel *To Kill A Mockingbird*.

Auberon

Old German, meaning 'royal bear'. Also the name for a fairy king. It is the French spelling for Oberon.

Aubrey

French, meaning 'elf ruler'. More popular for boys during the Middle Ages; now more usually given to girls.

Auden

Old English, meaning 'old friend'. W.H. Auden is considered to be one of the most influential 20th-century poets.

Audie

Old English, meaning 'noble strength'. Audie L. Murphy was one of the most decorated and honoured American soldiers of World War II.

Augustus
(alt. Augustas)

Latin, meaning 'venerated'. The first Roman emperor. Also a character in Roald Dahl's *Charlie and the Chocolate Factory*.

Aurelien

French, meaning 'golden'. Also the name of a Roman emperor.

Austin

Latin, meaning 'venerated'. Austin Healey played rugby union for England. Also the name of a classic car.

Avery
(alt. Avrie, Averey, Averie)

English, meaning 'wise ruler'. Can also be derived from the name Alfred, or the ancient English word for elf.

Avi

Hebrew, meaning 'father of a multitude of nations'. Name of an author of popular children's and teens' fiction.

Awnan

Irish, meaning 'little Adam'.

Axel

German and Scandinavian, a Germanised form of the Hebrew Absalom, meaning 'father is peace'. Made famous by Guns 'n' Roses front man Axl Rose.

Ayers
(alt. Ayer, Aires, Aire)

English, meaning 'heir to a fortune'.

Azarel
(alt. Azaryah)

Hebrew, meaning 'helped by God'. Also the name of an evil spirit in the Bible.

Azriel

Hebrew, meaning 'God is my help'. Name is often used to describe the angel of death in many religions, including Christianity and Judaism.

Azuko

African, meaning 'past glory'. Most commonly found in Japan.

 Boys' names

Baden

German, meaning 'battle'. Also the name of a city in Switzerland known for its hot springs.

Bailey

English, meaning 'bailiff'.

Baird

Scottish, meaning 'poet' or 'one who sings ballads'. John Logie Baird was a Scottish engineer credited with inventing the world's first working television.

Bakari

Swahili, meaning 'hope' or 'promise'.

Baker

English, from the word 'baker'.

Baldwin

Old French, meaning 'bold, brave friend'. The Baldwin family is a well-known acting dynasty in Hollywood, with brothers Alec, Stephen, William, and Daniel.

Balin

Old English. Balin was one of the Knights of the Round Table.

Balthazar

Babylonian, meaning 'protect the King'. A name commonly attributed to one of the Three Wise Men in the Christian Nativity story.

Balwinder
(alt. Balvinder)

Hindi, meaning 'merciful, compassionate'. Balwinder Singh Sandhu is a well-known former Indian Test cricketer.

Bannon

Irish, meaning 'descendant of O'Banain'. Also a river in Wales.

Barack

African, meaning 'blessed'. Made popular by US President Barack Obama.

Barclay

Old English, meaning 'birch tree meadow'.

Barker

Old English, meaning 'shepherd'.

Barnaby
(abbrev. Barney)

Greek, meaning 'son of consolation'. *Barnaby Rudge* is one of Charles Dickens's novels.

Barnard

English, meaning 'strong as a bear'.

Baron
(alt. Barron)

Old English, meaning 'young warrior'. Baron is a title given to men of nobility.

Barrett

English, meaning 'strong as a bear'.

Barry
(abbrev. Baz)

Irish Gaelic, meaning 'fair haired'. Famous Barrys include Barry Humphries, best known as the comedian behind Dame Edna Everage. Also Baz Luhrmann, the Australian film director.

Bartholomew
(abbrev. Bart)

Hebrew, meaning 'son of the farmer'. The name of one of Jesus' apostles. Bart is the name of the eldest child of the cartoon family the Simpsons.

Barton

Old English, meaning 'barley settlement'. One of the more popular names of towns in England, with at least 25 on record.

Baruch

Hebrew, meaning 'blessed'. Also a term for a Jewish blessing.

Barzillai

Hebrew, meaning 'made of iron'. A minor character in the Bible, Barzillai supposedly teaches youngsters not to be afraid of old age.

Bashir

Arabic, meaning 'well educated' and 'wise'.

Basil

Greek, meaning 'royal, kingly'. Basil is the lead character in the TV comedy *Fawlty Towers*. Also the name of a herb.

Basim

Arabic, meaning 'smile'.

Bastien

Greek, meaning 'revered'. Bastien Pagez was one of the most important servants to Mary, Queen of Scots.

Baxter

Old English, meaning 'baker'.

Bay

From the bay tree or the indentation in the coastline. Also a girls' name.

Bayard

French, meaning 'auburn haired'. Bayard Rustin was one of Martin Luther King Jr's mentors and advisors during the American Civil Rights movement.

Bayo
(alt. Baio)

Nigerian, meaning 'to find joy'.

Bayre

American, meaning 'beautiful'.

Beau

French, meaning 'handsome'. Beau Bridges is an American actor. Beau Brummell was a fashionable figure in Regency England and friend of the future King George IV. Beau was not the given name of either man, but an adopted name.

Beck

Old Norse, meaning 'stream'.

Beckett

Old English, meaning 'beehive' or 'bee cottage'. Associated with the Irish writer Samuel Beckett.

Beckham

English, meaning 'homestead by the stream'. Made famous by David and Victoria Beckham.

Béla

Hungarian, meaning 'within'. Famously associated with the actor Bela Lugosi, now more commonly used for girls, particularly after the success of the character Bella from the *Twilight* series.

Belarius

Shakespearean, meaning 'a banished lord'. From Shakespeare's play *Cymbeline*.

Benedict
(abbrev. Ben)

Latin, meaning 'blessed'. Benedict Cumberbatch is currently enjoying mega stardom thanks to his role in *Sherlock*. Ben Ainslie is the most successful Olympic sailor ever.

Benicio

Spanish, meaning 'benevolent'. Benicio del Toro is an Oscar-winning actor from Puerto Rico.

Benjamin
(abbrev. Ben, Benjie, Benny)

Hebrew, meaning 'son of the south'. Benjamin Franklin, American inventor and discoverer of electricity was one of the Founding Fathers of the United States. Ben Affleck, actor, and Ben Fogle, adventurer and TV personality, are both Benjamins.

Bennett

French/Latin vernacular form of Benedict, meaning 'blessed'.

Benoit

French form of Benedict, meaning 'blessed'.

Benson

English, meaning 'son of Ben'. Also linked to the village of Benson in Oxfordshire.

Bentley

Old English, meaning 'bent grass meadow'. Usually associated with the British luxury car company.

Benton

Old English, meaning 'town in the bent grass'. Derived from the towns of Long Benton and Little Benton in Northumberland.

Beriah

Hebrew, meaning 'in fellowship' or 'in envy'. Beriah was a son of Asher in the Bible.

Bernard
(abbrev. Bernie)

Germanic, meaning 'strong, brave bear'.

Berry

Old English, meaning 'berry'.

Berton

Old English, meaning 'bright settlement'. Guitartist Berton Averre was part of the band The Knack, known for its hit 'My Sharona'.

Bertrand
(alt. Bertram; abbrev. Bert, Bertie)

Old English, meaning 'illustrious'. Bertrand Russell was a British philosopher and social critic. Bertram (Bertie) Wooster was one of P.G. Wodehouse's most beloved characters. Bert is also a shortened form of Albert.

Bevan

Welsh, meaning 'son of Evan'.

Bilal

Arabic, meaning 'wetting, refreshing'. Popular in many Muslim communities.

Bill
(alt. Billy)

English, from William, meaning 'strong protector'.

Birch

Old English, meaning 'bright' or 'shining'. Also a type of tree.

Birger

Norwegian, meaning 'rescue'.

Bishop

Old English, meaning 'bishop'.

Bjorn

Old Norse, meaning 'bear'. Bjorn Ulvaeus was one of the founding members of Swedish pop supergroup ABBA, and is still a prolific songwriter with partner Benny Andersson.

Blaine

Irish Gaelic, meaning 'yellow'. Blaine Anderson is a fictional character from TV hit comedy *Glee*.

Blair

Scottish Gaelic, meaning 'plain'. Can be used as a boys' or a girls' name.

Blaise

French, meaning 'lisp' or 'stutter'. St Blaise was an Armenian bishop who was beaten and beheaded for his faith. Also commonly used as a girls' name.

Blake

Old English, meaning 'dark, black'.

Blas

(alt. Blaze)

German, meaning 'firebrand'. Also a mountain in the Alps.

Bo

Scandinavian, short form of Robert, meaning 'bright fame'. Rock and roll pioneer and musician Ellas Otha Bates was known by his stage name Bo Diddly.

Boaz

Hebrew, meaning 'swiftness' or 'strength'. A character in the Bible, found in the Book of Ruth.

Bob

(alt. Bobby)

Old German, from Robert, meaning 'bright fame'.

Boden

(alt. Bodie)

Scandinavian, meaning 'shelter'. In some translations Boden also means 'messenger'.

Bogumil

Slavic, meaning 'God's favour'. Usually associated with Bogomil Cove in the Shetland Islands.

Bolívar

Spanish, meaning 'the bank of the river'. Simón Bolívar was a leader in Latin America's struggle for independence from Spain. The bolívar is the currency of Venezuela.

Bond

Old English, meaning 'peasant farmer'. Usually associated with novel and film character James Bond.

Boris

Slavic, meaning 'battle glory'. London's current mayor is Boris Johnson.

Bosten

English, meaning 'town by the woods'.

Botolf

English, meaning 'wolf'. St Botwulf of Thorney is the patron saint of travellers and farming.

Bowen

Welsh, meaning 'son of Owen'. The Bowen knot is a common heraldic symbol, and looks like a square with loops at each corner.

Boyd

Scottish Gaelic, meaning 'yellow'. Famous Boyds include English historian Boyd Hilton, designer and star of *American Hot Rod* Boyd Coddington and cricketer Boyd Rankin.

Bradley

(abbrev. Brad)

Old English, meaning 'broad' or 'wide'. Brad Pitt is one of America's most famous modern actors. Sir Bradley Wiggins is the most famous modern cyclist, winner of both multiple Olympic medals and the Tour de France.

Brady

Irish, meaning 'large-chested'.

Bradyn

Gaelic, meaning 'descendant of Bradan'.

Bram

Gaelic, meaning 'raven'.

Brandon

Old English, meaning 'gorse'. Brandon Stark is a character in the TV series *Game of Thrones*.

Brandt

(alt. Brant)

Old English, meaning 'beacon'.

Brannon

Gaelic, meaning 'raven'. Brannon Braga is a TV producer.

Branson

English, meaning 'son of Brand'. Sir Richard Branson is an entrepreneur and adventurer, the founder of the Virgin Group of companies.

Braulio

Spanish, meaning 'shining'.

Brendan

Gaelic, meaning 'prince'. Actor Brendan Fraser is known for his role in the 'Mummy' film series.

Brennan

Gaelic, meaning 'teardrop'. The Brennan family are Ireland's most successful musical family, selling over 100 million records worldwide.

Brenton

English, from Brent, meaning 'hill'. Actor Brenton Thwaites is known for his role in soap opera *Home and Away*.

Brett

English, meaning 'a brewer'. Singer Brett Michaels is the lead singer of rock group Poison, known for the hit 'Every Rose Has Its Thorn'.

Brewster

(alt. Brew, Brewer)

English, meaning 'a brewer'.

Brian

(alt. Bryan, Bryant)

Gaelic, meaning 'high' or 'noble'. Famous Brians include physicist and TV star Professor Brian Cox, actor Brian Blessed and Queen guitar legend Brian May.

Brice

(alt. Bryce)

Latin, meaning 'speckled'.

Brier

French, meaning 'heather'.

Brock

Old English dialect, meaning 'badger'.

Broderick

English, meaning 'ruler'.

Brody

Gaelic, meaning both 'ditch' and 'brother'. It can be used for girls but more commonly for boys.

Brogan

Irish, meaning 'sturdy shoe'. A very old name, being mentioned in texts from the ninth century.

Bronwyn

Welsh, meaning 'white breasted'. More commonly used as a girls' name.

Brook

English, meaning 'stream'.

Brooklyn

From the name of the New York borough. Commonly associated with David and Victoria Beckham's eldest child.

Bruce

Scottish, meaning 'high' or 'noble'. Television presenter Sir Bruce Forsyth holds the Guinness World Record for the longest television career for a male entertainer.

Bruno

Germanic, meaning 'brown'. Bruno Tonioli is a judge on *Strictly Come Dancing*, and its American counterpart *Dancing With The Stars*.

Brutus

Latin, meaning 'dim-wit'. The name of Julius Caesar's assassin.

Bryant

English variant of Brian, meaning 'high' or 'noble'.

Bryden

(alt. Brydon)
Irish, meaning 'strong one'.

Bryn

Welsh, meaning 'mount' or 'hill'.

Bryson

(alt. Bryce, Brycen)
Welsh, meaning 'descendant of Brice'.

Bubba

American, meaning 'boy'. Associated with the character Bubba in *Forrest Gump*.

Buck

American, meaning 'goat' or 'deer', specifically a male deer.

Bud

(alt. Buddy)
American, meaning 'friend'.

Burdett

Middle English, meaning 'bird'.

Burgess

(alt. Burges, Burgiss, Berje)
English, meaning 'business'.

Burke

French, meaning 'fortified settlement'.

Burl

French, meaning 'knotty wood'.

Buzz

American, shortened form of Busby, meaning 'village in the thicket'. The US astronaut Buzz Aldrin was the second person to set foot on the moon.

Byron

Old English, meaning 'barn'. Made famous by the poet Lord Byron.

 Boys' names

Cabot
Old English, meaning 'to sail'.

Cadby
(alt. Cadbey, Cadbee, Cadbie)
English, meaning 'soldiers' colony'.

Cade
(alt. Caden)
English, meaning 'round, lumpy'. A character in the novel *Gone With The Wind*.

Cadence
Latin, meaning 'with rhythm'. Can be used as a girls' or a boys' name.

Cadogan
Welsh, meaning 'battle glory and honour'. Sir Cadogan is a knight who constantly challenged Gryffindors to duels in J.K. Rowling's 'Harry Potter' series.

Caedmon
Celtic, meaning 'wise warrior'. An early English poet.

Caelan
Gaelic, meaning 'slender'.

Caerwyn
(alt. Carwyn, Gerwyn)
Welsh, meaning 'white fort' or 'settlement'. Carwyn Jones is the First Minister of Wales.

Caesar
Disputed origin. The Roman military leader and dictator Gaius Julius Caesar favoured the Moorish meaning 'elephant'.

Caetano
Portuguese, meaning 'from Gaeta, Italy'.

Cagney
Irish, meaning 'successor of the advocate'.

Caiden
Arabic, meaning 'companion'. A variant of the name Caden.

Caillou

French, meaning 'pebble'. Name of the main character in a Canadian children's cartoon.

Cain

Hebrew, meaning 'full of beauty'. Brother of Abel in the biblical Book of Genesis.

Cainan

Hebrew, meaning 'possessor' or 'purchaser'.

Cairo

Egypt's capital city. Located near Giza, home of the great pyramids.

Calder

Scottish, meaning 'rough waters'.

Caleb

(alt. Calen; abbrev. Cal)

Hebrew, meaning 'dog'. Caleb was one of twelve spies sent by Moses into Caanan.

Calhoun

Irish, meaning 'slight woods'.

Calix

Greek, meaning 'very handsome'.

Callahan

Irish, meaning 'contention' or 'strife'.

Callum

(alt. Calum)

Gaelic, meaning 'dove'. Often associated with St Columba, one of the Twelve Apostles of Ireland. Has seen a big rise in popularity outside of Scotland and Ireland in recent years.

Calvin

(alt. Kalvin)

French, meaning 'little bald one'. Name of popular fashion designer Calvin Klein.

Camden

Gaelic, meaning 'winding valley'. Also an area of north London.

Cameron

Scottish Gaelic, meaning 'crooked nose'. Name of a Scottish Clan.

Camillo

Latin, meaning 'free born' or 'noble'. A popular Italian name.

Campbell

Scottish Gaelic, meaning 'crooked mouth'. Was first used as a nickname.

Canaan

Hebrew, meaning 'to be humbled'. A region in the Middle East that existed during biblical times.

Candido

Latin, meaning 'candid' or 'honest'. Candido Jacuzzi is the inventor of the jacuzzi tub.

Canon

(alt. Cannon)

French, meaning 'of the church'.

Canton

French, meaning 'dweller of corner'.

Canute
(alt. Cnut, Cnute)
Scandinavian, meaning 'knot'. Name of an eleventh-century King of England.

Cappy
Italian, meaning 'lucky'. A nickname for someone with the rank of Captain.

Carden
Old English, meaning 'wool carder'. Carding is the process of combing the raw wool fibres to remove tangles and impurities.

Carey
Gaelic, meaning 'love'. Becoming more popular as a girls' as well as a boys' name.

Carl
(alt. Carlo, Carlos)
Old Norse, variant of Charles, meaning 'free man'.

Carlton
Old English, meaning 'free peasant settlement'.

Carmelo
Latin, meaning 'garden' or 'orchard'. Its variant, Carmel, refers to Mount Carmel in Israel, which in biblical times was known for its fruitfulness.

Carmen
Latin/Spanish, meaning 'song'. Name of one of the most famous French operas.

Carmine
Latin, meaning 'song'. Also a bright red pigment used in the manufacture of ruby-red juice.

Carnell
English, meaning 'defender of the castle'.

Carson
(alt. Carsten)
Scottish, meaning 'marsh-dwellers'.

Carter
Old English, meaning 'transporter of goods'.

Cary
Old Celtic river name. Also means 'love'. Cary Grant was a legendary romantic lead actor in films; Cary Elwes is a modern British actor.

Case
(alt. Casey)
Irish Gaelic, meaning 'alert' or 'watchful'.

Casimer
Slavic, meaning 'famous destroyer of peace'.

Casper
Persian, meaning 'treasurer'. The name of a friendly ghost in a comic book.

Caspian
English, meaning 'of the Caspy people'. From the Caspian Sea. A literary character from the C.S. Lewis book *Prince Caspian*.

Cassidy

Irish, meaning 'clever' or 'curly haired'. Originated from the surname, Caiside.

Cassius

(alt. Cassio, Cason, Cash)

Latin, meaning 'empty, hollow'. A name popular during the Roman era. Cassius Clay was the original name of legendary American boxer Muhammad Ali.

Cathal

Celtic, meaning 'battle rule'.

Cato

Latin, meaning 'all-knowing'. Cato the Younger was a Roman politician who opposed Caesar.

Cecil

Latin, meaning 'blind'. Name of famous American movie director Cecil B. DeMille.

Cedar

English, from the name of an evergreen tree.

Cedric

Welsh, meaning 'spectacular bounty'. First appeared in Sir Walter Scott's 1819 novel, *Ivanhoe*.

Celesto

(alt. Celestino, Celindo)

Latin, meaning 'heaven sent'.

Chad

(alt. Chadrick)

Old English, meaning 'warlike, warrior'. Use of this name was rare until it sprang to popularity in the 1960s.

Chaim

(alt. Chayyim)

Hebrew, meaning 'life'.

Champion

English, from the word 'champion', meaning 'warrior'.

Chandler

Old English, meaning 'candle maker and seller'.

Charles

(abbrev. Chas, Charlie)

Old German, meaning 'free man'. Popularised by Charles the Great (a.k.a. Charlemagne). Prince Charles is heir to the throne of England. Charles Dickens was one of the finest and most enduringly popular English authors.

Chaska

Sioux name usually given to first son.

Chauncey

(alt. Chance)

English, from the word 'chance' meaning 'good fortune'.

Che

Spanish, shortened form of José. Made famous by Che Guevara.

Chesley

Old English, meaning 'camp on the meadow'.

Chesney

English, meaning 'place to camp'. Also used as a girls' name.

Chester

Latin, meaning 'camp of soldiers'. The name of an English city.

Chilton

(alt. Chillron, Chilly, Chilt)
English, meaning 'tranquil'.

Chima

Old English, meaning 'hilly land'.

Christian

English, from the word 'Christian'. Christian Bale is an actor and Christian Louboutin a famous shoe designer.

Christopher

(alt. Christophe; abbrev. Chris, Christy)
Greek, meaning 'Christ bearer'. Name of the famous explorer Christopher Columbus.

Cian

Irish, meaning 'ancient'. Father of Lug in Irish mythology.

Ciaran

Irish, meaning 'black'. Was the name of two Irish saints.

Cicero

Latin, meaning 'chickpea'. Famous Roman philosopher and orator.

Cimarron

City in western Kansas. Also the name of a novel by Edna Ferber.

Ciprian

Latin, meaning 'from Cyprus'. Popular in Romanian heritage.

Ciro

Spanish, meaning 'sun'. Name of an opera by Francesco Cavalli dating back to 1654.

Clancy

Old Irish, meaning 'red warrior'. Evolved from the surname Mac Fhlannchaidh.

Clarence

Latin, meaning 'one who lives near the river Clare'.

Clark

Latin, meaning 'clerk'. The human identity of the famed superhero Superman (Clark Kent).

Claude

(alt. Claudie, Claudio, Claudius)
Latin, meaning 'lame'. Has been in use since the Middle Ages.

Claus

Variant of Nicholas, meaning 'victorious'.

Clay

English, from the word 'clay'.

Clement
(alt. Clem)
Latin, meaning 'merciful'. Has been used as the name for 14 different popes.

Cleo
Greek, meaning 'glory'. Most commonly used as a name for girls, but also for boys.

Cletus
Greek, meaning 'illustrious'. Used to refer to the third pope, Anacletus.

Clifford
(alt. Clifton; abbrev. Cliff)
English, from the word 'cliff'.

Clint
(alt. Clinton)
Old English, meaning 'fenced settlement'. Name of famous actor/writer/director Clint Eastwood.

Clive
Old English, meaning 'cliff' or 'slope'. Famous Clives include actor Clive Owen and author and broadcaster Clive James.

Clyde
Scottish, from the river that passes through Glasgow. Name of famous American bank robber Clyde Barrow of the duo Bonnie and Clyde.

Coby
(alt. Cody, Colby)
Irish, meaning 'son of Oda'.

Cody
English, meaning 'pillow'. Also a girls' name.

Colden
Old English, meaning 'dark valley'.

Cole
(alt. Coley)
Old French, meaning 'coal black'.

Colin
Gaelic, meaning 'young creature'. Famous Colins include actor Colin Firth and champion rally driver Colin McRae.

Colson
Old English, meaning 'coal black'.

Colton
English, meaning 'swarthy'. Evolved from the Old English name, Cola.

Columbus
Latin, meaning 'dove'. Name of Italian explorer Christopher Columbus.

Colwyn
Welsh, from the river in Wales.

Conan
Gaelic, meaning 'wolf'. Middle name of 'Sherlock Holmes' author, Sir Arthur Conan Doyle.

Conley
Gaelic, meaning 'sensible'.

Connell
(alt. Connolly)
Irish, meaning 'high' or 'mighty'.

Connor
(alt. Conor, Conrad, Conroy)
Irish, meaning 'lover of hounds'.
Evolved from the name Conchobhar
(King of Ulster).

Constant
(alt. Constantine)
English, from the word 'constant'.
A name widely used by Christians
as early as the seventeenth
century.

Cooper
Old English, meaning 'barrel
maker'.

Corban
Hebrew, meaning 'dedicated and
belonging to God'.

Corbett
(alt. Corbin, Corby)
Norman French, meaning 'young
crow'.

Cordell
Old English, meaning 'cord maker'.

Corey
(alt. Cory)
Gaelic, meaning 'hill hollow'.
Thought to have originated from the
Old Norse name Kori.

Corin
Latin, meaning 'spear'. A variant of
the German given name Quirin.

Corliss
(alt. Corlis, Corlyss, Corlys)
English, meaning 'benevolent'.

Cormac
Gaelic, meaning 'impure son'. Name
given to a third-century Irish king.

Cornelius
(alt. Cornell)
Latin, meaning 'horn'. The head
of the Ministry of Magic (Cornelius
Fudge) in J.K. Rowling's 'Harry Potter'
series.

Cortez
Spanish, meaning 'courteous'.

Corwin
Old English, meaning 'heart's friend'
or 'companion'.

Cosimo
(alt. Cosme, Cosmo)
Italian, meaning 'order' or 'beauty'.
Given name of Pope Innocent VII
(1339–1406).

Coty
French, meaning 'riverbank'.
Surname of people who lived near
a coast.

Coulter
English, meaning 'young horse'.

Courtney
Old English, meaning 'domain of
Curtis'. A given name that has been
in use since the seventeenth century.
Used for both boys and girls.

Covey

English, meaning 'flock of birds'.

Cowan

Gaelic, meaning 'hollow in the hill'.

Craig

Welsh, meaning 'rock'. Originally used as a surname by people who lived near a cliff. Craig David is a singer-songwriter and there are two famous sporting Craig Bellamys, one a Welsh footballer and the other an Australian rugby league star.

Crispin

Latin, meaning 'curly haired'. Name of a third-century saint, twin brother of St Crispinian. Patron saints of shoemakers.

Croix

French, meaning 'cross'.

Cruz

Spanish, meaning 'cross'. Made famous by David and Victoria Beckham's son.

Cullen

Gaelic, meaning 'handsome'. Made famous by the *Twilight* book series.

Curran

Gaelic, meaning 'dagger' or 'hero'.

Curtis

(alt. Curt)

Old French, meaning 'courteous'. Commonly used in the Middle Ages as a name of a courteous person.

Cutler

Old English, meaning 'knife maker'.

Cyprian

English, meaning 'from Cyprus'.

Cyril

Greek, meaning 'master' or 'Lord'. Name of St Cyril, one of the inventors of the Glagolitic alphabet, the precursor to the Cyrillic alphabet.

Cyrus

Persian, meaning 'Lord'. Cyrus the Great conquered Babylon in 539 BC.

 Boys' names

Dabeel
(alt. Dabee, Dabie, Daby)
Indian, meaning 'warrior'.

Daelan
English, meaning 'aware'. Also a girls' name.

Dafydd
(alt. Dai)
Welsh, meaning 'beloved'. Welsh version of David.

Daichi
Japanese, meaning 'great wisdom'.

Daire
(alt. Daer, Daere, Dair)
Irish, meaning 'wealthy'.

Daisuke
Japanese, meaning 'lionhearted'.

Dakari
African, meaning 'happy'.

Dale
Old English, meaning 'valley'.

Dallin
English, meaning 'dweller in the valley'.

Dalton
English, meaning 'town in the valley'.

Daly
Gaelic, meaning 'assembly'.

Damarion
Greek, meaning 'gentle'.

Damian
(alt. Damien, Damon)
Greek, meaning 'to tame, subdue'. Name of a fourth-century patron saint of physicians. Damien is the name of the Devil's son in 'The Omen' series of films. Damon Hill is British champion racing driver and Damon Albarn is a musician and the lead singer of Blur.

Dane
Old English, meaning 'from Denmark'.

Daniel
(alt. Dan, Danny)

Hebrew, meaning 'God is my judge'. Daniel was a prophet during biblical times. An enduringly popular name for boys.

Dante

Latin, meaning 'lasting'. Associated with the thirteenth-century Italian poet Dante Alighieri, author of *The Divine Comedy*.

Darby

Irish, meaning 'without envy'.

Darcy

Gaelic, meaning 'dark'. Associated with Jane Austen's Mr Darcy, and the parody of this character in *Bridget Jones' Diary*. A name more commonly used for girls in modern times.

Dario
(alt. Darius)

Greek, meaning 'kingly'. Associated with Dario Argento, an Italian film director.

Darnell

Old English, meaning 'the hidden spot'.

Darragh
(alt. Dara)

Irish, meaning 'dark oak'. A popular name in Ireland, now being seen in England and Wales.

Darrell
(alt. Daryl)

Old English, meaning 'open'. Originated from the Norman French surname d'Airelle.

Darren
(alt. Darrian)

Gaelic, meaning 'great'. Darren Aronofsky is an American film-maker. In the UK the name is well connected with sport, including Darren Gough (cricket), Darren Bent and Darren Fletcher (football) and Darren Barker (boxing).

Darrick

Old German, meaning 'power of the tribe'.

Darshan

Hindi, meaning 'vision'.

Darwin

Old English, meaning 'dear friend'. Often associated with the naturalist Charles Darwin.

Dash
(alt. Dashawn)

American, meaning 'enlightened one'. Associated with one of the characters in Disney Pixar's *The Incredibles*.

Dashiell

French, meaning 'page boy'. Dashiell Hammett was an American author, famous for hard-boiled detective fiction.

Dason
Native American, meaning 'chief'.

David
(alt. Dave, Davey, Davie, Davin)
Hebrew, meaning 'beloved'.
Associated with the King of Israel
who killed Goliath the giant as a boy.

Davis
Old English, meaning 'son of David'.

Dawson
Old English, meaning 'son of David'.
Associated with the main character in
the TV show *Dawson's Creek*

Dax
(alt. Daxton)
French, once a town in south-
western France.

Dayal
Indian, meaning 'kind'.

Dayton
Old English, meaning 'David's place'.
A city in the US state of Ohio.

Dean
Old English, meaning 'valley'. Dean
Koontz is an American author and
Dean Martin was a hugely popular
singer and entertainer, known as the
'King of Cool'.

Declan
Irish, meaning 'full of goodness'.
Associated with St Declan, who was
born in the fifth century.

Dedric
Old English, meaning 'gifted ruler'.

Deepak
(alt. Deepan)
Indian, meaning 'illumination'.
Associated with doctor and spiritual
author Deepak Chopra.

Del
(alt. Delano, Delbert, Dell)
Old English, meaning 'bright shining
one'. Associated with the main
character in *Only Fools and Horses*, a
BBC comedy.

Delaney
Irish, meaning 'dark challenge'.

Demetrius
Greek, meaning 'harvest lover'.
Name of a fourth-century Greek
sculptor.

Dempsey
Irish, meaning 'proud'.

Denham
(alt. Denholm)
Old English, meaning 'valley
settlement'.

Dennis
(alt. Denis, Denny, Denton)
English, meaning 'follower of
Dionysius'. Associated with the
boy in the comic strip *Dennis the
Menace*. Other famous Dennises
include actors Dennis Hopper and
Dennis Quaid and footballer Dennis
Bergkamp.

Denzil
(alt. Denzel)
English, meaning 'fort'. Most commonly associated with Oscar-winning actor Denzel Washington.

Deon
Greek, meaning 'of Zeus'.

Derek
English, meaning 'power of the tribe'. Short form for the given name Diderik.

Dermot
Irish, meaning 'free man'. Dermot Morgan portrayed Father Ted, and Dermot O'Leary is a prolific TV and radio presenter.

Desmond
Irish, meaning 'from south Munster'. Associated with South African social rights activist Archbishop Desmond Tutu.

Destin
French, meaning 'destiny'.

Devyn
(alt. Devin)
Irish, meaning 'poet'.

Dewey
Welsh, from Dewi (David). One of Disney character Donald Duck's three nephews.

Dexter
(alt. Dex)
Latin, meaning 'right-handed'. The main character from the US TV show *Dexter*.

Diallo
(alt. Dialo)
African, meaning 'bold'.

Dick
(alt. Dickie, Dickon, Diccon)
From Richard, meaning 'powerful leader'. Dick is one of Enid Blyton's *Famous Five* and Dickon is a character in Frances Hodgson Burnett's *The Secret Garden*.

Didier
French, meaning 'much desired'. St Didier is a saint honoured in the Catholic Church. Famous Didiers include footballers Didier Deschamps and Didier Drogba.

Diego
Spanish, meaning 'supplanter'. Has been in use since the eleventh century.

Dietrich
Old German, meaning 'power of the tribe'.

Diggory
English, meaning 'dyke'.

Dilbert
English, meaning 'day bright'. Popularised by the American comic strip of the same name.

Dimitri
(alt. Dimitrios, Dimitris)
Greek, meaning 'prince'. A popular name in Russia.

Dino

Diminutive of Dean, meaning 'valley'. Used as short form for names ending with -dino.

Dion

Greek, short form of Dionysius, the Greek god of wine. Dionysius was the son of Zeus and Semele.

Dirk

Variant of Derek, meaning 'power of the tribe'. A name also used to refer to a dagger.

Divakar

Sanskrit, meaning 'the sun'.

Dominic

Latin, meaning 'Lord'.

Donald

(alt. Don, Donal, Donaldo)

Gaelic, meaning 'great chief'. Famous Donalds include actor Donald Sutherland, business giant Donald Trump and ever-popular Disney character Donald Duck.

Donato

Italian, meaning 'gift'. Given name of Italian sculptor Donatello.

Donnell

(alt. Donnie, Donny)

Gaelic, meaning 'world fighter'.

Donovan

Gaelic, meaning 'dark-haired chief'. Associated with Scottish singer Donovan.

Doran

Gaelic, meaning 'exile'.

Dorian

Greek, meaning 'descendant of Doris'. Name of the title character in Oscar Wilde's *The Picture of Dorian Gray*.

Douglas

(alt. Dougal, Dougie)

Scottish, meaning 'black river'. Douglas Adams was the author of *The Hitchhiker's Guide to the Galaxy*.

Doyle

Irish, meaning 'foreigner'.

Draco

(alt. Drake)

Latin, meaning 'dragon'. Made popular by the character Draco Malfoy in J.K. Rowling's 'Harry Potter' series.

Drew

Shortened form of Andrew, meaning 'man' or 'warrior'.

Dryden

English, meaning 'dry town'.

Dudley

Old English, meaning 'people's field'. Also the name of Harry Potter's cousin.

Duff

Gaelic, meaning 'swarthy'.

Duke

Latin, meaning 'leader'. The title of a nobleman ruling over a duchy.

Duncan

Scottish, meaning 'dark warrior'. King Duncan is a character in Shakespeare's *Macbeth*.

Dustin
(alt. Dusty)

French, meaning 'brave warrior'. Popularised by American actor Dustin Hoffman.

Dwayne
(alt. Duwayne, Duane)

Irish Gaelic, meaning 'swarthy'.

Dwight

Flemish, meaning 'blond'. Associated with the 34th President of the United States, Dwight D. Eisenhower.

Dwyer

Gaelic, meaning 'dark wise one'.

Dyani

Native American, meaning 'eagle'.

Dylan
(alt. Dillon)

Welsh, meaning 'son of the sea'. Name of the famous Welsh poet Dylan Thomas.

Less common three-syllable names

Alastair	Elliot
Barnaby	Lancelot
Dominic	Roberto
Dorian	Theodore
Elijah	

E Boys' names

Eagan
Irish, meaning 'fiery'.

Eamon
(alt. Eamonn, Eames)

Irish, meaning 'wealthy protector'. TV presenter Eamon Holmes is known for early-morning programmes.

Earl
(alt. Earle, Errol)

English, meaning 'nobleman, warrior, prince'. Earl is a title of nobility, used since Anglo-Saxon times.

Ebenezer
(abbrev. Ebb)

Hebrew, meaning 'stone of help'. Ebenezer Scrooge is the main character in Charles Dickens' novel *A Christmas Carol*.

Edgar
(alt. Elgar)

Old English, meaning 'wealthy spear'. Poet and writer Edgar Allan Poe is known for works such as *The Raven*.

Edison
English, meaning 'son of Edward'. Thomas Edison was one of America's greatest and most well-known inventors.

Edmund
(abbrev. Ed)

English, meaning 'wealthy protector'. Edmund Blackadder is the title character in the historical comedy series *Blackadder*, starring Rowan Atkinson.

Edric
Old English, meaning 'rich and powerful'.

Edsel
Old German, meaning 'noble'. Henry Ford, the automobile magnate, named his son Edsel.

Edward

(alt. Eduardo; abbrev. Ed, Edd, Eddie, Eddy)

Old English, meaning 'wealthy guard'. Edward has become extremely popular since the release of the *Twilight* series. Ed Miliband was the leader of the Labour Party.

Edwin

English, meaning 'wealthy friend'.

Efrain

Hebrew, meaning 'fruitful'. Normally used in Spanish-speaking cultures.

Egan

Irish, meaning 'fire'. Egan, derived from the name Aedhagan, is one of the oldest surnames in Europe.

Eilif

(alt. Elif, Eilyg, Elyf)

Norse, meaning 'immortal'. Eilif Paterssen was an influential Norwegian painter and artist in the early 20th century.

Einar

Old Norse, meaning 'battle leader'. Still a popular name in Iceland.

Eladio

Greek, meaning 'Greek'. Related to the name Heladio.

Elam

Hebrew, meaning 'eternal'. Elam is mentioned in the Bible as being a son of Shem, and son of Noah.

Elbert

Old English, meaning 'famous'. Variation of the name Albert.

Eldon

Old English, meaning 'Ella's hill'. Also refers to the town in County Durham, England.

Eldred

(alt. Eldridge)

Old English, meaning 'old venerable counsel'.

Elgin

Old English, meaning 'high minded'. Also refers to the town of the same name in Scotland.

Eli

(alt. Eliah)

Hebrew, meaning 'high'. Eli is a character in the Old Testament of the Bible.

Elias

(alt. Elijah, Elio)

Hebrew, meaning 'the Lord is my God'. Walt Disney's father was Elias Disney. Actor Elijah Wood played Frodo Baggins in the *Lord of the Rings* films.

Ellery

Old English, meaning 'elder tree'. Ellery Hanley is a former rugby league player and coach for Great Britain.

Elliott

English variant of Elio, meaning 'the Lord is my God'. Made popular by the lead character in the film *E.T.*

Ellis

Welsh, variant of Elio, meaning 'the Lord is my God'.

Ellison

English, meaning 'son of Ellis'.

Elmer
(alt. Elmo)

Old English, meaning 'noble'; Arabic, meaning 'aristocratic'. Elmer the elephant features in a number of children's picture books by author David McKee.

Elmo
(alt. Ellmo, Elmon)

Greek, meaning 'gregarious'. One of the characters in the children's TV series *Sesame Street*.

Elmore

Old English, meaning from 'elm tree' and 'moor'. Elmore Leonard was an American author.

Elon
(alt. Alon)

Hebrew, meaning 'oak tree'. A very old name, it is now not used much outside of Hebrew-speaking communities.

Elroy

French, meaning 'king'. Elroy Jetson was the youngest member of the cartoon Jetson family.

Elton

Old English, meaning 'Ella's town'. Singer and songwriter Sir Elton John's real name is Reg Dwight.

Elvin

English, meaning 'elf-like'. Elvin Bale was a big performer with circuses, known for human cannonball acts and high-wire daredevil work.

Elvis

Figure in Norse mythology. Made famous by the singer Elvis Presley.

Emanuel

Hebrew, meaning 'God is with us'. Features in hymns and carols.

Emeric

German, meaning 'work rule'. St Emeric of Hungary was known for a pure and pious life.

Emile
(alt. Emil, Emiliano, Emilio)

Latin, meaning 'eager'. Emile is Remy the rat's older brother in Disney's film *Ratatouille*.

Emlyn

Welsh. The name of a town, Newcastle Emlyn, in west Wales. Emlyn Hughes was a famous footballer of the 1970s turned TV presenter.

Emmett

English, meaning 'universal'. Emmett Scanlan played a villain in *Hollyoaks* for many years.

Emrys

Welsh, meaning 'immortal'. The legendary magician Merlin is said to have been given the name Emrys at birth, and only later adopted his more famous moniker.

Eneco

Spanish, meaning 'fiery one'.

Enoch

Hebrew, meaning 'dedicated'. Enoch was the great-great-grandfather of Noah in the Bible.

Enrico

(alt. Enrique)

Italian, form of Henry, meaning 'home ruler'. Extremely popular name in Italy for boys.

Enzo

Italian, short for Lorenzo, meaning 'laurel'. Enzo Ferrari was the founder of the Ferrari automobile company.

Eoghan

(alt. Eoin)

Irish form of Owen, meaning 'well born' or 'noble'. Eoghan was an Irish king in the fifth century. Eoin Colfer is the author of the young adult fiction series Artemis Fowl.

Ephron

(alt. Effron)

Hebrew, meaning 'dust'.

Erasmo

(alt. Erasmus)

Greek, meaning 'to love'. Erasmus was a Dutch humanist and theologian during the Renaissance period.

Eric

Old Norse, meaning 'ruler'. Often associated with singer and guitarist Eric Clapton.

Ernest

(alt. Ernesto, Ernie, Ernst)

Old German, meaning 'serious'. Author Ernest Hemingway is known for his influential novels A Farewell to Arms and The Old Man and the Sea.

Errol

English, meaning 'boar wolf'. Actor Errol Flynn is best known for his swashbuckler roles and the lead role in The Adventures of Robin Hood.

Erskine

Scottish, meaning 'high cliff'. Also a place in Scotland.

Erwin

Old English, meaning 'boar friend'.

Eryx

Greek, meaning 'boxer'. Sometimes used as an alternative spelling for Eric.

Ethan

(alt. Etienne)

Hebrew, meaning 'long lived'. Ethan Coen and Joel Coen are influential director brothers known for films such as Fargo and True Grit. Ethan Hawke is an Oscar-nominated actor.

Eugene
Greek, meaning 'well born'.

Evan
Welsh, meaning 'God is good'.

Evelyn
German, meaning 'hazelnut'. Evelyn Waugh is the author of *Brideshead Revisited*, *Decline and Fall* and *Scoop*.

Everard
(alt. Everett)

Old English, meaning 'strong boar'. Also the name of an old English ale.

Everly
(alt. Everleigh, Everley)

English, meaning 'grazing meadow'. Used as a name for boys and girls.

Ewald
(alt. Ewan, Ewen, Ewell)

Old English, from Owen, meaning 'well born' or 'noble'. Actor Ewan McGregor is known for his roles in *Trainspotting*, *Moulin Rouge* and *Star Wars*.

Exton
English, meaning 'on the River Exe'.

Ezra
Hebrew, meaning 'helper'. Ezra Pound was an American poet.

Famous male drummers

Dave (Grohl)

John (Bonham)

Keith (Moon)

Lars (Ulrich)

Mick (Fleetwood)

Phil (Collins)

Ringo (Starr – real name Richard Starkey)

Stewart (Copeland)

Tommy (Lee)

Travis (Barker)

Boys' names

Faber
(alt. Fabir)

Latin, meaning 'blacksmith'. Faber and Faber is a well-known UK publishing house.

Fabian
(alt. Fabien, Fabio)

Latin, meaning 'one who grows beans'. Also associated with the teen pop sensation Fabian in the 1950s and 1960s.

Fabrice
(alt. Fabrizio)

Latin, meaning 'works with his hands'. Popular in France. Fabrice Muamba is a former football player who survived an on-pitch heart attack.

Faisal

Arabic, meaning 'resolute'. Faisal II was the last King of Iraq, whose reign ended during the revolution of 1958.

Falco
(alt. Falcon, Falconer, Falke, Faulkner)

Latin, meaning 'falconer'.

Faron

Spanish, meaning 'pharaoh'. Also derived from a Gaelic word for 'thunder'.

Farrell

Gaelic, meaning 'hero'.

Faustino

Latin, meaning 'fortunate'.

Fela
(alt. Felah, Fella, Fellah)

African, meaning 'a man who is warlike'. The name of the famous Nigerian musician Fela Kuti.

Felipe
(alt. Filippo)

Spanish, meaning 'lover of horses'. Formula One driver Felipe Massa has driven for Ferrari and Williams.

Felix
(alt. Felice)

Italian/Latin, meaning 'happy'. Felix the Cat was a popular twentieth-century cartoon character.

Fennel

Latin, name of a herb. More commonly used as a girls' name.

Ferdinand
(alt. Fernando)

Old German, meaning 'bold voyager'.

Fergus
(alt. Ferguson)

Gaelic, meaning 'supreme man'.

Ferris

Gaelic, meaning 'rock'. *Ferris Bueller's Day Off* was a runaway hit film during the 1980s.

Fiachra

Irish, meaning 'raven'. St Fiachra is the patron saint of gardeners.

Fidel

Latin, meaning 'faithful'. Fidel Castro was President of Cuba from 1976 to 2008.

Finbarr

Gaelic, meaning 'fair head'. St Finbarr is the patron saint of the City of Cork.

Finian
(alt. Finnian)

Gaelic, meaning 'fair'. St Finnian is an important Irish saint, and a founder of the theory of monasticism.

Finlay
(alt. Finley, Finn)

Gaelic, meaning 'fair-haired courageous one'.

Finn

Finnish, meaning 'from Finland'. Now usually associated with the character of Finn in *Glee*.

Finnegan

Gaelic, meaning 'fair'. Author James Joyce wrote *Finnegans Wake* as a complex work of comedy.

Fintan

Gaelic, meaning 'little fair one'. A seer in Irish mythology called Fintan supposedly saved one of Noah's granddaughters from the flood.

Fitzroy

English, meaning 'the king's son'. Usually associated with Vice-Admiral Robert Fitzroy, who accompanied Charles Darwin on his famous voyages.

Flavio

Latin, meaning 'yellow hair'. The opera *Flavio* was composed by Handel.

Florencio
(alt. Florentino)

Latin, meaning 'from Florence'.

Florian
(alt. Florin)

Slavic/Latin, meaning 'flower'. St Florian is the patron saint of chimney sweeps, soapmakers and firefighters.

Floyd

Welsh, meaning 'grey haired'.

Flynn

Gaelic, meaning 'with a ruddy complexion'.

Forbes

(alt. Forbs, Forb, Forbe)

Gaelic, meaning 'of the field'.

Fortunato

Italian, meaning 'lucky'.

Foster

Old English, meaning 'woodsman'.

Fotini

(alt. Fotis)

Greek, meaning 'light'.

Francis

(alt. Francesco, Francisco, Franco, François)

Latin, meaning 'from France'. After the election of Pope Francis, Francesco has become the most popular name for boys in Italy.

Frank

(alt. Frankie, Franklin, Franz)

Middle English, meaning 'free landholder'. Also a diminutive of Francis. Famous Franks include footballer Frank Lampard, crooner Frank Sinatra, and film director Frank Capra.

Fraser

(alt. Fraiser)

Scottish, meaning 'of the forest men'.

Frederick

(alt. Friedrich; abbrev. Freddie, Fred)

Old German, meaning 'peaceful ruler'. There is a spelling or pronunciation variation of Frederick in practically every European language.

Furman

Old German, meaning 'ferryman'.

Fyfe

(alt. Fife, Fyffes)

Scottish, meaning 'from Fifeshire'.

 Boys' names

Gabino
Latin, meaning 'God is my strength'.

Gabriel
(abbrev. Gabe)
Hebrew, meaning 'hero of God'.
One of the archangels in the Bible.

Gael
(alt. Gale)
English, old reference to the Celts.
Gale has become a highly recognised
name since the release of 'The
Hunger Games' trilogy.

Gaius
(alt. Gaeus)
Latin, meaning 'rejoicing'. Julius
Caesar's full name was Gaius Julius
Caesar.

Galen
Greek, meaning 'healer'. Galen
of Pergamon was a well-respected
ancient Greek and Roman
philosopher and physician.

Galileo
Italian, meaning 'from Galilee'.
Galileo Galilei was an important and
influential physicist and astronomer
during the Scientific Revolution.

Ganesh
Hindi, meaning 'lord of the horde'.
One of the Hindu deities.

Gannon
Irish, meaning 'fair skinned'. More
commonly used as a surname,
particularly in Ireland.

Gareth
(alt. Garth, Garthe, Gart, Garte)
Welsh, meaning 'gentle'.

Garfield
Old English, meaning 'spear field'.
Also the name of the cartoon cat.

Garland
English, as in 'garland of flowers'.

Garnet

English, precious stone, red in colour. Occasionally used for boys, although not as frequently as for girls.

Garrett

Old German, meaning 'spear' or 'ruler'. Ireland's Garret the Great was known as 'the uncrowned King of Ireland' during his time of political power in the fifteenth century.

Gary
(alt. Garry, Geary)

Old English, meaning 'spear'. Some of Britain's best-loved Garys include Take That member Gary Barlow and football pundit Gary Lineker.

Gaspar
(alt. Gaspard)

Persian, meaning 'treasurer'. *Gaspar and Lisa* is a popular children's television programme, broadcast by Disney, about two dogs living in Paris.

Gaston

From the Gascony region in the south of France.

Gavin
(alt. Gawain)

Scottish/Welsh, meaning 'little falcon'.

Gene

Greek, shortened form of Eugene, meaning 'well born'. Famous Genes include actors Gene Kelly and Gene Hackman, and Kiss guitarist Gene Simmons.

Genkei

Japanese, meaning 'honoured'. One of Japan's most famous botanists is Genkei Masamune, who is credited with identifying hundreds of new species.

Gennaro

Italian, meaning 'of Janus'.

Geoffrey
(abbrev. Geoff)

Old German, meaning 'peace'.

George
(alt. Giorgio)

Greek, meaning 'farmer'. Chosen by the Duke and Duchess of Cambridge for their son, born in July 2013, and third in line to the throne.

Gerald
(alt. Geraldo, Gerard, Gerardo, Gerhard; abbrev. Gerry)

Old German, meaning 'spear ruler'. Former President of the United States Gerald Ford is the only person to have served as both President and Vice President without being elected to either position, thanks to two infamous resignations before him.

Geronimo

Italian, meaning 'sacred name'. Originally the name of a prominent Apache Indian, this has now become a word for 'go-get-'em!'

Gert

Old German, meaning 'strong spear'.

Gervase

Old German, meaning 'with honour'. Gervase Phinn is a widely read author of several humorous books describing his life as a school inspector in Yorkshire.

Giacomo

Italian, meaning 'God's son'. Legendary womaniser Casanova's full name was Giacomo Girolamo Casanova.

Gibson

English, meaning 'son of Gilbert'.

Gideon

Hebrew, meaning 'tree cutter'. Gideon is a figure in the Bible.

Gilbert
(alt. Gilberto)
French, meaning 'bright promise'.

Giles

Greek, meaning 'small goat'.

Gino

Italian, meaning 'well born'.

Giovanni

Italian form of John, meaning 'God is gracious'.

Giri
(alt. Gririe, Giry, Girey)
Indian, meaning 'from the mountain'.

Giulio

Italian, meaning 'youthful'. Composer Giulio Caccini was active during the Baroque era.

Giuseppe

Italian form of Joseph, meaning 'Jehovah increases'.

Glen
(alt. Glenn, Glyn)
English, from the word 'glen'.

Godfrey

German, meaning 'peace of God'.

Gordon

Gaelic, meaning 'large fortification'. Famous Gordons include chef Gordon Ramsay, former England goalkeeper Gordon Banks, and former prime minister Gordon Brown.

Gottlieb

German, meaning 'good love'. One of Mozart's names at birth was Gottlieb; others included Joannes, Chrisostomus and Wolfgang.

Gower

Area of the Welsh coast, by the Bristol Channel.

Graeme
(alt. Graham)
English, meaning 'gravelled area'.

Grant

English, from the word 'grant'.

Granville

English, meaning 'gravelly town'. Probably the most famous Granville is the character portrayed by David Jason in sitcom *Open All Hours*.

Gray
(alt. Grey)
English, from the word 'grey'.

Grayson
English, meaning 'son of gray'. Grayson Perry is an artist who won the Turner Prize in 2003.

Green
English, from the word 'green'.

Gregory
(alt. Gregorio; abbrev. Greg, Greig)
English, from the word 'griffin'. Actor Gregory Peck was best known for his role in *To Kill A Mockingbird*.

Griffin
English. A griffin is a mythical creature with the body of a lion and the head and wings of an eagle.

Groves
English, meaning 'inhabits near grove of trees'.

Grylfi
(alt. Gylfie, Gylfee, Gylffi)
Scandinavian, meaning 'king'. Gylfi was the first Nordic king in Scandinavia.

Guido
Italian, meaning 'guide'.

Guillaume
French form of William, meaning 'strong protector'. William the Conqueror is known as Guillaume le Conquérant in France.

Gulliver
English, meaning 'glutton'. *Gulliver's Travels*, by Jonathan Swift, tells the story of a surgeon who sets sail for adventure.

Gunther
German, meaning 'warrior'.

Gurpreet
Indian, meaning 'love of the teacher'. More commonly used in Punjabi-speaking communities.

Gustave
(abbrev. Gus)
Scandinavian, meaning 'royal staff'. Gustave Flaubert is the author of classics including *Madame Bovary*. Also the name given to a legendary crocodile in Burundi, whose length is said to be over 20ft and that has killed as many as 300 humans.

Guy
English, from the word 'guy'. Guy Fawkes is the character most associated with the Gunpowder Plot of 1605, which was an attempt to blow up the Houses of Parliament.

Gwyn
Welsh, meaning 'white'. Commonly used as a name for girls as well as for boys.

Boys' names

Habib

Arabic, meaning 'beloved one'.

Hackett

(alt. Hacket, Hackit, Hackitt)

German, meaning 'small hacker'.

Haden

(alt. Haiden)

English, meaning 'hedged valley'. Also a popular type of mango.

Hades

Greek, meaning 'sightless'. Name of the god of the underworld in Greek mythology.

Hadrian

From Hadria, a north Italian city. Hadrian's Wall in northern England is named after the Roman Emperor Hadrian.

Hadwin

Old English, meaning 'friend in war'.

Hakeem

Arabic, meaning 'wise and insightful'. Actor Hakeem Kae-Kazim is known for his role in the film *Hotel Rwanda*.

Hal

(alt. Hale, Hallie)

English, nickname for Henry, meaning 'home ruler'. Used in this context in Shakespeare's Henry IV plays.

Halim

Arabic, meaning 'gentle'. Al-Halim is one the names of God in Islam.

Hallam

Old English, meaning 'the valley'.

Hamid

Arabic, meaning 'praiseworthy'. Hamid Karzai was the elected president of Afghanistan from 2001 to 2014.

Hamilton

Old English, meaning 'flat-topped hill'.

Hamish

Scottish form of James, meaning 'he who supplants'.

Hamlet

(alt. Hamlett, Hammet, Hamnet)

German, meaning 'village'. A variation of the Danish Amleth, and often associated with Shakespeare's tragedy *Hamlet*.

Hampus

Swedish form of Homer, meaning 'pledge'. Hampus Lindholm is an international ice hockey player, originally from Sweden.

Hamza

Arabic, meaning 'lamb'. Also a letter in the Arabic alphabet.

Han

(alt. Hannes, Hans)

Scandinavian, meaning 'the Lord is gracious'.

Hanif

(alt. Haneef, Haneaf, Haneif)

Arabic, meaning 'devout'. Usually refers to people who submitted entirely to their religion in Islam.

Hank

German, form of Henry, meaning 'home ruler'.

Hansel

German, meaning 'the Lord is gracious'. One of the most famous Grimm fairy tales is the story of Hansel and Gretel.

Hardy

English, meaning 'tough'. Often associated with the author Thomas Hardy, or comedic duo Laurel and Hardy.

Harlan

English, meaning 'dweller by the boundary wood'. Harlan Coben is the author of several mystery novels.

Harland

Old English, meaning 'army land'. Fast food chain KFC was founded by Colonel Harland David Sanders. The *Titanic* was built at Belfast shipyard Harland and Wolff.

Harley

Old English, meaning 'hare meadow'.

Harmon

Old German, meaning 'soldier'.

Harold

Scandinavian, meaning 'army ruler'. The last Anglo-Saxon King of England was Harold II, whose reign ended after he lost the Battle of Hastings.

Harry

Old German, form of Henry, meaning 'home ruler'. Famous Harrys include Prince Harry, Harry Potter and One Direction singer Harry Styles.

Hart

Old English, meaning 'stag'.

Harvey

Old English, meaning 'strong and worthy'. The film *Harvey*, starring Jimmy Stewart and Josephine Hull, is about a man whose best friend is an enormous invisible rabbit.

Haskell

Hebrew, meaning 'intellect'.

Hassan

Arabic, meaning 'handsome'. Hassan Rouhani is the current President of Iran.

Haydn

(alt. Hayden, Haydon)

Old English, meaning 'hedged valley'. Also a composer, Franz Joseph Hadyn, was one of the most influential and popular of the classical period.

Heart

English, from the word 'heart'.

Heath

English, meaning 'heath' or 'moor'. Heath Ledger was a prolific actor, known for his roles in *A Knight's Tale*, *10 Things I Hate About You* and *The Dark Knight*.

Heathcliff

English, meaning 'cliff near a heath'. Made famous by Emily Brontë's novel *Wuthering Heights*.

Heber

Hebrew, meaning 'partner'.

Hector

Greek, meaning 'steadfast'. A Trojan prince and historic fighter in ancient Greek mythology.

Henry

(alt. Henri, Hendrik, Hendrix)

Old German, meaning 'home ruler'. There have been eight Kings of England named Henry, and in the unlikely event that Prince Harry found himself on the throne he would become Henry IX.

Henson

English, meaning 'son of Henry'.

Herbert

(alt. Heriberto; abbrev. Bert, Herb)

Old German, meaning 'illustrious warrior'. Herbert Hoover was a President of the United States and founder of the FBI.

Herman

(alt. Herminio, Hermon)

Old German, meaning 'soldier'.

Hermes

Greek, meaning 'messenger'. The messenger of the gods in Greek mythology.

Herschel

(alt. Hirsch)

Yiddish, meaning 'deer'.

Hezekiah
Hebrew, meaning 'God gives strength'. The 13th king of Judah was King Hezekiah.

Hideki
Japanese, meaning 'excellent trees'. The prime minister of Japan during World War II was Hideki Tojo.

Hideo
Japanese, meaning 'excellent name'. One of Japan's most prolific comedians is Hideo Higashikokubaru.

Hilario
Latin, meaning 'cheerful, happy'. Goalkeeper Henrique Hilario Meireles Sampaio is usually known just as Hilario.

Hilary
(alt. Hillary)
English, meaning 'cheerful'. Most used now as a girls' name although it can be used for boys, as with politician Hilary Benn.

Hildred
German, meaning 'battle counsellor'.

Hillel
Hebrew, meaning 'greatly praised'. Rabbi Hillel was an important leader in the Jewish faith.

Hilliard
Old German, meaning 'battle guard'.

Hilton
Old English, meaning 'hill settlement'.

Hiram
Hebrew, meaning 'exalted brother'.

Hiro
Spanish, meaning 'sacred name'.

Hiroshi
Japanese, meaning 'generous'.

Hobart
English, meaning 'bright and shining intellect'. Also the name of the capital of Tasmania.

Hodge
English, meaning 'son of Roger'.

Hogan
Gaelic, meaning 'youth'. Wrestling superstar Terry Bollea is better known as Hulk Hogan.

Holden
English, meaning 'deep valley'.

Hollis
Old English, meaning 'holly tree'.

Homer
Greek, meaning 'pledge'. Name of the Greek poet – and of the TV character Homer Simpson.

Honorius
Latin, meaning 'honourable'. Honorius was a Roman emperor in the fifth century BC.

Horace
Latin, common name of the Roman poet Quintus Horatius Flaccus.

Houston

Old English, meaning 'Hugh's town'. Also a city in the state of Texas, USA.

Howard

Old English, meaning 'noble watchman'. Howard Hughes was a businessman, film-maker and aviator and one of the wealthiest men on the planet. Howard Donald is a founder member of enduringly successful boy band Take That.

Howell

Welsh, meaning 'eminent and remarkable'. Also the name of a town in Lincolnshire.

Hoyt

Norse, meaning 'spirit' or 'soul'. Also believed to be an Old English name, meaning someone who lives on a hill.

Hristo

From Christo, meaning 'follower of Christ'. Hristo Stoichkov is acknowledged to be one of the best footballers of his generation, and the best Bulgarian footballer ever.

Hubbell
(alt. Hubble)

English, meaning 'brave hearted'.

Hubert

German, meaning 'bright and shining intellect'.

Hudson

Old English, meaning 'adventurous' or 'son of Hugh'. Also one of the largest rivers in the USA.

Hugh
(alt. Hubert, Hugo, Huw)

Old German, meaning 'soul, mind and intellect'. Famous Hughs include actors Hugh Grant, Hugh Laurie and Hugh Jackman. The founder of fashion house Givenchy was Count Hubert de Givenchy. Huw Stephens is a Welsh radio presenter.

Humbert

Old German, meaning 'famous giant'. Be warned: it's the name and surname of the paedophile protagonist of Vladimir Nabokov's novel *Lolita*.

Humphrey

Old German, meaning 'peaceful warrior'. Actor Humphrey Bogart is best known for his role in the film *Casablanca*.

Hunter

English, from the word 'hunter'. Popular name in the USA for boys, yet to take off in the UK.

Hurley

Gaelic, meaning 'sea tide'.

Huxley

Old English, meaning 'Hugh's meadow'.

Hyrum
(alt. Hiram, Hyram)

Hebrew, meaning 'exalted brother'. Hyrum Smith was one of the founders of the Church of Jesus Christ of Latter Day Saints; also known as the Mormons.

I

Boys' names

Iago
Spanish, meaning 'he who supplants'. Name of the villain in Shakespeare's *Othello*.

Ian
(alt. Ion, Iain)

Gaelic, variant of John, meaning 'God is gracious'. Famous Ians include former cricketer Sir Ian Botham, novelists Ian Fleming and Iain Banks and journalist and satirist Ian Hislop.

Ianto
Welsh, meaning 'gift of God'. Ianto Jones is a featured character in sci-fi drama series *Torchwood*.

Ibaad
Arabic, meaning 'a believer in God'.

Ibrahim
Arabic, meaning 'father of many'. Also the Arabic name for the prophet and father of Islam, Abraham.

Ichabod
Hebrew, meaning 'glory is good'. The protagonist in Washington Irving's short story 'The Legend of Sleepy Hollow' is called Ichabod Crane.

Ichiro
Japanese, meaning 'firstborn son'. A current Japanese superstar baseball player is Ichiro Suzuki.

Idan
Hebrew, meaning 'place in time'.

Idris
Welsh, meaning 'fiery leader'. Actor Idris Elba is known for his roles in *The Wire*, *Luther* and *Mandela: Long Walk to Freedom*.

Ifan
Welsh variant of John, meaning 'God is gracious'.

Ignacio
Latin, meaning 'ardent' or 'burning'. More commonly found in South America, particularly Uruguay and Argentina.

Ignatz
German, meaning 'fiery'.

Igor
Russian or Norse origin, meaning 'warrior'.

Ikaika
Hawaiian, meaning 'strong'.

Iku
Japanese, meaning 'nourishing'.

Ilan
(alt. Elan)

Hebrew, meaning 'tree'. Composer Ilan Eshkeri is known for his scores of several films, including Layer Cake and Kick-Ass.

Ilias
Greek variant of Hebrew Elijah, meaning 'the Lord is my God'.

Imanol
Basque-language variant of Immanuel, meaning 'God is with us'.

Indiana
Latin, meaning 'from India'. Also the film character Indiana Jones and the American state.

Indigo
English, describing a deep blue colour derived from a plant. Used as a boys' and girls' name.

Indio
Spanish, meaning 'indigenous people'.

Ingo
Danish, meaning 'meadow'. Also the name of a tropical plant.

Inigo
Spanish, meaning 'fiery'. Famous Inigos include the sixteenth-century English architect Inigo Jones and a character in the film The Princess Bride.

Ioannis
Greek, meaning 'the Lord is gracious'.

Iovianno
Native American, meaning 'yellow hawk'. More common as a spelling alternative for Giovanni.

Ira
Hebrew, meaning 'full grown and watchful'. In the Hindu faith, Ira-putra is Hanuman the monkey god. Ira Gershwin was a famous 20th-century American lyricist.

Irvin
(alt. Irving, Irwin)

Gaelic, meaning 'green and fresh water'. Composer Irving Berlin is known for songs such as 'White Christmas' and 'Alexander's Ragtime Band'.

Isaac
(alt. Isaak; abbrev. Ike)

Hebrew, meaning 'laughter'. Isaac was the son of Abraham and Sarah in the Bible and the Qur'an. Famous Ikes include singer Ike Turner and former US president Dwight D. Eisenhower (known as Ike).

Isadore
(alt. Isidore, Isidro)

Greek, meaning 'gift of Isis'. Popular name in both ancient Greece and ancient Egypt.

Isai
(alt. Isaiah, Isaias, Izaiah)

Arabic, meaning 'protection and security'.

Iser

Yiddish, meaning 'God wrestler'. Most common in Germany.

Ishedus

Native American, meaning 'on top'.

Ishmael
(alt. Ismael)

Hebrew, meaning 'God listens'. Ishmael was the son of the prophet Abraham and his wife Hagar.

Israel

Hebrew, meaning 'God perseveres'. Also the name of the country.

Istvan

Hungarian variant of Stephen, meaning 'crowned'. Very common in Eastern Europe.

Itai

Hebrew, meaning 'the Lord is with me'. One of the most common names in Israel.

Ivan

Hebrew, meaning 'God is gracious'. Russian Grand Prince Ivan the Terrible is credited for conquering so much land that Russia has ended up the size it is today.

Ivanhoe

Russian, meaning 'God is gracious'. Also name of the novel by Walter Scott.

Ivey

English, variant of Ivy usually reserved for boys.

Ivo

French, from the word 'yves', meaning 'yew tree'. Dr Ivo Robotnik is the villain in Sonic the Hedgehog video games.

Ivor

Scandinavian, meaning 'yew'. Composer Ivor Novello was such an influential performer that there is an entire awards series named after him: the Ivor Novello Awards (the Ivors) are given out for songwriting and composing.

Ivory

English, from the word 'ivory'. More commonly used as a girls' name.

Izar

Basque, meaning 'star'. The izar is also a piece of Ihram clothing worn during the Islamic Hajj pilgrimage.

Boys' names

Jabari
Swahili, meaning 'valiant'.

Jabez
Hebrew, meaning 'borne in pain'. Jabez is a well-respected ancestor of Judah in the Bible.

Jabulani
(alt. Jabulanie, Jabulany, Jabulaney)

African, meaning 'happy one'. The Jabulani is also a name for a type of Adidas football used in most professional Association games.

Jace
(alt. Jaece, Jase, Jayce)

Hebrew, meaning 'healer'. Sometimes used as a shortened version of Jason.

Jacek
Polish, meaning 'hyacinth'. Derived from the Greek name Hyakinthos, which comes from an ancient myth about a beautiful boy.

Jacinto
Spanish or Portuguese, meaning 'hyacinth'.

Jack
(alt. Jackie, Jacky)

From the Hebrew John, meaning 'God is gracious'. The UK's most popular boy's name for 14 years until 2011.

Jackson
(alt. Jaxon)

English, meaning 'son of Jack'. Jackson Pollock was an abstract expressionist artist, known for his large-scale paintings of splashes and drips.

Jacob
(alt. Jacobo, Jaco, Jago; abbrev. Jake)

Hebrew, meaning 'he who supplants'. Ancestor of the tribes of Israel in the Bible.

Jacques
(alt. Jaquez)

French form of James, meaning 'he who supplants'. Famous Jacques include Jacques Cousteau, the marine explorer, writer and film-maker, and Jacques Villeneuve, the racing driver.

Jaden
(alt. Jadyn, Jaeden, Jaiden, Jaidyn, Jayden, Jaydin)

Hebrew, meaning 'Jehovah has heard'. Actor Will Smith's eldest child is called Jaden Smith, and has begun an acting career of his own.

Jaeger
(alt. Jager, Jaecer, Jaegar)

German, meaning 'mighty hunter'. Also the name of a designer clothing line in Britain.

Jafar

Arabic, meaning 'stream'. The name of the villain in Disney's *Aladdin*.

Jagger

Old English, meaning 'one who cuts'. Sir Mick Jagger is the lead singer of the Rolling Stones.

Jaheem
(alt. Jaheim)

Hebrew, meaning 'raised up'. R&B singer Jaheim Hoagland goes by the stage name Jaheim.

Jahir

Hindi, meaning 'jewel'.

Jair
(alt. Jairo)

Hebrew, meaning 'God enlightens'. Also the name of a minor character in the Bible.

Jalen
(alt. Jalon, Jaylon, Jaylan)

American, meaning 'healer' or 'tranquil'. The original spelling was probably Galen, in Greek.

Jali

Gujarati, meaning 'latticed screen'. Popular form of architectural detailing throughout India.

Jamar
(alt. Jamarcus, Jamari, Jamarion, Jamir)

Modern variant of Jamaal, meaning 'handsome'. More common in the USA than in Britain.

Jamel
(alt. Jamal, Jamaal, Jamil)

Arabic, meaning 'handsome'. Actor Jamel Debbouze is a French and Moroccan film star.

James
(alt. Jaime; abbrev. Jamie, Jamey, Jim, Jimmy)

English, meaning 'he who supplants'. An enduringly popular name. Famous actors with this name include James Coburn, James Franco, James Corden, Jamie Bell and Jamie Foxx.

Jameson
(alt. Jamison)

English, meaning 'son of James'.

Jamin
(alt. Yamin)

Hebrew, meaning 'son of the right hand'.

Jan
(alt. Janko, János)

Slavic, from John, meaning 'the Lord is gracious'. Jan is also a term of endearment in Arabic, meaning 'dear'. Used for boys and also girls.

Janesh

Hindi, meaning 'leader of people'.

Janus

Latin, meaning 'gateway'. The two-faced Roman god of doors, beginnings and endings.

Japheth
(alt. Japhet)

Hebrew, meaning 'comely'. One of the sons of Noah in the Bible.

Jared
(alt. Jarem, Jaren, Jaret, Jarod, Jarrod)

Hebrew, meaning 'descending'. Actor Jared Leto is known for his roles in *Fight Club*, *American Psycho* and *Dallas Buyers Club*.

Jarlath

Gaelic, from Iarlaith, from St Iarlaithe mac Loga.

Jarom

Greek, meaning 'to raise and exalt'. One of the prophets in the Book of Mormon.

Jarrell

Variant of Gerald, meaning 'spear ruler'.

Jarrett

Old English, meaning 'spear-brave'. Sometimes used as an alternative spelling to Garrett.

Jarvis

Old German, meaning 'with honour'. Jarvis Cocker is the singer with the band Pulp.

Jason

Greek, meaning 'healer'. Famous Jasons include actor Jason Statham, and the ancient Greek myth of Jason and the Argonauts.

Jasper

Greek, meaning 'treasure holder' or 'speckled stone'. The stone jasper has been used for thousands of years for carved ornaments and jewellery. Jasper Conran is a modern fashion designer.

Javen
(alt. Javan)

Arabic, meaning 'youth'. Javan was one of Noah's grandsons in the Bible.

Javier

Spanish, meaning 'bright'. Actor Javier Bardem is known for his roles in *No Country for Old Men* and the James Bond movie *Skyfall*.

Jay

Latin, meaning 'jaybird'. Jays are a group of bird species in the crow family.

Jeevan

Indian, meaning 'life'. Often used with a prefix like 'har', to form other names (such as Harjeevan).

Jefferson

English, meaning 'son of Jeffrey'.

Jeffrey
(abbrev. Jeff)

Old German, meaning 'peace'. Famous Jeffreys include author Jeffrey Archer, and actors Jeff Bridges and Jeff Daniels.

Jensen
(alt. Jenson)

Scandinavian, meaning 'son of Jan'. Has increased in popularity in the UK in recent years, probably linked to the rise of Jenson Button, Formula One racing driver.

Jeremiah
(alt. Jeremia, Jeremias, Jeremiya)

Hebrew, meaning 'the Lord exalts'. One of the main prophets in the Bible.

Jeremy
(alt. Jem)

Hebrew, meaning 'the Lord exalts'. Famous Jeremys include actor Jeremy Irons, presenter Jeremy Clarkson and actor Jeremy Renner.

Jeriah

Hebrew, meaning 'Jehovah has seen'. Minor character in the Bible.

Jericho

Arabic, meaning 'city of the moon'. An ancient and religious city in the Palestinian West Bank.

Jermaine

Latin, meaning 'brotherly'. Jermaine Jackson was one of the original members of the Jackson 5.

Jerome

Greek, meaning 'sacred name'. Famous Jeromes include actor Jerome Flynn, and St Jerome, who was a medieval priest and theologian.

Jerry

English, from Gerald, meaning 'spear ruler'. Famous Jerrys include presenter Jerry Springer, comedian Jerry Seinfeld and the film *Jerry Maguire*.

Jesse

Hebrew, meaning 'the Lord exists'. Jesse James was a Wild West outlaw and train robber in the 1870s.

Jesus

Hebrew, meaning 'the Lord is Salvation' and the Son of God.

Jet
(alt. Jelt)

English, meaning 'black gemstone'. Jet is a minor gemstone, formed of fossilised wood.

Jethro

Hebrew, meaning 'eminent'. Famous Jethros include Jethro Tull, the agricultural pioineer, who gave his name to a 1970s rock band, and the father-in-law of Moses in the Bible.

Jim

(alt. Jimmy)

From James, meaning 'he who supplants'. Jim is one of the leading characters in Mark Twain's classic novel *Huckleberry Finn*.

Jiri

(alt. Jiro)

Czech, meaning 'farmer'. More commonly used in Czech-speaking communities as an alternative to George.

Joachim

(alt. Joaquin)

Hebrew, meaning 'established by God'. Also the name of the Virgin Mary's father in the Bible. Actor Joaquin Phoenix is known for his roles in *Gladiator*, *Walk the Line* and *Her*.

Joah

(alt. João)

Hebrew, meaning 'God is gracious'. The name of several minor characters in the Bible.

Joe

(alt. Joey, Jomar)

From Joseph, meaning 'Jehovah increases'. Usually used as a nickname for Joseph, Joel or Josiah, as well as a name in its own right.

Joel

Hebrew, meaning 'Jehovah is the Lord'.

John

(alt. Johan, Johannes, Johnny)

Hebrew, meaning 'God is gracious'. John the Baptist and the apostle John are major characters in the New Testament of the Bible.

Jolyon

English, meaning 'young'. One of the more prominent characters in the 'Tintin' comic series is Jolyon Wagg.

Jonah

(alt. Jonas)

Hebrew, meaning 'dove'. A character in the Bible who was swallowed by a whale.

Jonathan

(alt. Johnathan, Johnathon, Jonathon; abbrev. Jon, Jonny, Jonty)

Hebrew, meaning 'God is gracious'. Famous Jonathans include comedian and TV presenter Jonathan Ross, author Jonathan Swift and actor Jonathan Pryce.

Jordan

(alt. Jory, Judd)

Hebrew, meaning 'down-flowing'. Can be used as a girls' name or a boys' name.

Jorge

Spanish or Portuguese version of George, meaning 'farmer'. Actor Jorge Garcia is known for his role as Hurley in *Lost*.

José

Spanish variant of Joseph, meaning 'God increases'. José Mourinho is the football manager known as 'the special one'.

Joseph
(alt. Joss)

Hebrew, meaning 'Jehovah increases'. Famous Josephs include two Biblical Josephs: the wearer of the many-coloured coat and the father of Jesus Christ. Others include actor Joseph Gordon-Levitt.

Joshua
(abbrev. Josh)

Hebrew, meaning 'God is salvation'. Joshua was the leader of the Israelites after Moses' death in the Bible.

Josiah

Hebrew, meaning 'God helps'. One of the kings of Judah in the Bible.

Josué

Spanish variant of Joshua, meaning 'God is salvation'.

Jovan

Latin, meaning 'the supreme God'. More commonly used in Serbia and Macedonia.

Joweese

Native American, meaning 'chirping bird'. Originally used more commonly for girls, it has now become a boys' name.

Joyce

Latin, meaning 'joy'. More commonly used as a girls' name but can be used for boys.

Juan

Spanish variant of John, meaning 'God is gracious'. It is also becoming a popular name for girls in China, with the meaning of 'chapter or scroll' in Mandarin.

Jubal

Hebrew, meaning 'ram's horn'. Also the name of the 'father of music' in the Bible.

Jude
(alt. Judson)

Hebrew, meaning 'praise' or 'thanks'. Famous Judes include St Jude, the patron saint of lost causes, actor Jude Law and Thomas Hardy's novel *Jude the Obscure*.

Julian
(alt. Julio, Julien; abbrev. Jules, Jools)

Greek, meaning 'belonging to Julius'. The original calendar in the Roman empire was called the Julian calendar. Famous Juleses include author Jules Verne, DJ Judge Jules and pianist/presenter Jools Holland.

Julius

Latin, meaning 'youthful'. Julius Caesar was dictator of Rome and the first Roman emperor, ruling in the first century BC.

Junior

Latin, meaning 'the younger one'. Can also be used as a suffix to names to denote a name that has been passed down from father to son (such as Steve Jones Sr and Steve Jones Jr).

Junius

Latin, meaning 'young'. The pseudonym of an anonymous and prolific political writer in the eighteenth century.

Jupiter

Latin, meaning 'the supreme God'. Jupiter was king of the Roman gods and the god of thunder. Jupiter is also the largest planet in the solar system.

Juraj

Hebrew, meaning 'God is my judge'. More popular in Eastern Europe.

Jurgen

German form of George, meaning 'farmer'. Former football player Jurgen Klinsmann is now the manager of the US national team.

Justice

English, from the word 'justice', meaning a set of moral values, ethics and law.

Justin
(alt. Justus)

Latin, meaning 'just and upright'. Famous Justins include singers Justin Timberlake and Justin Bieber, and children's TV presenter Justin Fletcher.

Juwan

Hebrew, meaning 'the Lord is gracious'.

K Boys' names

Kabelo

African, meaning 'gift'. Popular name in Botswana.

Kade

Scottish, meaning 'from the wetlands'. More commonly used as a spelling alternative to Cade.

Kadeem

Arabic, meaning 'one who serves'. Actor Kadeem Hardison is known for his role on *A Different World*.

Kaden

(alt. Kadin, Kaeden, Kaedin, Kaiden)
Arabic, meaning 'companion'. Also the name of a town in Germany.

Kadir

Arabic, meaning 'capable and competent'.

Kafka

Czech, meaning 'bird-like'. Often associated with the author Franz Kafka.

Kahekili

Hawaiian, meaning 'the thunder'. Also the name of several kings of Maui.

Kahlil

(alt. Kalil)
Arabic, meaning 'friend'. The Lebanese author Kahlil Gibran is known for his work *The Prophet*.

Kai

Greek, meaning 'keeper of the keys'. Kai has meanings in several languages, including 'dog' in Cornish, 'ocean water' in Hawaiian and 'food' in Maori.

Kaito

Japanese, a combination of the words 'sea, ocean' and 'soar, fly'.

Kalani

Hawaiian, meaning 'sky'.

Kale

German, meaning 'free man'.
Also the name of a leafy green
vegetable.

Kaleb

(alt. Caleb)

Hebrew, meaning 'dog' or
'aggressive'. Kaleb was also the
most prominent King of Aksum, the
capital of Abyssinia, in the
sixth century.

Kalen

Gaelic, meaning 'uncertain'.

Kaleo

Hawaiian, meaning 'the voice'.
Kaleo Kanahele is a silver medal-
winning American paralympian in
volleyball.

Kamari

Indian, meaning 'the enemy of
desire'. Also the name of a popular
tourist destination in Greece.

Kamden

English, meaning 'winding valley'.
Also a spelling alternative for
Camden.

Kamil

(alt. Kaamil)

Arabic, meaning 'perfection'. Also
a Polish and Slovak name meaning
'religious service attender'.

Kane

Gaelic, meaning 'little battler'.

Kani

Hawaiian, meaning 'sound'.

Kanye

A town in Botswana. Made popular
by rapper Kanye West.

Kareem

(alt. Karim)

Arabic, meaning 'generous'.

Karl

(alt. Karson)

Old German, meaning 'free man'.

Kasey

Irish, meaning 'alert'.

Kaspar

Persian, meaning 'treasurer'.

Kavon

Gaelic, meaning 'handsome'. More
commonly used in the USA.

Kayden

Arabic, meaning 'companion'. Also
used as a spelling alternative for
Caden.

Kazimierz

Polish, meaning 'declares peace'.
Also the name of a town in
Poland.

Kazuki

Japanese, meaning 'radiant hope'.
Kazuki Takahashi is a well-known
Japanese artist and video game
creator.

Kazuo

Japanese, meaning 'harmonious man'. Depending on the characters/spellings used, Kazuo can also mean 'first son' or 'first in leadership'.

Keagan
(alt. Keegan, Kegan)

Gaelic, meaning 'small flame'.

Keane

Gaelic, meaning 'fighter'.

Keanu

Hawaiian, meaning 'breeze'. Actor Keanu Reeves is known for his roles in *Bill & Ted's Excellent Adventure*, *Speed* and 'The Matrix' trilogy.

Keary

Gaelic, meaning 'black-haired'. Also used as a girls' name.

Keaton

English, meaning 'place of hawks'. Buster Keaton was a famous American actor and director of silent films.

Keefe
(alt. Keef, Keeffe, Kief, Kiefe)

Gaelic, meaning 'beautiful and graceful'.

Keeler

Gaelic, meaning 'beautiful and graceful'. Also a term used for a small, shallow tub for bathing.

Keenan
(alt. Kenan)

Gaelic, meaning 'little ancient one'.

Keiji

Japanese, meaning 'govern with discretion'. Also a term sometimes used for police officers.

Keir

Gaelic, meaning 'dark-haired' or 'dark-skinned'. James Keir Hardie was a Scottish socialist and labour leader in the nineteenth and twentieth centuries.

Keith

Gaelic, meaning 'woodland'. Famous Keiths include Rolling Stones band member Keith Richards, presenter Keith Chegwin and chef Keith Floyd.

Kekoa

Hawaiian, meaning 'brave one' or 'soldier'.

Kelby

Old English, meaning 'farmhouse near the stream'.

Kell
(alt. Kellan, Kellen, Kelley, Kelly, Kiel)

Norse, meaning 'spring'. Usually associated with the ancient and lavishly illustrated Book of Kells (as well as the cartoon movie).

Kelsey

Old English, meaning 'victorious ship'. Actor Kelsey Grammer is known for his roles in *Cheers* and *Frasier*.

Kelton

Old English, meaning 'town of the keels'. Singer Roy Orbison (of 'Oh, Pretty Woman' fame) had the middle name Kelton.

Kelvin

Old English, meaning 'friend of ships'. A kelvin is a unit of measurement for temperature, using the Kelvin scale.

Kemenes

Hungarian, meaning 'maker of furnaces'. More commonly used in Eastern Europe.

Kendal

Old English, meaning 'the Kent river valley'.

Kendon

Old English, meaning 'brave guard'.

Kendrick

Gaelic, meaning 'royal ruler'. Fairly popular in the USA, including hip hop artist Kendrick Lamar and record producer Kendrick Dean.

Kenelm

Old English, meaning 'bold'. St Kenelm was a boy king and martyr, mentioned in *The Canterbury Tales*.

Kenji

Japanese, meaning 'intelligent second son'. Also the name of a period in Japanese history in the thirteenth century.

Kennedy

Gaelic, meaning 'helmet head'. The Kennedy family are a prominent American-Irish Catholic dynasty, whose members have included President John F. Kennedy. Used for girls as well as boys in the USA.

Kenneth
(abbrev, Ken, Kenny, Kenney)

Gaelic, meaning 'born of fire'. Famous Kenneths include comedian Kenneth Williams, actor Kenneth Branagh and designer brand Kenneth Cole.

Kennison

English, meaning 'son of Kenneth'.

Kent

English, meaning 'rim or border'. From the county of the same name in England.

Kenton

English, meaning 'town of Ken'. Kenton Cool is a British mountaineer and mountain guide. He has climbed Mount Everest 11 times.

Kenya

From the country and mountain in Africa.

Kenzo

Japanese, meaning 'wise'. Kenzo Takada is the Japanese designer who founded the fashion brand Kenzo.

Keola

Hawaiian, meaning 'life'.

Keon

(alt. Kean, Keoni)

Persian, meaning 'King of Kings'. In Hawaiian, the same spelling means 'God is gracious'.

Kepler

German, meaning 'hat maker'.

Kerr

English, meaning 'wetland'. Kerr Smith is an American actor.

Kerry

Irish, from the county of the same name. More commonly a girls' name.

Kerwin

(alt. Kermit)

Gaelic, meaning 'without envy'. Most popular in the USA.

Keshav

Indian, meaning 'beautiful-haired'. One of the names for Vishnu in the Hindu religion.

Kevin

Gaelic, meaning 'handsome beloved'. Famous Kevins include former footballer Kevin Keegan and actors Kevin Kline and Kevin Bacon.

Khalid

(alt. Khaled, Khalif, Khalil)

Arabic, meaning 'immortal'. Actor Khalid Abdalla is known for his roles in United 93 and The Kite Runner.

Kian

(alt. Keyon, Kyan)

Persian, meaning 'king or realm'. In Ireland, the same spelling means 'ancient'.

Kiefer

German, meaning 'barrel maker'. Actor Kiefer Sunderland is best known for his role in the series 24.

Kieran

(alt. Kiaran, Kieron, Kyron)

Gaelic, meaning 'black'. Famous Kierans include gymnast Kieran Behan and actor Kieran Culkin.

Kijana

Swahili, meaning 'youth'.

Kilby

From the English 'Cilebi', a place in Leicestershire.

Kilian

Irish, meaning 'bright headed'. St Kilian was a bishop in Ireland in the seventh century.

Kimani

African, meaning 'beautiful and sweet'. Kenyan Kimani Maruge held the Guinness World Record for being the oldest person to start primary school, at the ripe old age of 84.

King

English, from the word 'male ruler of state'.

Kingsley

English, meaning 'the king's meadow'. Kingsley Shacklebolt is a key character in J.K. Rowling's 'Harry Potter' series. Sir Kingsley Amis was an English novelist.

Kirby

German, meaning 'settlement by a church'. Also the name of a small, pink, bubble-like video game character.

Kirk

Old German, meaning 'church'.

Klaus

German, meaning 'victorious'. Also a shortened form of Nikolaus.

Knightley
(alt. Knightly)

English, meaning 'of the knight's meadows'. An English place name in Staffordshire.

Kobe
(alt. Koda, Kody)

Japanese, meaning 'a Japanese city'.

Kofi

Ghanaian, meaning 'born on Friday'. Kofi Annan was the Secretary General of the United Nations from 1997 to 2006.

Kohana

Japanese, meaning 'little flower'. The Kohana cat is a hairless breed of cat.

Kojo

Ghanaian, meaning 'Monday'. Kojo is also a type of computer programming language.

Kolby

Norse, meaning 'settlement'. Often used as a spelling alternative for Colby.

Komal

Hindi, meaning 'soft and tender'.

Korben
(alt. Korbin)

Gaelic, meaning 'a steep hill'. Korben Dallas is the protagonist in the sci-fi film The Fifth Element.

Kramer

German, meaning 'shopkeeper'. Usually associated with the character Kramer on the 1990s sitcom Seinfeld.

Kris
(alt. Krish)

From Christopher, meaning 'Christ bearer'. Can be a short form of Kristopher, Kristian or (for girls) Kristen.

Kurt

German, meaning 'courageous advice'. Famous Kurts include Glee character Kurt, actor Kurt Russell and singer Kurt Cobain.

Kurtis

French, meaning 'courtier'.

Kwame

Ghanaian, meaning 'born on Saturday'. Kwame Nkrumah was the first president of Ghana.

Kyden

English, meaning 'narrow little fire'. Sometimes used as a spelling alternative for Caden.

Kyle

(alt. *Kylan, Kyleb, Kyler*)
Scottish Gaelic, meaning 'narrow and straight'. Originated from the place name in Scotland.

Kyllion

Irish, meaning 'war'.

Kyree

From Cree, a Canadian tribe. More commonly used in the USA.

Kyros

Greek, meaning 'legitimate power'. Kyros of Constantinople was an important figure in the Orthodox Church in the eighth century.

Long names

Alexander

Bartholomew

Christopher

Demetrius

Giovanni

Montgomery

Obadiah

Roberto

Salvatore

Zachariah

L Boys' names

Laban

Hebrew, meaning 'white'. Laban is the brother of Rebekah in the Bible.

Lachlan

Gaelic, meaning 'from the land of lakes'. A popular name in Australia.

Lacy

Old French, after the place in France. The feminine equivalent is Lacey.

Laertes

English, meaning 'adventurous'. Ophelia's brother in Shakespeare's *Hamlet*.

Lalit

Hindi, meaning 'beautiful'. The Lalit is one of the melodic aspects of Indian classical music.

Lamar

(alt. Lemar)

Old German, meaning 'water'. Singer Lemar is known for his songs 'Dance (With U)' and 'If There's Any Justice'.

Lambert

(alt. Lambros)

Scandinavian, two elements meaning 'land' and 'brilliant'. The name has been in use since Roman times.

Lamont

Old Norse, meaning 'law man'.

Lancelot

(abbrev. Lance)

Variant of Lance, meaning 'land'. The name of one of the Knights of the Round Table. Cyclist Lance Armstrong won the Tour de France seven times before being stripped of his titles for cheating.

Landen

(alt. Lando, Landon, Langdon, Landen)

English, meaning 'long hill'. Also the name of a town in Belgium.

Lane

(alt. Layne)

English, from the common word meaning 'narrow road'.

Lang

(alt. Langston)

Norse, meaning 'long meadow'.

Lannie

(alt. Lanny)

German, meaning 'precious'. Sometimes used as a nickname for Rowland or Orlando, as well as a name in its own right.

Larkin

Gaelic, meaning 'rough' or 'fierce'. Poet Philip Larkin was known for his works *The Whitsun Weddings* and *High Windows*.

Laron

French, meaning 'thief'.

Larry

Latin, variant of Lawrence, meaning 'man from Laurentum'. Famous Larrys include actor Larry Hagman, presenter Larry King and comedian Larry Grayson.

Lars

Scandinavian variant of Lawrence, meaning 'man from Laurentum'. The founder of Swedish electronics brand Ericsson was called Lars Magnus Ericsson.

Lasse

Finnish, meaning 'girl'. (Still, ironically, a boy's name.) Men with the name Lars are sometimes called Lasse as a nickname in Scandinavia. Finn Lasse Viren was one of the greatest long-distance runners of all time. Lasse Hallström is a Swedish film director.

Laszlo

Hungarian, meaning 'glorious rule'. Derived from the name of King/St Ladislaus I of Hungary.

Lathyn

Latin, meaning 'fighter'. Sometimes also used as a name for girls.

Latif

Arabic, meaning 'gentle'. The female equivalent for girls is Latifa.

Laurel

Latin, meaning 'bay'. One of the founders of Jamaican ska music was Laurel Aitken.

Laurence

(alt. Lawrence; abbrev. Larry)

Latin, meaning 'man from Laurentum'. Actor Laurence Olivier was known for his roles in dozens of Shakespeare productions and Hollywood films.

Laurent

French form of Lawrence, meaning 'man from Laurentum'. Laurent-Perrier is a champagne brand.

Lazarus

Hebrew, meaning 'God is my help'. Also the name of a minor character in the Bible, said to have been raised from the dead by Jesus Christ.

Leandro

Spanish, meaning 'lion man'. More commonly used in South America.

Lear

German, meaning 'of the meadow'. Shakespeare's play *King Lear* tells the story of a wealthy king decending into madness.

Lee
(alt. Leigh)

English, meaning 'pasture' or 'meadow'. Famous Lees include comedian Lee Mack, 'Harry Potter' character Lee Jordan and assassin Lee Harvey Oswald.

Leib

Yiddish, meaning 'lion'.

Leif
(alt. Liev)

Scandinavian, meaning 'heir'. Actor Liev Schreiber is known for his roles in *X-Men Origins: Wolverine*, the 'Scream' trilogy and *Ray Donovan*.

Leith

From the name of a busy port town in Scotland.

Lennox

Gaelic, meaning 'with many elm trees'. Lennox Lewis is a retired world heavyweight boxing champion.

Lenny

Shortened form of Lennox or Leonard, as well as a name in its own right. Lenny Kravitz is a musician and Lenny Godber was a much-loved character in the classic TV series *Porridge*.

Leo
(alt. Leon)

Latin, meaning 'lion'. Also the star sign.

Leonard
(alt. Leonardo)

Old German, meaning 'lion strength'. Famous Leonards and Leonardos include actors Leonard Nimoy and Leonardo DiCaprio, and artist and inventor Leonardo da Vinci.

Leopold

German, meaning 'brave people'. Prince Leopold was Queen Victoria and Prince Albert's eighth child, who was known to suffer from the blood disorder haemophilia.

Leroy

French, meaning 'king'. The song 'Bad Bad Leroy Brown' was a hit for R&B singer Jim Croce in 1973.

Leslie
(abbrev. Les)

Scottish Gaelic, from the name of the prominent clan. Also meaning 'holly garden'. Used as a name for girls (more commonly spelt Lesley) and for boys equally.

Lester

English, meaning 'from Leicester'. Lester Piggott is one of England's most successful jockeys.

Lewis

English form of French Louis, meaning 'famous warrior'. Famous Lewises include the Formula One racing driver Lewis Hamilton, comedian Lewis Black and *Alice in Wonderland* author Lewis Carroll.

Lex

English variant of Alexander, meaning 'defending men'. Lex Luthor is the villain of the *Superman* stories.

Liam

German, meaning 'helmet'. Famous Liams include actor Liam Neeson, singer Liam Gallagher and One Direction member Liam Payne.

Lincoln

English, meaning 'lake colony'.

Linden

European, from the tree of the same name. Less commonly used for girls.

Lindsay

Scottish, meaning 'linden tree'. In recent times used more for girls than for boys.

Linus

Latin, meaning 'lion'. Usually associated with the *Peanuts* cartoon strip character, who is known for carrying a blanket everywhere.

Lionel

English, meaning 'lion'. Famous Lionels include dancer/actor Lionel Blair, singer Lionel Richie and composer Lionel Bart.

Llewellyn

Welsh, meaning 'like a lion'.

Lloyd

Welsh, meaning 'grey-haired and sacred'. Famous Lloyds include actor Roger Lloyd Pack, former prime minister David Lloyd George and composer Andrew Lloyd Webber.

Logan

Gaelic, meaning 'hollow'. Usually associated with sci-fi novel *Logan's Run*. Has risen in popularity in recent years. Logan Lerman is the American actor playing the title role in the *Percy Jackson* films.

Lonnie

English, meaning 'lion strength'.

Lorcan

Gaelic, meaning 'little fierce one'. Also the name of several kings of Leinster in Ireland.

Louis

(alt. *Lou, Louie, Luigi, Luis*)

French, meaning 'famous warrior'. Famous Louises include One Direction singer Louis Tomlinson, music manager Louis Walsh and designer brand Louis Vuitton.

Lucas
(alt. Lukas, Luca)

English, meaning 'man from Luciana'. Popular in Brazil – there are several Brazilian footballers with this first name.

Lucian
(alt. Lucio)

Latin, meaning 'light'. Lucian of Samosata was an ancient Greek writer. Lucian Freud was a painter.

Ludwig

German, meaning 'famous warrior'. Ludwig van Beethoven was a hugely influential Classical and Romantic composer.

Luke
(alt. Luc, Luka)

Latin, meaning 'from Lucanus'. Famous Lukes include a primary character in the Bible, the author of the Gospel of Luke, *Star Wars* protagonist Luke Skywalker and actor Luke Perry.

Lupe

Latin, meaning 'wolf'. Rapper Lupe Fiasco is known for his songs 'Superstar' and 'The Show Goes On'.

Luther

German, meaning 'soldier of the people'. Famous Luthers include the German church reformer Martin Luther, US civil rights activist Martin Luther King Jr and Luther Vandross, the multi-award-winning singer.

Lyle

French, meaning 'the island'. Lyle Lovett is an American country singer.

Lyn
(alt. Lyndon)

Spanish, meaning 'pretty'. More commonly used as a name for girls.

Lynton

English, meaning 'town of lime trees'. Also a girls' name.

M

Boys' names

Mabon
(alt. Maban, Mabery)
Welsh, meaning 'our son'. A character in the King Arthur legend.

Mac
(alt. Mack, Mackie)
Scottish, meaning 'son of'.

Macaulay
Scottish, meaning 'son of the phantom'. Actor Macaulay Culkin shot to fame as a child actor in the *Home Alone* films.

Mace
English, meaning 'heavy staff' or 'club'. Can also be a nickname for Mason.

Mackenzie
Scottish, meaning 'the fair one'. Actor Mackenzie Crook is known for his roles in *The Office*, *Pirates of the Caribbean*, and *Game of Thrones*.

Mackland
Scottish, meaning 'land of Mac'.

Macon
French, name of towns in France and Georgia (USA).

Macsen
Scottish, meaning 'son of Mac'.

Madden
(abbrev. Mads)
Irish, meaning 'descendant of the hound'.

Maddox
English, meaning 'good' or 'generous'. Derived from Madoc, a legendary Welsh Prince who supposedly discovered America years before Christopher Columbus. Maddox Jolie-Pitt is the eldest son of Angelina and Brad.

Madison
(alt. Madsen)
Irish, meaning 'son of Madden'.

Magnus
(alt. Manus)

Latin, meaning 'great'. Famous Magnuses include Magnus Carlsen the chess grand master and TV presenter Magnus Magnusson.

Maguire

Gaelic, meaning 'son of the beige one'.

Mahabala

Indian, meaning 'great strength'. Also the name of a Buddhist guardian.

Mahesh

Hindi, meaning 'great ruler'. Also one of the names of Lord Shiva in the Hindu faith.

Mahir

Arabic, meaning 'skilful'.

Mahlon

Hebrew, meaning 'sickness'. Found in the Bible.

Mahmoud

Arabic, meaning 'praiseworthy'. Mahmoud Ahmadinejad was the president of Iran until 2013.

Mahoney

Irish, meaning 'bear'.

Major

English, from the word 'major'.

Makal

Alternative to Michael or Mikael, meaning 'close to God'.

Makani

Hawaiian, meaning 'wind'. Also a popular name in Arabic-speaking communities.

Makis

Hebrew, meaning 'gift from God'.

Mako

Hebrew, meaning 'God is with us'. Mako Iwamatsu was a prominent voice-over artist known for his roles in *Avatar: The Last Airbender* and *Conan the Barbarian*.

Malachi
(alt. Malachy)

Hebrew, meaning 'messenger of God', the name of a Jewish prophet in the Bible. Also an Irish name.

Malcolm

English, meaning 'Columba's servant'. Famous Malcolms include activist Malcolm X, actor Malcolm McDowell and bestselling author and journalist Malcolm Gladwell.

Mali

Arabic, meaning 'full and rich'. Also the name of a West African republic.

Manfred

Old German, meaning 'man of peace'. The band Manfred Mann is known for the song 'Blinded by the Light'.

Manish
(alt. Manesh)

English, meaning 'manly'. Extremely popular name in large parts of India.

Manley

English, meaning 'manly and brave'.
Also the name of a Cornish village.

Mannix

Gaelic, meaning 'little monk'.
Usually associated with the detective
series *Mannix*.

Manoi
(alt. Manos)

Japanese, meaning 'love springing
from intellect'. Also the name of a
Laotian king.

Manuel

Spanish variation of Hebrew
Emanuel, meaning 'God is with us'.
Usually associated with the character
of Manuel in the sitcom *Fawlty
Towers*.

Manzi

Italian, meaning 'steer'. Also the old
name for parts of southern China.

Marc
(alt. Marco, Marcos, Marcus, Markel)

French, meaning 'from the god
Mars'. Famous Marcs include
designer brand Marc Jacobs, singer
Marc Bolan and drummer Marc Bell.

Marcel
(alt. Marcelino, Marcello)

French, meaning 'little warrior'. One
of the most famous mimes of all time
was Frenchman Marcel Marceau.

Marek

Polish variant of Mark, meaning 'from
the god Mars'.

Mariano

Latin, meaning 'from the god Mars'.
Other theories suggest that Mariano
is a tribute to the Virgin Mary.

Mario
(alt. Marius)

Latin, meaning 'manly'. Mario is
a popular Nintendo video game
character, alongside his brother Luigi.
Mario Andretti is a retired Formula
One world champion racing driver.

Mark
(alt. Markus)

English, meaning 'from the god
Mars'. Famous Marks include the
Gospel of Mark from the Bible, actors
Mark Hamill and Mark Wahlberg and
author Mark Twain.

Marley
(alt. Marlin)

Old English, meaning 'meadow near
the lake'. Sometimes used as a short
form of Marlon. Famous Marleys
include singer Bob Marley and a
naughty Labrador dog called Marley.

Marlo

American, meaning 'bitter'.

Marlon

English, meaning 'like little hawk'.
Famous Marlons include actor Marlon
Brando, singer Marlon Jackson and
comedian Marlon Wayans.

Marshall

Old French, meaning 'caretaker of
horses'. Also the name of a group of
islands in the Pacific Ocean.

Martin
(abbrev. Marty)

Latin, meaning 'dedicated to Mars'. Famous Martins include actors Martin Freeman and Martin Sheen and director Martin Scorsese.

Marvel

English, from the word 'marvel'. Also the name of the long-running comic book company.

Marvin

Welsh, meaning 'sea friend'. Famous Marvins include singer Marvin Gaye, composer Marvin Hamlish and cartoon character Marvin the Martian.

Mason

English, a mason is a craftsman in either stonework or brickwork.

Massimo

Italian, meaning 'greatest'. The Massimo family were an ancient Roman family with great influence.

Mathias
(alt. Matthias)

Hebrew, meaning 'gift of the Lord'. Matthias was the apostle chosen to replace Judas in the Bible.

Mathieu

French form of Matthew, meaning 'gift of God'.

Matthew
(alt. Mathew)

Hebrew, meaning 'gift of the Lord'. Famous Matthews include the Gospel of Matthew and actors Matthew McConaughey and Matthew Perry.

Maurice
(alt. Mauricio)

Latin, meaning 'dark skinned' or 'Moorish'. Children's author Maurice Sendak was best known for his work *Where the Wild Things Are*.

Maverick

American, meaning 'non-conformist leader'. Usually associated with the character Maverick from the film *Top Gun*.

Maximillian
(alt. Maximilian; abbrev. Max, Maxie, Maxim)

Latin, meaning 'greatest'. The name of several Roman emperors. Famous Maxes include actor Max Greenfield, the film *Mad Max*, and cosmetics brand Max Factor.

Maximino

Latin, meaning 'little Max'. More commonly used in Spanish-speaking communities.

Maxwell

Latin, meaning 'Maccus' stream'.

Maynard

Old German, meaning 'brave'. The name of a character in *Desperate Housewives*. John Maynard Keynes was a highly influential British economist.

Mearl

English, meaning 'my earl'. Was used widely in the nineteenth century.

Mederic

French, meaning 'doctor'. Most commonly used in Quebec, Canada.

Mekhi

African, meaning 'who is God?' Actor Mekhi Phifer is known for his roles in *ER*, *8 Mile* and *Lie To Me*.

Melbourne

From the city of the same name in Victoria, Australia.

Melchior

Persian, meaning 'king of the city'. The name of one of the three kings in the biblical story of the birth of Jesus.

Melton

English, meaning 'town of Mel'.

Melville

Scottish, meaning 'town of Mel'.

Melvin

(alt. Melvyn; abbrev. Mel)

English, meaning 'smooth brow'. Famous Melvins include DJ Melvin O'Doom, presenter Melvyn Bragg and actor Melvyn Douglas. Famous Mels include director Mel Brooks and comedian Mel Smith.

Memphis

Greek, meaning 'established and beautiful'. Also the name of a city in Tennessee, USA.

Mercer

English, a mercer was a man who traded or dealt in textiles.

Meredith

Welsh, meaning 'great ruler'. Used equally for girls and boys.

Merle

(alt. Merl, Murl)

French, meaning 'blackbird'.

Merlin

Welsh, meaning 'sea fortress'. Merlin was a magician and wise man in the King Arthur legend.

Merrick

Welsh, meaning 'Moorish'.

Merrill

Gaelic, meaning 'shining sea'.

Merritt

English, from the word 'merit'. Can be used for both boys and girls.

Merton

Old English, meaning 'town by the lake'. Also the name of a London borough.

Meyer

(alt. Mayer)

Hebrew, meaning 'bright farmer'.

Michael
(abbrev. *Mick, Micky, Mickey, Mike*)
Hebrew, meaning 'resembles God'. Famous Michaels include one of the archangels, Formula One racing legend Michael Schumacher, singer Michael Jackson and, reportedly the highest-paid comedian in the world, Michael McIntyre.

Michalis
Greek form of Michael, meaning 'resembles God'. Singer Michalis Hatzigiannis is popular in Greece and Cyprus.

Michel
French form of Michael, meaning 'resembles God'. Deutscher Michel is also the cartoon personification of Germany (in the same way that Uncle Sam represents the USA).

Michelangelo
Italian, meaning 'Michael's angel'. Name of the famous painter whose work can still be seen in the Sistine Chapel in Rome.

Michele
Italian form of Michael, meaning 'resembles God'. Elsewhere, more commonly used as a girls' name.

Michio
Japanese, meaning 'a man with the strength of three thousand men'. Michio Kaku is a leading theoretical physicist.

Miguel
Spanish form of Michael, meaning 'resembles God'.

Miklos
Greek form of Nicholas, meaning 'victorious'. Sometimes used as an alternative to Michael as well.

Milan
From the name of the Italian city. Also the name of singer-songwriter Shakira's son.

Miles
(alt. *Milo, Milos, Myles*)
English, from the word 'miles'. Famous Mileses include trumpeter Miles Davies, singer Miles Kane and *Star Trek: Next Generation* character Miles O'Brien.

Milton
English, meaning 'miller's town'.

Miro
Slavic, meaning 'peace'.

Misha
Russian, meaning 'resembles God'. Its English equivalent is often thought to be Mike, and the feminine version is Mischa.

Mitchell
(abbrev. *Mitch*)
English, meaning 'who is like God'. Mitchell Mark was a pioneer in motion picture technology.

Modesto

Italian, meaning 'modest'. Also the name of a town in California, USA.

Mohamed

(alt. Mohammad, Mohamet, Mohammed, Muhammad; abbrev. Mo)

Arabic, meaning 'praiseworthy'. Acknowledged as the prophet and founder of Islam. The name is extremely popular in large parts of the world. British runner Mo Farah is the Olympic and world record holder for the 5,000 and 10,000 metres.

Monroe

Gaelic, meaning 'mouth of the river Rotha'.

Monserrate

Latin, meaning 'jagged mountain'. A mountain in Colombia.

Montague

(abbrev. Monty)

French, meaning 'pointed hill'.

Montana

Latin, meaning 'mountain'. Also a state in the USA.

Monte

Italian, meaning 'mountain'. Also the name of a popular card game.

Montgomery

(abbrev. Monty)

Variant of Montague, meaning 'pointed hill'. Actor Montgomery Clift was known for his roles in From Here to Eternity, A Place in the Sun and The Misfits.

Moody

English, from the word 'moody'. Mad Eye Moody is a prominent character in J.K. Rowling's 'Harry Potter' series.

Mordecai

Hebrew, meaning 'little man'. Also a character in the Bible.

Morgan

Welsh, meaning 'great and bright'. Can be used for both boys and girls. Famous Morgans include actor Morgan Freeman, film maker Morgan Spurlock and musician Morgan Nicholls.

Moritz

Latin, meaning 'dark skinned and Moorish'. Also the German equivalent of Maurice.

Moroccan

Arabic, meaning 'from Morocco'. Also the name of one of Mariah Carey's twins.

Morpheus

Greek, meaning 'shape'. The name of the god of dreams in the epic poem Metamorphoses by Roman poet Ovid. Also a character in The Matrix.

Morris

Welsh, meaning 'dark skinned and Moorish'.

Morrison

English, meaning 'son of Morris'.

Mortimer

French, meaning 'dead sea'.

Morton

Old English, meaning 'moor town'. The name of several English towns.

Moses

(alt. Moshe, Moshon)

Hebrew, meaning 'saviour'. In the Bible, Moses receives the Ten Commandments from God.

Moss

English, meaning 'near a peat bog'.

Muir

Gaelic, meaning 'of the moor'.

Mungo

Gaelic, meaning 'most dear'.

Murphy

Irish, meaning 'sea warrior'.

Murray

Gaelic, meaning 'lord and master'. Famous Murrays include legendary Formula One commentator Murray Walker and Nobel Prize-winning physicist Murray Gell-Mann.

Mustafa

Arabic, meaning 'chosen'. Also a name for the prophet Muhammad in the Muslim faith.

Mwita

Swahili, meaning 'humorous one'.

Myron

Greek, meaning 'myrrh'. Myron was a popular sculptor in ancient Greece.

Boys' names

Nairn

Scottish, meaning 'alder-tree river'. From the Scottish town of the same name.

Najee

Arabic, meaning 'dear companion'. Also the name of an influential jazz musician.

Nakia

Arabic, meaning 'pure'. Also used as a name for girls.

Nakul

Indian, meaning 'mongoose'. Choreographer Nakul Dev Mahajan has made a name for himself choreographing both Bollywood and Hollywood films.

Naphtali
(alt. Naftali)

Hebrew, meaning 'wrestling'. One of Joseph's brothers in the Bible.

Napoleon

Italian, meaning 'man from Naples'. The French general Napoleon Bonaparte became emperor of France.

Narciso

Latin, from the myth of Narcissus, who drowned after falling in love with his own reflection.

Nash

English, meaning 'at the ash tree'.

Nasir

Arabic, meaning 'helper'.

Nathan
(alt. Nathaniel; abbrev. Nat, Nate)

Hebrew, meaning 'God has given'. Name of many characters in the Bible.

Naval

Indian, meaning 'wonder'.

Naveen

Indian, meaning 'new'. Actor Naveen Andrews is known for his roles in *Lost*, *The English Patient* and *Rollerball*.

Ned

Used as a short form of Edward, meaning 'wealthy guard', but can be used in its own right. A character in *Game of Thrones* and *The Simpsons* and the chosen name of Ned Rocknroll, most famous for being married to Kate Winslet.

Nehemiah

Hebrew, meaning 'comforter'. A prominent character in the Bible.

Neil
(alt. Neal, Niall)

Irish, meaning 'champion'.

Neilson

Irish, meaning 'son of Neil'. Also the name of a prominent train manufacturer in Scotland.

Nelson

Variant of Neil, meaning 'champion'. Admiral Horatio Nelson commanded the British navy at the Battle of Trafalgar. Nelson Mandela was the first black president of South Africa.

Nemo

Latin, meaning 'nobody'. Made famous by the Disney animation *Finding Nemo*.

Neo

Latin, meaning 'new'. Neo is the protagonist in *The Matrix* trilogy.

Nephi

Greek, meaning 'cloud'. The Books of Nephi are some of the subdivisions of the Book of Mormon.

Nessim
(alt. Nasim)

Arabic, meaning 'breeze'. Sham el-Nessim is also the first day of spring in Egypt.

Nestor

Greek, meaning 'traveller'. Nestor was the king of Pylos in ancient Greek mythology.

Neville

Old French, meaning 'new village'. Famous Nevilles include former prime minister Neville Chamberlain and Harry Potter character Neville Longbottom.

Newland
(alt. Newlands, Newland, Neuland)

English, meaning 'from a new land'. Also the name of several towns in the UK.

Newton

English, meaning 'new town'.

Nicholas
(alt. Nicolas, Niklas; abbrev. Nick, Nicky, Niko, Nikos, Nico)

Greek, meaning 'victorious'. An enduringly popular name. Famous Nicholases include St Nicholas (the original Santa Claus), actor Nicolas Cage and the alchemist Nicholas Flamel.

Nigel

Gaelic, meaning 'champion'. Famous Nigels include actor Nigel Hawthorne, photographer Nigel Barker and producer/presenter Nigel Lythgoe.

Nikhil

Sanskrit, meaning 'whole' or 'entire'. Often associated with former *Emmerdale* character Nikhil Sharma.

Nikita

Greek, meaning 'unconquered', also Russian. Nikita Khrushchev was leader of the Soviet Union from 1953 to 1964. Also used as a girls' name.

Nikolai
(alt. Nikolay)

Russian variant of Nicholas, meaning 'victorious'. Several Russian emperors were known as either Nicholas or Nikolai.

Nimrod

Hebrew, meaning 'we will rebel'. Character in the Bible. Also the title of a piece of music by Elgar and the name of a type of aircraft.

Ninian

Gaelic, associated with the fifth-century saint of the same name.

Nissim

Hebrew, meaning 'wonderful things'.

Noah

Hebrew, meaning 'peaceful'. In the Bible, Noah is said to have built an ark to save two of every animal from a flood that covered the earth.

Noel

French, meaning 'Christmas'. Famous Noels include actor/composer Noel Coward, TV and radio presenter Noel Edmonds and musician Noel Gallagher.

Nolan

Gaelic, meaning 'champion'.

Norbert

Old German, meaning 'Northern brightness'. Norbert is also the name of Hagrid's pet dragon in J.K. Rowling's 'Harry Potter' series.

Norman

Old German, meaning 'Northerner'.

Normand

French, meaning 'from Normandy'.

Norris

Old French, meaning 'Northerner'. Norris McWhirter was the co-author with his brother, Ross, of *The Guiness Book of Records*.

Norton

English, meaning 'Northern town'.

Norval

French, meaning 'Northern town'.

Norwood

English, meaning 'Northern forest'. Also the name of several towns in the UK.

Nova

Latin, meaning 'new'.

Nuno

Latin, meaning 'ninth'.

Nunzio

Italian, meaning 'messenger'. A fairly popular name in Italy.

Nyoka

Swahili, meaning 'like a snake'. Nyoka Meredith was the *Jungle Girl* in the novel by Edgar Rice Burroughs, later adapted into a cinema serial.

Names of poets

Andrew (Marvell)

Geoffrey (Chaucer)

Hugo (Williams)

John (Donne, Keats, Milton)

Percy (Bysshe Shelley)

Robert (Burns)

Siegfried (Sassoon)

Ted (Hughes)

Walt (Whitman)

William (Blake, Wordsworth)

Boys' names

Oakley

English, meaning 'from the oak meadow'. Also the name of a clothing brand.

Obadiah

Hebrew, meaning 'God's worker'. Used throughout the Bible to indicate a servant of God.

Obama

African, meaning 'crooked'. Made famous by the current President of the USA Barack Obama.

Obed

Hebrew, meaning 'servant of God'. Obed was the grandfather of David in the Bible.

Oberon
(abbrev. Obie)

Old German, meaning 'royal bear'. The Fairy King in Shakespeare's *A Midsummer Night's Dream*. Obie

is the name of an overweight dachshund that achieved internet notoriety in 2014.

Obijulu
(alt. Obiajulu)

Nigerian, meaning 'one who has been consoled'.

Octave
(alt. Octavian, Octavio)

Latin, meaning 'eight'. An octave is a group of eight notes in a musical scale.

Oda
(alt. Odell, Odie, Odis)

Hebrew, meaning 'praise God'. Oda of Canterbury was archbishop in the tenth century.

Ogden

Old English, meaning 'oak valley'. Ogden Nash was an American humorous poet.

Oisin

(alt. Ossian)

Celtic, meaning 'fawn'. The name of an ancient Irish poet.

Ola

Norse, meaning 'precious'. Ola Nordmann is the personification of Norway, in the same way Uncle Sam represents the USA.

Olaf

(alt. Olan)

Old Norse, meaning 'ancestor'. Also the name of the snowman in Disney's *Frozen*.

Oleander

Hawaiian, meaning 'joyous'. Also the name of a highly poisonous flowering shrub.

Oleg

(alt. Olen)

Russian, meaning 'holy'. Oleg the Seer was a Grand Prince of Rus', who ruled large parts of eastern Europe in the tenth century.

Olin

Russian, meaning 'rock'.

Oliver

(abbrev. Ollie)

Latin, meaning 'olive tree'. The UK's most popular boys' name in several recent years.

Olivier

French form of Oliver, meaning 'olive tree'.

Omar

(alt. Omari, Omarion)

Arabic, meaning 'speaker'. Extremely popular name in Sunni communities.

Ondrej

Czech, meaning 'manly'. The English equivalent is Andrew.

Ora

Latin, meaning 'hour'.

Oran

(alt. Oren, Orrin)

Gaelic, meaning 'light and pale'.

Orange

English, from the word 'orange', applied to both the fruit and the colour.

Orion

Greek, from the legend of a massive hunter, who was sent to spend eternity as a star constellation.

Orlando

(alt. Orlo)

Old German, meaning 'old land'. Famous Orlandos include actor Orlando Bloom, the Shakespearean character Orlando in *As You Like It* and the city of Orlando in Florida, USA.

Orpheus

Greek, meaning 'beautiful voice'. Orpheus was an ancient Greek musician and charmer, who tried to rescue his wife from the underworld.

Orrick

English, meaning 'sword ruler'.

Orson

Latin, meaning 'bear'. Film director Orson Welles was known for his radio play *The War of the Worlds*, and films *Citizen Kane* and *Touch of Evil*.

Orville

Old French, meaning 'gold town'. Orville and Wilbur Wright were the American brothers credited with building the first successful aeroplane.

Osaka

From the Japanese city.

Osborne
(alt. Osbourne)

Norse, meaning 'bear god'.

Oscar

Old English, meaning 'spear of the Gods'. Oscar Wilde was an Irish poet and writer, best known for his ready wit.

Osias

Hebrew, meaning 'salvation'. Osias Beert was an influential still-life painter in the seventeenth century.

Oswald

German, meaning 'God's power'. Oswald the Lucky Rabbit was Walt Disney's original cartoon creation before Mickey Mouse was born.

Othello

Old German, meaning 'wealth'. From the character in Shakespeare's play *Othello*.

Otis

German, meaning 'wealth'. Singer Otis Redding was known for his songs '(Sittin' on) The Dock of the Bay', 'Respect' and 'Try A Little Tenderness'.

Otten

German, meaning 'son of Otto'.

Otto
(alt. Otha, Otho)

German, meaning 'wealthy'. Famous Ottos include Anne Frank's father, Otto Frank, and Prussian leader Otto von Bismarck.

Ovid

Latin, meaning 'sheep'. Associated with the Roman poet, author of *Metamorphoses*.

Owain
(alt. Owen)

Welsh, meaning 'noble-born'. Owain Ddantgwyn was a prince of Wales and a contender to be the real King Arthur.

Oz

Hebrew, meaning 'strength'. As well as the fictional land of Oz in the story *The Wizard of Oz*, this is also a slang term for Australia.

Boys' names

Pablo
Spanish, meaning 'little'. Spanish painter and sculptor Pablo Picasso was one of the most influential artists of the twentieth century.

Paco
Native American, meaning 'eagle'. Also a Spanish alternative for Francisco.

Padma
Sanskrit, meaning 'lotus'. Also used as a name for girls.

Padraig
Irish, meaning 'noble'. The English equivalent is Patrick.

Panos
Greek, meaning 'all holy'.

Paolo
(alt. Paulo)
Italian, meaning 'little'. Paolo Nutini is a singer and Paulo Coelho is a Brazilian author.

Paresh
Sanskrit, meaning 'supreme spirit'.

Paris
From France's capital city. Also the Trojan prince in Homer's *Iliad* and Juliet's suitor in Shakespeare's *Romeo and Juliet*. Originally a boys' name, but now also used as a name for girls.

Pascal
Latin, meaning 'Easter child'.

Patrice
French form of Patrick, meaning 'noble'. Also a name given to girls.

Patrick
(abbrev. Pat, Paddy)
Irish, meaning 'noble'. The patron saint of Ireland. Patrick Stewart is an English actor whose long and distinguished career has included many spells with the Royal Shakespeare Company and playing Captain Jean-Luc Picard on *Star Trek*.

Patten

English, meaning 'noble'.

Paul

Hebrew, meaning 'small'. Paul the Apostle is a key character in the Bible. Famous Pauls include singers Paul Simon and Paul McCartney and artist Paul Cézanne.

Pavel

Latin, meaning 'small'. The English equivalent is Paul.

Pax

Latin, meaning 'peace'. From the Roman goddess of peace.

Paxton

English, meaning 'town of peace'.

Payne

Latin, meaning 'peasant'.

Payton

Latin, meaning 'peasant's town'.

Pedro

Spanish form of Peter, meaning 'rock'. Several kings of Portugal and Aragon have been named Pedro.

Penn

English, meaning 'hill'. Famous Penns include magician Penn Jillette. English Quaker William Penn was the founder of the state of Pennsylvania in the USA.

Percival

(abbrev. Percy)

French, meaning 'pierce the valley'. One of the Knights of the Round Table. Percy Weasley is a character in J.K. Rowling's 'Harry Potter' series.

Perez

Hebrew, meaning 'breach'. One of Judah's sons in the Bible.

Pericles

Greek, meaning 'far-famed'. Pericles was an influential ancient Greek general and statesman.

Perrin

Greek, meaning 'rock'.

Perry

English, meaning 'rock'. Perry is an alcoholic drink made from pears.

Pervis

English, meaning 'purveyor'.

Pesah

(alt. Pesach, Pesasch)

Hebrew, meaning 'spared'. Pesach the Hebrew name for the Jewish festival of Passover.

Peter

(abbrev. Pete)

Greek, meaning 'rock'. St Peter was one of Jesus's disciples in the Bible. Famous Peters include Peter Pan, film director Sir Peter Jackson, actor Peter Sellers and Russian emperor Peter the Great.

Petros

Greek form of Peter, meaning 'rock'.

Peyton

Old English, meaning 'fighting man's estate'.

Philemon

Greek, meaning 'affectionate'. A character in the New Testament of the Bible.

Philip

(alt. Phillip; abbrev. Phil, Phill, Pip)

Greek, meaning 'lover of horses'. Famous Philips include Prince Philip, Philip the Apostle in the Bible and author Philip Pullman. Pip is usually associated with the character of the same name in Charles Dickens' novel Great Expectations

Philo

Greek, meaning 'love'. Philo of Alexandria was an ancient Roman Jewish philiosopher.

Phineas

(alt. Pinchas)

Hebrew, meaning 'oracle'. Phineas was an ancient Greek king of Thrace.

Phoenix

Greek, meaning 'dark red'. In ancient Greek mythology, a phoenix is a bird that has the power to regenerate itself from its ashes.

Pierre

French form of Peter, meaning 'rock'. A popular French name.

Piers

Old English form of Peter, meaning 'rock'. Journalist and TV presenter Piers Morgan is known for his work with various tabloid newspapers and Britain's Got Talent.

Pierson

Variant of Piers, meaning 'son of Piers'.

Placido

Latin, meaning 'placid'. Tenor opera singer Placido Domingo is known for his vast array of operatic roles and performances with Luciano Pavarotti and José Carreras.

Pradeep

Hindi, meaning 'light'.

Pranav

Sanskrit, meaning 'spiritual leader'. Pranava is another way of saying 'Om' in Sanskrit.

Presley

Old English, meaning 'priest's meadow'. Usually associated with legend Elvis Presley.

Preston

Old English, meaning 'priest's town'. Also the name of a town in England. Preston Sturges was an Oscar-winning playwright.

Primo

Italian, meaning 'first'. Also used as a slang term for 'good' or 'excellent'.

Primus

Latin, meaning 'first'. Primus is often used in cartoons and comic books as a name for villains or superheroes, including in *Transformers* and Marvel comics.

Prince

English, from the word 'prince'. As well as a title of nobility, this name is often associated with the singer Prince.

Proctor

(alt. Prockter, Procter)
Latin, meaning 'steward'.

Prospero

Latin, meaning 'prosperous'. Prospero is the protagonist in Shakespeare's play *The Tempest*.

Pryor

English, meaning 'first'.

Ptolemy

Greek, meaning 'aggressive' or 'warlike'. Claudius Ptolemy was an ancient Greek mathematician and astronomer.

Purvis

(alt. Purves, Purviss)
French, meaning 'purveyor'.

 Boys' names

Qabil
(alt. Quabil)
Arabic, meaning 'able'. Qabil is the Arabic name for Cain, who was one of the sons of Adam and Eve in the Bible.

Qino
(alt. Quino)
Chinese, meaning 'handsome'. Also used in Spanish-speaking communities.

Quadim
Arabic, meaning 'able'. Often used with the prefix 'al', to form Al-Quadim.

Quadir
Arabic, meaning 'powerful'.

Quaid
Irish, meaning 'fourth'.

Qued
Old English, meaning 'bad or ugly'. Also an old name for the devil.

Quemby
Norse, meaning 'from the woman's estate'.

Quentin
(alt. Quinten, Quintin, Quinton, Quintus)
Latin, meaning 'fifth'. Famous Quentins include illustrator Quentin Blake and film director Quentin Tarantino.

Quillan
Gaelic, meaning 'sword'.

Quillon
Gaelic, meaning 'club'. The quillon is the bar on a sword where the handle meets the blade.

Quincy

Old French, meaning 'estate of the fifth son'. Jazz and soul legend Quincy Jones is known for his long career of music production, songwriting and performing.

Quinlan

Gaelic, meaning 'fit, shapely and strong'.

Quinn

Gaelic, meaning 'counsel'. Usually associated with the character from *Glee*.

Quinton

English, meaning 'queen's community'.

Old name, new fashion

Bertrand	Norris
Dexter	Pierce
Felix	Reginald
Hector	Ulysses
Jefferson	Winston

R Boys' names

Radames

Slavic, meaning 'famous joy'.
A character in the Verdi opera
Aïda.

Rafael

(alt. Raphael; abbrev. Rafa, Rafe,
Rafer, Raffi)

Hebrew, meaning 'God has healed'.
One of the archangels in the Bible.
Rafael Nadal is a Spanish tennis
player who has held the world No. 1
ranking.

Ragnar

Old Norse, meaning 'strong
counsellor'. Very popular name in
Scandinavia and Germany.

Raheem

(alt. Rahim)

Arabic, meaning 'merciful and
kind'.

Rahm

Hebrew, meaning 'mercy'.

Rahul

(alt. Raoul, Raul)

Indian, meaning 'efficient'. Rahul
was Buddha's son.

Raiden

(alt. Rainen)

From the Japanese god of thunder.
It also refers to the combination of
lightning and thunder.

Rainer

Old German, meaning 'warrior from
the gods'. Rainer Hersch is a British
classical music comedian.

Raj

Sanskrit, meaning 'kingdom'. Also a
Polish term for 'heaven'.

Rajesh

(alt. Ramesh)

Indian, meaning 'ruler of kings'.
Popular in both India and
Nepal.

Raleigh

Old English, meaning 'deer's meadow'. Sir Walter Raleigh was an Elizabethan explorer and politician.

Ralph

Old English, meaning 'wolf'. Famous Ralphs include actor Ralph Fiennes, fashion brand Ralph Lauren and cartoon character Ralph from *The Simpsons*.

Ram

English, from the word for a male sheep.

Ramiro

Spanish, meaning 'judicious'. A popular name for boys in Argentina.

Ramone

Spanish, meaning 'wise supporter' or 'romantic'. The Ramones were an American rock band who all had the stage surname Ramone.

Ramsey
(alt. Ramsay)

Old English, meaning 'wild garlic island'. Ramsay MacDonald was the UK's first-ever Labour prime minister.

Randall
(alt. Randal, Randolph; abbrev. Randy)

Old German, meaning 'wolf shield'. Randy Newman is an American singer-songwriter and film composer. In modern English, randy can also mean amorous.

Raniel

English, meaning 'God is my happiness'. Can also be used as an alternative to Daniel.

Ranjit

Indian, meaning 'influenced by charm'. Several Indian cricketers have been called Ranjit.

Rannoch

Gaelic, meaning 'fern'. Also an area in the Scottish Highlands.

Rashad

Arabic, meaning 'good judgement'.

Rashid
(alt. Rasheed)

Indian, meaning 'rightly guided'. Ar-Rashid, meaning The Guide, is one of God's names in the Islamic tradition.

Rasmus

Greek, meaning 'beloved'. Usually used as a shortened form of Erasmus.

Raven

English, from the word 'raven', referring to the black bird.

Ravi

Hindi, meaning 'sun'. Ravivar is the Hindi word for Sunday.

Rawlins

French alternative of Roland, meaning 'renowned land'.

Ray

English, from the word 'ray'. Also a short form of Raymond. Famous Rays include singer Ray Charles and actors Ray Liotta and Ray Winstone.

Raymond
(alt. Rayner; abbrev. Ray)

English, meaning 'advisor'. Illustrator and author Raymond Briggs is known for *The Snowman*.

Raz

Hebrew, meaning 'secret' or 'mystery'.

Reagan

Irish, meaning 'little king'.

Reginald
(abbrev. Reggie)

Latin, meaning 'regal'. Singer Elton John's birth name was Reginald Kenneth Dwight. Reggie Yates is a British actor and TV and radio presenter.

Regis

Latin, meaning 'of the king'.

Reid

Old English, meaning 'by the reeds'.

Reilly
(alt. Riley)

Irish, meaning 'courageous'. A very common first name and surname in Ireland.

Remington

English, meaning 'ridge town'.

Remus

Latin, meaning 'swift'. Famous Remuses include the ancient Roman myth of Romulus and Remus, and the character of Remus Lupin in J.K. Rowling's 'Harry Potter' series.

Rémy

French, meaning 'from Rheims'.

Ren

Shortened form of Reginald, meaning 'regal'. According to Confucianism, Ren is also the feeling of satisfaction or pleasure after doing something nice for someone else.

Renato

Latin, meaning 'rebirth'.

René

French, meaning 'rebirth'. Traditionally only a name for boys, René is now often given to girls as well – in place of Renée.

Reno

Latin, meaning 'renewed'. Also a gambling city in Nevada, USA.

Reuben
(alt. Ruben)

Spanish, meaning 'a son'. The son of Jacob and eldest brother of Joseph in the Bible.

Reuel

Hebrew, meaning 'friend of God'. The name of several characters in the Bible.

Rex

Latin, meaning 'king'.

Rey

Spanish, meaning 'king'. In Telugu, Rey also means 'friend'.

Reynold

Latin, meaning 'king's advisor'. As a surname, Reynold can be traced back to pre-Norman times.

Rhodes

German, meaning 'where the roses grow'. Also the name of the Greek island and city.

Rhodri

Welsh, meaning 'ruler of the circle'. Rhodri the Great was a Welsh king in the ninth century.

Rhys

(alt. Reece)

Welsh, meaning 'enthusiasm'. Famous Rhyses include actors Rhys Ifans, Griff Rhys Jones and Jonathan Rhys Meyers.

Ricardo

Spanish form of Richard, meaning 'powerful leader'.

Richard

(abbrev. Rich, Richie, Ritchie, Rick, Ricki, Ricky, Dick, Dicky)

Old German, meaning 'powerful leader'. A popular name through many decades, it has dropped off in usage in recent years. Famous Richards include three Kings of England, the first of whom is known as Richard the Lionheart. Famous Ritchies include singer Ritchie Valens and Happy Days character Richie Cunningham.

Ridley

English, meaning 'cleared wood'. Film director Sir Ridley Scott is known for his films Alien, Thelma & Louise and Gladiator.

Rigby

English, meaning 'valley of the ruler'.

Ringo

English, meaning 'ring'. Usually associated with Beatles drummer Ringo Starr, whose birth name is Richard Starkey.

Rio

Spanish, meaning 'river'. Footballer Rio Ferdinand has played for Manchester United and England.

Riordan

Gaelic, meaning 'bard'.

Rishi

Sanskrit, meaning 'scribe'. In ancient India, Rishis were the scribes who kept records of hymns and scientific advancement.

River

English, from the body of water. Actor River Phoenix was known for his roles in Stand By Me, Indiana Jones and the Last Crusade and My Own Private Idaho.

Roald

Scandinavian, meaning 'ruler'. Author Roald Dahl is one of the best-loved children's authors of all time, penning books such as *Charlie and the Chocolate Factory*, *Matilda* and *The Witches*.

Robbie

Shortened form of Robert, meaning 'bright fame'. Famous Robbies include singer Robbie Wiliams, actor Robbie Coltrane and poet Robert 'Robbie' Burns.

Robert

(abbrev. Rob, Robbie, Bob, Bobby, Dobbin)

Old German, meaning 'bright fame'. Famous Roberts include Scottish king Robert the Bruce and actors Robert Pattinson and Robert de Niro. Famous Robs include actor Rob Lowe and comedian Rob Brydon.

Roberto

Italian form of Robert, meaning 'bright fame'.

Robin

English, from the word for the small, flame-breasted bird. Famous Robins include comedian Robin Williams, singer Robin Thicke and outlaw legend Robin Hood.

Robinson

English, meaning 'son of Robin'. Usually associated with the novel and title character *Robinson Crusoe*, by Daniel Defoe.

Rocco

(alt. Rocky)

Italian, meaning 'rest'. Famous Roccos include Madonna's son Rocco Ritchie.

Rockwell

English, meaning 'of the rock well'.

Rod

Shortened form of Rhodri, Roderick and Rodney. Famous Rods include singer Rod Stewart and journalist Rod Liddle.

Roderick

(abbrev. Rod, Roddy)

German, meaning 'famous power'. Impressionist Rory Bremner's real name is Roderick Bremner.

Rodney

(abbrev. Rod, Roddy)

Old German, meaning 'island near the clearing'. Also a much-loved character in *Only Fools And Horses*.

Rodrigo

Spanish form of Roderick, meaning 'famous power'.

Roger

Old German, meaning 'spear man'. Famous Rogers include athlete Roger Bannister, The Who singer Roger Daltrey and tennis player Roger Federer.

Roland

Old German, meaning 'renowned land'. Also puppet character Roland Rat.

Rolf

Old German, meaning 'wolf'.

Rollie

(alt. Rollo)

Old German, meaning 'renowned land'. Often used as a shortened version of Rolf or Roland.

Roman

Latin, meaning 'from Rome'.

Romeo

Latin, meaning 'pilgrim to Rome'. Made famous by Shakespeare's play *Romeo and Juliet*. Romeo is the second son of David and Victoria Beckham.

Ronald

(abbrev. Ron, Ronnie)

Norse, meaning 'mountain of strength'. Hollywood actor Ronald Reagan became 40th president of the United States.

Ronan

Gaelic, meaning 'little seal'. Singer Ronan Keating is known for his career with boy band Boyzone.

Rory

English, meaning 'red king'. Famous Rorys include comedian Rory Bremner, actor Rory MacGregor and comedian Rory McGrath.

Ross

(alt. Russ)

Scottish, meaning 'cape'. Famous Rosses include actor Ross Kemp and comedian Ross Noble.

Rowan

(alt. Roan)

Gaelic, meaning 'little red one'. Also reference to the rowan tree. Rowan Atkinson is the comedian, writer and actor best known for his roles in *Blackadder* and as *Mr Bean*.

Roy

Gaelic, meaning 'red'. Famous Roys include England football manager Roy Hodgson and singer Roy Orbison.

Rudolph

(abbrev. Rudy)

Old German, meaning 'famous wolf'. Usually associated with the Christmas reindeer with a shiny red nose.

Rufus

Latin, meaning 'red-haired'. Famous Rufuses include presenter Rufus Hound, actor Rufus Sewell and singer Rufus Wainwright.

Rupert

Variant of Robert, meaning 'bright fame'.

Ruslan

Russian, meaning 'like a lion'.

Russell

Old French, meaning 'little red one'. Famous Russells include comedian Russell Brand, screenwriter Russell T. Davies and astrologer Russell Grant.

Rusty

English, meaning 'ruddy'. Most commonly used in the USA as a name for boys.

Ryan

Gaelic, meaning 'little king'. Famous Ryans include actor Ryan Gosling, footballer Ryan Giggs and comedian Ryan Stiles.

Ryder

English, meaning 'horseman'.

Rye

English, from the word 'rye'. Also a type of grain.

Ryker

From Richard, meaning 'powerful leader'.

Rylan

English, meaning 'land where rye is grown'. Presenter Rylan Clark is known for several reality TV programmes, including *Celebrity Big Brother*.

Ryley

Old English, meaning 'rye clearing'. More commonly used as a spelling alternative to Riley.

Ryu

Japanese, meaning 'dragon'. A Ryu can also refer to a discipline, such as a martial art, or school of thought.

S

Boys' names

Saar
Hebrew, meaning 'tempest'.

Saber
(alt. Sabre)
French, meaning 'sword'.

Sagar
Bengali, meaning 'sea'.

Sage
English, meaning 'wise'. Also a herb.

Sakari
Native American, meaning 'sweet'.
Most commonly used in Finnish-
speaking communities.

Salil
Indian, meaning 'from the water'.
Salil Shetty is the current Secretary
General of Amnesty International.

Salim
(alt. Saleem)
Arabic, meaning 'secure'. The Salim
Khan family are a Bollywood dynasty,
with dozens of members involved as
actors, directors, producers or writers.

Salvador
Spanish, meaning 'saviour'. Artist
Salvador Dali was known for his
surrealist paintings.

Salvatore
Italian, meaning 'saviour'.

Samir
Arabic, meaning 'pleasant
companion'.

Samson
Hebrew, meaning 'son of Sam'.
Character with supernatural strength
in the Bible.

Samuel
(abbrev. Sam, Sama, Sammie, Sammy)
Hebrew, meaning 'God is heard'.
Famous Samuels include a prophet in
the Bible, author Samuel Langhorne
Clemens (known as Mark Twain) and
actor Samuel L. Jackson.

Sandeep
(alt. Sundeep)

Hindi, meaning 'lighting the way'. Popular in Hindu and Sikh communities.

Sandro

Italian, a shortened form of Alessandro, meaning 'defending men'.

Sandy

Shortened form of Alexander, meaning 'defender of mankind'. Famous Sandys include TV presenter Sandy Gall and pro golfer Sandy Lyle.

Sanjay

Hindi, meaning 'victory'. Famous Sanjays include *The Simpsons* character Sanjay, politician Sanjay Gandhi and Hindu narrative *Mahabharata* character Sanjaya.

Santiago

Spanish, meaning 'St James'. Also the name of the capital city of Chile.

Santino

Spanish, meaning 'little St James'. Santino was also the name of the first chimpanzee recognised to have forward-planning skills, in 2009.

Santo
(alt. Santos)

Latin, meaning 'saint'. Also the name of at least 10 separate football clubs around the world, including in Brazil, Mexico and Cape Town.

Sasha
(alt. Sacha)

Shortened Russian form of Alexander, meaning 'defending men'. DJ Sasha is known for his remixes of popular songs by Madonna and The Chemical Brothers.

Scott
(alt. Scottie)

English, meaning 'from Scotland'. Scott Mills is a radio DJ and TV presenter.

Seamus

Irish variant of James, meaning 'he who supplants'. Irish poet and playwright Seamus Heaney was awarded the Nobel Prize for literature.

Sean
(alt. Shaun, Shawn)

Variant of John, meaning 'God is gracious'. The name originated in the Middle Ages, when French invaders reached Ireland and the Irish began pronouncing the French name Jean as Sean. Famous Seans include legendary Bond actor Sean Connery.

Sebastian
(alt. Sébastien)

Greek, meaning 'revered'. Famous Sebastians include the crab character in Disney's *The Little Mermaid*, novelist Sebastian Faulks and Sebastian Vettel, the Formula One world champion racing driver.

Sergio
(alt. Serge)

Latin, meaning 'servant'. Popular name for boys in parts of Cameroon, Belgium and Haiti.

Seth

Hebrew, meaning 'appointed'. Famous Seths include the third son of Adam and Eve in the Bible, and actors Seth MacFarlane and Seth Greene.

Severus

Latin, meaning 'severe'. Best known now as the character Severus Snape in J.K. Rowling's 'Harry Potter' series.

Seymour

English, from Saint-Maur in northern France. Famous fictional Seymours include Seymour of *The Little Shop of Horrors*, Principal Seymour Skinner in *The Simpsons* and the *Last of the Summer Wine* character.

Shalen

Arabic, meaning 'tribal leader'.

Shane

Variant of Sean, meaning 'God is gracious'. Famous Shanes include presenter Shane Richie, novelist Shane Briant and film director Shane Meadows.

Sharif

Arabic, meaning 'honoured'. Also a name for descendants of one of Muhammad's grandchildren.

Shea

Gaelic, meaning 'admirable'.

Shelby

Norse, meaning 'willow'. Also the name of a type of Mustang car.

Sherlock

English, meaning 'fair haired'. Usually associated with the character Sherlock Holmes.

Sherman

Old English, meaning 'shear man'. Also a type of World War II tank.

Shmuel

Hebrew, meaning 'his name is God'. The English equivalent is Samuel.

Shola

Arabic, meaning 'energetic'. Can be used for boys and girls. Shola Ameobi is a footballer who has played for England Under-21s and for Nigeria.

Sidney
(alt. Sydney; abbrev. Sid)

English, meaning 'wide meadow'. Actor Sidney Poitier is known for his roles in *Guess Who's Coming to Dinner* and *In The Heat of the Night*, as well as his work as a Bahamas diplomat.

Sigmund

Old German, meaning 'victorious hand'. Neurologist Sigmund Freud was known for his vast work of psychoanalysis.

Silvanus
(alt. Silvio)

Latin, meaning 'woods'. Silvanus was an ancient Roman deity of woods and fields.

Simba
(abbrev. Sim)

Swahili, meaning 'lion'. Usually associated with the character of Simba in Disney's *The Lion King*.

Simon
(alt. Simeon)

Hebrew, meaning 'to hear'. Famous Simons include music producer Simon Cowell and actor Simon Pegg.

Sinbad
(alt. Sindbad)

Persian, meaning 'Lord of Sages'. Also a literary merchant adventurer.

Sindri

Norse, meaning 'dwarf', from ancient Norse mythology.

Sipho

African, meaning 'the unknown one'.

Sire

English, from the word 'sire'. Used as a form of address or title for reigning kings.

Sirius

Hebrew, meaning 'brightest star'. Name of Harry Potter's godfather, Sirius Black, in J.K. Rowling's 'Harry Potter' series.

Skipper

English, meaning 'ship captain'.

Skyler
(alt. Skylar)

English, meaning 'scholar'. Can be a boys' or girls' name. Now often associated with female *Breaking Bad* character Skyler White.

Solomon
(alt. Shlomo)

Hebrew, meaning 'peace'. One of the most important kings in the Bible and Torah.

Sonny

American English, meaning 'son'. Singer Sonny Bono was half of the duo Sonny and Cher.

Soren

Scandinavian, meaning 'brightest star'. Also the name of a town in Germany.

Spencer

English, meaning 'guardian'. Actor Spencer Tracy was a star of Hollywood's golden era.

Spike

English, from the word 'spike'. Famous Spikes include film director Spike Lee and comedian and writer Spike Milligan (though neither was actually given the name Spike).

Stamos

Greek, meaning 'reasonable'.

Stanford

English, meaning 'stone ford'.
Stanford University in the USA is one of the most well-known Ivy League universities.

Stanley

(abbrev. Stan)

English, meaning 'stony meadow'.
Famous Stanleys include children's character Flat Stanley, film director Stanley Kubrick and actor Stanley Tucci.

Stavros

Greek, meaning 'cross'.

Stellan

Latin, meaning 'starred'. More commonly used in Swedish-speaking communities.

Steno

German, meaning 'stone'.

Stephen

(alt. Steven, Stefan, Stefano, Steffan; abbrev. Steve, Stevie)

English, meaning 'crowned'.
Famous Stephens include actor Stephen Fry, physicist Stephen Hawking and author Stephen King, while the Stevens include film director Steven Spielberg, Apple founder Steve Jobs and actor Steve Coogan.

Stewart

(alt. Stuart)

English, meaning 'steward'. The House of Stewart was the longest-surviving royal line in the Scottish monarchy. Stewart Lee is a British stand-up comedian. Famous Stuarts include DJ Stuart Maconie, football manager Stuart Pearce and film director Stuart Townsend.

Stoney

English, meaning 'stone like'. More commonly used as a surname.

Storm

English, from the word 'storm'.

Sven

Norse, meaning 'boy'. In the UK, Sven is usually associated with former England football manager Sven-Goran Eriksson.

Syed

(alt. Sayyid)

Arabic, meaning 'lucky'. Also a way of describing decendants of one of Muhammad's grandchildren.

Sylvester

Latin, meaning 'wooded'. Usually associated with the cartoon cat or actor Sylvester Stallone.

Syon

Indian, meaning 'followed by good'. Also the name of a large historical stately home in England.

T

Boys' names

Tacitus

Latin, meaning 'silent, calm'. From the ancient Roman historian and senator.

Tad

English, from the word 'tadpole'. Also a shortened form of Thaddeus.

Taine

Gaelic, meaning 'river'.

Taj

Indian, meaning 'crown'. Usually associated with the Indian palace the Taj Mahal.

Takashi

Japanese, meaning 'praiseworthy'.

Takoda

Sioux, meaning 'friend to everyone'. Most commonly used in the USA.

Talbot
(alt. Tal)

English, meaning 'command of the valley'. An aristocratic name.

Tamir

Arabic, meaning 'tall and wealthy'.

Taras
(alt. Tarez)

Scottish, meaning 'crag'. Taras was the son of Poseidon in ancient Greek mythology.

Tarek
(alt. Tarik, Tariq)

Arabic, meaning 'to strike'.

Tarian

Welsh, meaning 'shield'. Also the name of a breed of Welsh pony.

Tarquin

Latin, from the Roman clan name. Author Tarquin Hall is known for his works *To the Elephant Graveyard* and *Salaam Brick Lane*.

Tarun

Hindi, meaning 'young'. Bollywood star Tarun Kumar Bhatti is known simply as Tarun.

Tatanka

Lakota, meaning 'buffalo'. Legendary Native American leader Sitting Bull's Western name was Tatanka Lyotake.

Tate

English, meaning 'cheerful'.

Taurean

English, meaning 'bull like'. Also used as a term for people born under the Taurus star sign.

Tavares

English, meaning 'descendant of the hermit'. Also found as a last name in Portuguese-speaking communities.

Tave
(alt. Tavian, Tavis, Tavish)

French, from Gustave, meaning 'royal staff'. In Nordic cultures the name also means 'guarantor'.

Tavor

Hebrew, meaning 'misfortunate'. Also the name given to a type of assault rifle.

Taylor

English, meaning 'tailor'. Actor Taylor Lautner appeared in the Twilight films. Now used as often for girls as for boys.

Ted
(alt. Teddy)

Shortened form of Edward, meaning 'wealthy guard'. Famous Teds include Father Ted, and the Ted films.

Tennessee

Native American, meaning 'river town'. Also the name of a state in the USA.

Terence
(alt. Terrill; abbrev. Terry)

English, meaning 'tender'. Terence was an ancient Roman playwright of comedies.

Tex

English, meaning 'Texan'. More commonly used in the USA.

Thabo

African, meaning 'filled with happiness'. Thabo Mbeki was the president of South Africa from 1999 to 2008.

Thane
(alt. Thayer)

Scottish, meaning 'landholder'.

Thelonious

Latin, meaning 'ruler of the people'. Thelonious Monk was an influential jazz pianist and composer.

Theodore
(abbrev. Theo)

Greek, meaning 'God's gift'. St Theodore was a warrior and martyr of the Eastern Orthodox Church.

Theophile
(alt. *Theophilus*)
Latin, meaning 'God's love'.

Theron
Greek, meaning 'hunter'.

Thierry
French variant of Terence, meaning 'tender'. Striker Thierry Henry played for Arsenal and France.

Thomas
(abbrev. *Tom, Thom, Tommy*)
Aramaic, meaning 'twin'. An enduringly popular name. Thomas the Tank Engine is one of the most long-standing popular children's characters of book and screen.

Thomson
(alt. *Thomsen*)
English, meaning 'son of Thomas'. The spelling Thomsen also means 'twin' in Aramaic.

Thor
Norse, meaning 'thunder'. Thor was an ancient Nordic god of thunder and lightning.

Tiago
From Santiago, meaning 'St James'. Used as a shortened form of Santiago as often as a name in its own right, particularly in Portuguese-speaking communities.

Tibor
Latin, from the river Tiber. In Hungary, the name can also mean 'a short meeting'.

Tieman
(alt. *Tiemann*)
Gaelic, meaning 'lord'.

Tien
Vietnamese, meaning 'first'.

Timothy
(abbrev. *Tim, Timmy*)
Greek, meaning 'God's honour'. Famous Timothys include actors Timothy Spall, Timothy Olyphant and Timothy Dalton.

Tito
(alt. *Titus*)
Latin, meaning 'defender'. Usually associated with Tito Jackson, an original member of the Jackson 5.

Tobias
(alt. *Toby*)
Hebrew, meaning 'God is good'. Several characters in the Bible are named Tobias.

Tod
(alt. *Todd*)
English, meaning 'fox'. Several fictional characters are called Tod or Todd, including Todd Flanders in *The Simpsons*, Todd Alquist in *Breaking Bad* and Todd Grimshaw in *Coronation Street*.

Tonneau
French, meaning 'barrel'. A tonneau is also a word used for the rear section of a car, particularly old-fashioned cars.

Tony

Shortened form of Anthony, from the old Roman family name. Famous Tonys include footballer Tony Adams, former prime minister Tony Blair and comedian, historian and TV presenter Tony Robinson.

Torin

Gaelic, meaning 'chief'. Actor Torin Thatcher was known for his numerous stage roles and films, including *Great Expectations* and *Mutiny on the Bounty*.

Torquil

Gaelic, meaning 'helmet'. In Scandinavia the name is also derived from Thor, the god of thunder and lightning.

Tory
(alt. Torey)

Norse, meaning 'Thor'.

Toshi

Japanese, meaning 'reflection'. More commonly used in Japanese-speaking communities.

Travis

French, meaning 'crossroads'.

Trevelyan

Cornish, meaning 'of the house of Eden'.

Trevor

Welsh, meaning 'great settlement'. Famous Trevors include inventor Trevor Baylis, DJ Trevor Nelson and politician and presenter Trevor Phillips.

Trey
(alt. Tyree)

French, meaning 'three'. Sometimes used as a nickname for a third-born child or person whose name ends in III, such as Microsoft founder Bill Gates, whose birth name is William Henry Gates III.

Tristan
(alt. Tristram)

Celtic, from the Celtic hero. One of the knights of the Round Table.

Troy

Gaelic, meaning 'descended from the soldier'. Troy was a legendary city in ancient Greece.

Tudor

Variant of Theodore, 'God's gift'. The Tudors were a family dynasty who ruled England during the sixteenth century, including Henry VIII and Elizabeth I.

Tyler

English, meaning 'tile maker'. The name can be traced back to the fourteenth century and English rebel Wat Tyler, leader of the Peasants' Revolt.

Tyrell

French, meaning 'puller'. Usually associated with the House Tyrell from *Game of Thrones*.

Tyrone

Gaelic, meaning 'Owen's county'.
Also the name of a county in
Northern Ireland.

Tyson

English, meaning 'son of Tyrone'.
Became popular after the rise of
Mike Tyson, the boxer known for his
aggressive fighting style.

Prime ministers' names

Alexander (Alec) (Douglas-Home)

Andrew (Bonar Law)

Anthony (Eden, Blair)

Arthur (Wellesley, Balfour, Chamberlain)

Benjamin (Disraeli)

Clement (Attlee)

David (Lloyd George, Cameron)

Edward (Heath)

Gordon (Brown)

Harold (Macmillan, Wilson – though neither of their first names was
    Harold)

James (Callaghan – whose first name was Leonard)

John (Stuart, Russell, Major)

Neville (Chamberlain)

Ramsay (MacDonald – whose first name was James)

Spencer (Crompton, Perceval)

Stanley (Baldwin)

William (Cavendish, Pitt (Elder and Younger), Wyndham, Lamb,
    Gladstone)

Winston (Churchill)

– and Margaret (Thatcher) for a girl.

Boys' names

Uberto
(alt. Umberto)
Italian, variant of Hubert, meaning 'bright or shining intellect'. Several kings of Italy were called Umberto.

Udath
(alt. Udathel)
Indian, meaning 'noble'. More commonly used in Sanskrit-speaking communities.

Udo
German, meaning 'power of the wolf'.

Ugo
Italian form of Hugo, meaning 'soul, mind and intellect'. Also the name of a town in Japan.

Ulf
German, meaning 'wolf'. Also the name of a Danish Viking chief.

Ulrich
German, meaning 'noble ruler'.

Ultan
Irish, meaning 'from Ulster'. St Ultan was an Irish monk in the seventh century.

Ulysses
Greek, meaning 'wrathful'. Made famous by the mythological voyager of ancient Greece.

Unwyn
(alt. Unwin, Unwine)
English, meaning 'unfriendly'.

Upton
English, meaning 'high town'.

Urho
Finnish, meaning 'brave'.

Uri
(alt. Uriah, Urias)
Hebrew, meaning 'my light'. Magician Uri Geller is known for his illusions of psychokinesis and telepathy.

Uriel

Hebrew, meaning 'angel of light'. One of the archangels in the Bible.

Usher

English, from the word 'usher'. Made famous by the American R&B star.

Uttam

Indian, meaning 'best'. Actor Uttam Kumar is known as one of the great Bollywood actors of the twentieth century.

Uzi

(alt. Uzzi, Uzziah)

Hebrew, meaning 'God is my strength'. The name of several characters in the Bible. Also the name of an Israeli type of submachine gun.

Popular song names

Alfie ('Alfie' – Lily Allen)

Carmen ('Carmen' – Lana Del Ray)

Diana ('Diana' – One Direction)

George ('Oh George' – Foo Fighters)

Judas ('Judas' – Lady Gaga)

Maddie ('Alone With You (Maddie's Song)' – Ne Yo)

Mary ('Blind Mary' – Gnarls Barkley)

Simone ('Simone' – Goldfrapp)

Stephen ('Hey Stephen' – Taylor Swift)

Wyatt ('Lullaby for Wyatt' – Sheryl Crow)

V

Boys' names

Vaclav

Czech, meaning 'receives glory'. The English form is Wenceslaus.

Vadim

Russian, meaning 'scandal maker'. Vadim the Bold was a legendary warrior in Eastern Europe during the ninth century.

Valdemar

German, meaning 'renowned leader'. Valdemar was a king of Sweden during the thirteenth century.

Valente

Latin, meaning 'valiant'. More commonly used as a surname, particularly in Italy and Portugal.

Valentine

(alt. Valentin, Valentino; abbrev. Val)

English, from the word 'valentine'. St Valentine was a Roman saint associated with the tradition of courtly love, and whose day is celebrated on 14 February. The Spanish variant is Valentin and the Italian Valentino.

Valerio

Italian, meaning 'to be strong'. Originally a surname in Italy, Valerio is now also being given as a first name to boys.

Valia

Indian, meaning 'king of the monkeys'. Also used as a girls' name.

Van

Dutch, meaning 'son of'. Also a shortened form of Ivan, as with singer Van Morrison.

Vance

English, meaning 'marshland'. Usually associated with the comic book hero Justice, whose real name is Vance Astrovik.

Vangelis

Greek, meaning 'good news'. Vangelis is a modern Greek composer of various music, and is known for his work on films such as *Chariots of Fire*, *Blade Runner* and *Alexander*.

Varro

Latin, meaning 'strong'. There are several ancient Roman generals and poets known as Varro, most of whom were related to each other.

Varun

Hindi, meaning 'water god'. Shortened form of Varuna, who is the Hindu god of all water.

Vasilis

Greek, meaning 'kingly'.

Vaughan

(alt. Vaughn)

Welsh, meaning 'little'.

Vernell

French, meaning 'green and flourishing'. More commonly used in the USA.

Verner

Scandinavian form of the German Werner, meaning 'army defender'.

Vernon

(alt. Vernie)

French, meaning 'alder grove'.

Versilius

Latin, meaning 'flier'. Also the name of a fashionable part of Tuscany, Italy.

Vester

Latin, meaning 'wooded'. Also the name of a manufacturer of guitars.

Vibol

Cambodian, meaning 'man of plenty'.

Victor

(alt. Viktor)

Latin, meaning 'champion'. Author Victor Hugo is known for his novels *Les Miserables* and *The Hunchback of Notre-Dame*.

Vidal

(alt. Vidar)

Spanish, meaning 'life giving'. Hairdresser Vidal Sassoon owned a chain of salons and a range of styling products.

Vijay

Hindi, meaning 'conquering'. Bollywood star Joseph Vijay Chandrasekhar is known simply as Vijay.

Vikram

Hindi, meaning 'sun'. Bollywood star Vikram Kennedy Vinod Raj is known simply as Vikram.

Ville

French, meaning 'town'. The word is used to describe towns or cities throughout France and the UK, usually as a suffix – such as Carville in Yorkshire.

Vincent
(abbrev. Vin, Vince, Vinnie)
English, meaning 'victorious'.
Famous Vincents include actor Vince Vaughn, artist Vincent van Gogh and footballer-turned-actor Vinnie Jones.

Virgil
Latin, meaning 'staff bearer'. Ancient Roman poet of the same name.

Vito
Spanish, meaning 'life'. Usually associated with the character Vito Corleone from *The Godfather*.

Vittorio
Italian, meaning 'victory'. The English equivalent is Victor.

Vitus
Latin, meaning 'life'. St Vitus's day was traditionally celebrated with dancing, which led to naming a neurological condition that looks like uncontrolled dancing as 'St Vitus Dance'.

Vivek
Indian, meaning 'wisdom'. Bollywood star Vivekananthan is known simply as Vivek.

Vivian
Latin, meaning 'lively'. Commonly given to both boys and girls.

Vladimir
(abbrev. Vlad)
Slavic, meaning 'prince'. Famous Vladimirs include Russian President Vladimir Putin and legendary warrior Vlad the Impaler – who was also known as Dracula.

Volker
German, meaning 'defender of the people'.

Von
Norse, meaning 'hope'. In Germany, 'von' also means 'of' or 'from', and is used in names to denote origin, such as Ulrich von Liechtenstein.

Boys' names

Wade

English, meaning 'to move forward' or 'to go'. Wade Robson is a prolific choreographer of contemporary dance.

Waldemar

German, meaning 'famous ruler'. A common name for German princes during the Middle Ages.

Walden

English, meaning 'valley of the Britons'. Title of Henry Thoreau's famous book reflecting on simple living off the land.

Waldo

Old German, meaning 'rule'. Famous in the USA for the line of 'Where's Waldo?' books, known as 'Where's Wally?' in the UK.

Walker

English, meaning 'a fuller'. Most common in late 1800s and early 1900s in America.

Wallace

English, meaning 'foreigner' or 'stranger'. The man of the man-and-dog duo know to children everywhere as Wallace and Gromit.

Walter

(abbrev. Walt, Wally)

German, meaning 'ruler of the army'.

Ward

English, meaning 'guardian'.

Wardell

Old English, meaning 'watchman's hill'.

Warner

German, meaning 'army guard'. Best known for the movie studio Warner Brothers Entertainment, which has released blockbusters such as *Batman* and *Superman*.

Warren

German, meaning 'guard' or 'the game park'. An American businessman and philanthropist, Warren Buffett, is know as one of the richest people in the world.

Warwick

English, meaning 'farm near the weir'. The name of a historic town in England with a castle and a university.

Washington

English, meaning 'clever' or 'clever man's settlement'. The surname of the first president of the USA.

Wasim

Arabic, meaning 'attractive' or 'full of grace'.

Wassily

Greek, meaning 'royal' or 'kingly'. Wassily Kandinsky was an influential Russian painter of abstract art.

Watson

English, meaning 'son' or 'son of Walter'. The right-hand man of the famous fictional detective Sherlock Holmes.

Waverley

(alt. Waverly)

English, meaning 'meadow of aspens'. A common name for towns and cities in the USA.

Waylon

English, meaning 'land by the road'. American Waylon Jennings has been a popular country singer for decades.

Wayne

English, meaning 'a cartwright'. Famous Waynes include footballer Wayne Rooney, comedian Wayne Brady and rapper Lil Wayne.

Webster

English, meaning 'weaver'.

Weldon

English, meaning 'from the hill of well' or 'hill with a well'.

Wendell

(alt. Wendel)

German, meaning 'a wend'. American novelist and poet Wendell Berry has penned dozens of works throughout his career.

Werner

German, meaning 'army guard'.

Werther

German, meaning 'a soldier in the army'.

Weston

English, meaning 'from the west town'.

Wheeler

English, meaning 'wheel maker'.

Whitley

English, meaning 'white wood'.

Whitman

Old English, meaning 'white man'.

Whitney

Old English, meaning 'white island'. Can be used as a boys' or girls' name.

Wilber

(alt. Wilbur)

Old German, meaning 'bright will'. As one of the Wright brothers, Wilbur helped to invent the first powered aeroplanes.

Wildon

English, meaning 'wooded hill'.

Wiley

Old English, meaning 'beguiling' or 'enchanting'. The stage name of English rapper and songwriter Richard Kylea Cowie.

Wilford

Old English, meaning 'the ford by the willows'.

Wilfred

(alt. Wilfredo, Wilfrid; abbrev. Wilf)

English, meaning 'to will peace'.

Wilhelm

German, meaning 'strong-willed warrior'.

Wilkes

(alt. Wilkie)

Old English, meaning 'strong-willed protector' or 'strong and resolute protector'.

William

(abbrev. Will, Willie, Willy, Bill, Billy)

Old German, meaning 'strong-willed warrior'. Famous Williams include Prince William, playwright William Shakespeare and rapper Will.i.am.

Willis

English, meaning 'server of William'.

Willoughby

Old Norse and Old English, meaning 'from the farm by the trees'.

Wilmer

English (Teutonic), meaning 'famously resolute'. Wilmer Eduardo Valderrama is an American actor. Wilmer Allison was a tennis champion in the 1930s.

Wilmot

English, meaning 'resolute mind'.

Wilson

English, meaning 'son of William'. Wilson Pickett was an American R&B, soul and rock 'n' roll singer-songwriter.

Wilton

Old Norse and English, meaning 'from the farm by the brook' or 'from the farm by the streams'. A town in Wiltshire with a history dating back to the eighth century.

Windell

German, meaning 'wanderer' or 'seeker'. Windell Middlebrooks is an American actor.

Windsor

Old English, meaning 'river bank' or 'landing place'.

Winfield

English, meaning 'from the field of Wina'.

Winslow

Old English, meaning 'victory on the hill'.

Winter

Old English, meaning 'to be born in the winter'.

Winthrop

Old English, meaning 'village of friends'.

Winton

Old English, meaning 'a friend's farm'.

Wirrin

Aboriginal, meaning 'a tea tree'.

Wistan

Old English, meaning 'battle stone' or 'mark of the battle'. St Wistan was martyred in 840 AD and has his feast day on 1 June.

Wittan

Old English, meaning 'farm in the woods' or 'farm by the woods'. The Witan were a group of advisors to the king that operated from the seventh to eleventh centuries.

Wolf
(alt. Wolfe)

English, meaning 'strong as a wolf'.

Wolfgang

Teutonic, meaning 'the path of wolves'. Wolfgang Amadeus Mozart was one of the most important composers of the classical period.

Wolfrom

Teutonic, meaning 'raven wolf'.

Wolter

Dutch, a form of Walter, meaning 'ruler of the army'. Wolter Kroes is a Dutch singer.

Woodburn

Old English, meaning 'a stream in the woods'.

Woodrow

(abbrev. Woody)

English, meaning 'from the row of houses by the wood'. Woodrow Wilson was the 28th president of the USA. Woody Guthrie, named after the president, was an influential American folk singer. Woody is also the well-known cowboy in *Toy Story*.

Woodward

English, meaning 'guardian of the forest'.

Worcester

Old English, meaning 'from a Roman site'.

Worth

American, meaning 'worth much' or 'wealthy place' or 'wealth and riches'.

Wren

Old English, meaning 'tiny bird'. Often associated with the species of small birds found throughout the world.

Wright

Old English, meaning 'to be a craftsman' or 'from a carpenter'.

Wyatt

Teutonic, meaning 'from wood' or 'from the wide water'. Famous Wyatts include wild-west sheriff Wyatt Earp and comedian Wyatt Cenac.

Wyclef

(alt. Wycleff, Wycliff, Wycliffe)

English, meaning 'inhabitant of the white cliff'. Wyclef Jeanelle Jean is an American-Haitian rapper best known for his role in the Fugees.

Wynn

(alt. Wyn)

Welsh, meaning 'very blessed' or 'the fair blessed one'. Also used in old English to mean 'friend'.

X

Boys' names

Xadrian
American, a combination of X and Adrian, meaning 'from Hadria'.

Xander
Greek, meaning 'defender of the people'. A short form for Alexander.

Xannon
American, meaning 'descendant of an ancient family'.

Xanthus
Greek, meaning 'golden-haired'. One of the horses belonging to Achilles.

Xavier
Spanish, meaning 'the new house'. A name originating from the Catholic saint, Francis Xavier.

Xenon
Greek, meaning 'the guest'. Also one of the noble gases.

Xerxes
Persian, meaning 'ruler of the people' or 'respected king'. A king who attempted to invade the Greek mainland, but failed.

Xeven
Slavic, meaning 'lively'.

Xylander
Greek, meaning 'man of the forest'.

Boys' names

Yaal

Hebrew, meaning 'ascending' or 'one to ascend'.

Yadid

Hebrew, meaning 'the beloved one'.

Yadon

Hebrew, meaning 'against judgment'. Name of one of the many Pokemon characters.

Yahir

Spanish, meaning 'handsome one'. A Mexican singer.

Yaholo

Native American, meaning 'yells'.

Yair

Hebrew, meaning 'the enlightening one' or 'illuminating'.

Yakiya

Hebrew, meaning 'pure' or 'bright'.

Yanis
(alt. Yannis)

Greek, a form of John, meaning 'gift of God'.

Yarden

Hebrew, meaning 'to flow downward'. The Hebrew name Jordan comes from Yarden.

Ye

Chinese, meaning 'bright one' or 'light'.

Yehuda
(alt. Yehudi)

Hebrew, meaning 'to praise and exalt'. Often translated to mean Judah. Judah was a son of Jacob in the Bible.

Yered

Hebrew, a form of Jared, meaning 'descending'.

Yerik

Russian, meaning 'God-appointed one'.

Yerodin

African, meaning 'studious'.

Yervant

Armenian, meaning 'king of people'.

Yitzak
(alt. Yitzaak)

Hebrew, meaning 'laughter' or 'one who laughs'.

Ynyr

Welsh, meaning 'to honour'.

Yobachi

African, meaning 'one who prays to God' or 'prayed to God'.

Yogi

Indian, meaning 'master of oneself'. Popularised by the American cartoon character, Yogi Bear.

Yoloti

Aztec, meaning 'heart'.

Yona

Native American, meaning 'bear'; and also Hebrew, meaning 'dove'. A name used to refer to ancient people who spoke Greek.

York

Celtic, meaning 'yew tree' or 'from the farm of the yew tree'. Used as a surname by people originating from the city of York.

Yosef

Hebrew form of Joseph, meaning 'Jehovah increases'.

Yuri

Aboriginal, meaning 'to hear'; Japanese, meaning 'one to listen'; Russian, a form of George, meaning 'farmer'. Name of a South Korean pop singer.

Yuuta

Japanese, meaning 'excellent'.

Yves

French, meaning 'miniature archer' or 'small archer'. Yves Saint Laurent was a famous French fashion designer.

Z Boys' names

Zachariah
(alt. Zachary, Zecheriah; abbrev. Zac, Zach)
Hebrew, meaning 'remembered by the Lord' or 'God has remembered'.

Zad
Persian, meaning 'my son'.

Zada
(alt. Zadan, Zadin, Zadun)
Dutch, meaning 'a man who sowed seeds'.

Zadok
Hebrew, meaning 'righteous one'. The priest who anointed Solomon, made famous in Handel's anthem.

Zador
Hungarian, meaning 'violent demeanour'.

Zafar
Arabic, meaning 'triumphant'. Zafar Younis is a character from the BBC drama Spooks.

Zaid
African, meaning 'increase the growth' or 'growth'.

Zaide
Yiddish, meaning 'the elder ones'. An unfinished opera by Mozart.

Zain
(alt. Zane)
Arabic, meaning 'the handsome son'.

Zaire
African, meaning 'river'. Formerly the name of a country in Africa, now known as Democratic Republic of the Congo.

Zander

Greek, meaning 'defender of my people'.

Zarek

Persian, meaning 'God protect our king'. A Marvel comic book character created by Stan Lee and Gene Colan.

Zoltan

(alt. Zoltin)

Hungarian, meaning 'life'. Zoltan Karpathy is a character from the musical My Fair Lady.

Zuma

Arabic, meaning 'peace'.

Football players

Aaron (Lennon)

Alan (Shearer)

Ashley (Cole)

Daniel (Sturridge)

Darren (Fletcher)

David (Beckham)

Frank (Lampard)

Gareth (Bale)

Gary (Lineker)

Jack (Wilshere)

Joe (Cole)

Rio (Ferdinand)

Scott (Parker)

Steven (Gerrard)

Wayne (Rooney)

part three

Girls' Names

A Girls' names

Abigail
(alt. Abagail, Abbiegayle, Abbigail, Abigale, Abigayle; abbrev. Abbey, Abbi, Abi, Abie)

Hebrew, meaning 'my father's joy'. Found in the Bible. Abbey Clancy is the model and TV presenter who won *Strictly Come Dancing* in 2013. Abi Morgan is a screenwriter of films including *The Iron Lady*.

Abilene
(alt. Abilee)

Latin and Spanish for 'hazelnut'. Also from the Greek meaning 'plain' or 'meadow', it is the name of an ancient area of Syria.

Abina
(alt. Abena)

Ghanaian, meaning 'born on Tuesday'.

Abra
Sanskrit, meaning 'clouds'. Female variation of Abraham.

Abril
Spanish for the month of April.

Acacia
Greek, meaning 'point' or 'thorn'. Also a type of flowering tree and shrub.

Acadia
Variation of the Greek word arcadia meaning 'paradise'. Originally a French colony in Canada.

Ada
(alt. Adair)

Hebrew, meaning 'adornment'. The mathematician Ada Lovelace is generally considered to be the world's first computer programmer, in the nineteenth century.

Adalee
Derived from German, meaning 'noble'. Sometimes used as a contraction of Ada and Lee.

Adalia

Hebrew, meaning 'God is my refuge'.
Also the name of a type of ladybird.

Addison

(alt. Addisyn, Addyson; abbrev. Addie)
English, meaning 'son of Adam'.
Used equally for girls and boys.
Historically, more popular for boys in
the nineteenth century.

Adelaide

(alt. Adelaida; abbrev. Addie)
German, meaning 'noble'. Popular
after the rule of William IV and
Queen Adelaide of England in the
nineteenth century. Also an Australian
city and name of Australian actress
Adelaide Kane.

Adele

*(alt. Adela, Adelia, Adell, Adella,
Adelle; abbrev. Addie)*
German, meaning 'noble'. Award
winning singer-songwriter Adele
Laurie Blue Adkins is better known as
simply 'Adele'.

Adeline

*(alt. Adalyn, Adalynn, Adelina,
Adelyn)*
Variant of Adelaide, meaning 'noble'.

Adeola

(alt. Adeolah, Adeolla)
Nigerian, meaning 'weaver of a
crown of honour'.

Aderyn

Welsh, meaning 'bird'. Also the
name of several places in Wales.

Adesina

Nigerian, meaning 'she paves the
way'. Often given to a firstborn
daughter in Nigerian communities.

Adia

Variant of Ada, meaning
'adornment'. Usually associated with
the song 'Adia'.

Adina

(alt. Adena)
Hebrew, meaning 'high hopes' or
'precious'. Found in the Bible.

Adira

Hebrew, meaning 'noble' or
'powerful'.

Adrian

Latin, meaning 'from Hadria'.
Used more commonly for boys
than girls, although it did enjoy
a spell of popularity for girls in
the USA.

Adrienne

*(alt. Adriana, Adriane, Adrianna,
Adrianne)*
A feminine form of Adrian.

Aegle

Greek, meaning 'brightness' or
'splendour'. Also the name of
several characters in ancient Greek
mythology.

Aerin

Name of a character in J.R.R.
Tolkien's *Lord of the Rings* trilogy.

Aerith

American, from a character in the computer game *Final Fantasy VII*.

Aero

(alt. Aeron)
Greek, meaning 'flight'.

Aerolynn

Combination of the Greek Aero, meaning 'flight', and the English Lynn, meaning 'waterfall'.

Afia

(alt. Aafia, Aff, Affi)
Arabic, meaning 'a child born on Friday'. The name's profile rose while Afia Masoon was a character in *EastEnders*.

Africa

Celtic, meaning 'pleasant', as well as the name of the continent.

Afsaneh

Iranian, meaning 'a fairy tale'.

Afsha

Persian, meaning 'one who sprinkles light'. Actress Afsha Azad is known for her role as Padma Patil in the 'Harry Potter' film series.

Afton

Originally the name of a river in Aryshire, Scotland, or a town on the Isle of Wight.

Agatha

(abbrev. Aggie)
Greek and Latin, meaning 'good'. St Agatha was a third-century Christian saint, patron saint of fire, earthquakes and bells, amongst other things. Crime writer Agatha Christie is the world's best-selling novelist.

Aglaia

(alt. Aglaya, Aglaja)
Greek, meaning 'brilliance'. In Greek mythology, one of the Three Graces. Also the name of a kind of mahogany tree, an opera, an eighteenth-century British ship and a saint.

Agnes

Greek, meaning 'virginal' or 'pure'. St Agnes of Rome is the patron saint of chastity and girls, amongst other things.

Agrippina

Latin, meaning 'born feet first'. The name of several influential women of ancient Rome.

Aida

Arabic, meaning 'reward' or 'present'. Also the name of an opera by Giuseppe Verdi.

Aidanne

(alt. Aden, Aidan, Aidanne, Aiden, Aidenne)
Gaelic, meaning 'fire'. A feminine variation of Aidan. Aidan is used most commonly for boys but also for girls.

Ailbhe

Irish, meaning 'noble' or 'bright'. Has also been used as a boys' name.

Aileen
(alt. Aelinn, Aleen, Aline, Alline, Eileen)

Gaelic variant of Helen, meaning 'light'. Aileen Cust was the first female veterinarian in Great Britain.

Ailith
(alt. Ailish)

Old English, meaning 'seasoned warrior'. Rare since the Middle Ages.

Ailsa

Scottish, meaning 'pledge from God'. Also the name of a Scottish island, Ailsa Craig.

Aimee
(alt. Aimie, Amie)

French form of Amy, meaning 'beloved'. Famous Aimees include actress Aimee Garcia, singer Aimee Mann, and Aimee Osbourne of the Osbourne Family.

Aina

Scandinavian, meaning 'forever'.

Aine
(alt. Aino)

Celtic, meaning 'happiness'. Aine was a Celtic goddess of summer and prosperity.

Ainsley
(alt. Ansley)

Old English, meaning 'meadow' or 'clearing'. Also variant of an old Scottish last name used as a first name. Ainsley is used as both a girls' and a boys' name. Ainsley Hayes was a leading character in TV hit *The West Wing*.

Aisha
(alt. Aeysha, Aysha)

Arabic, meaning 'woman'; also Swahili, meaning 'life'. Aisha was one of the prophet Muhammad's wives.

Aishwarya

Variant of the Arabic Aisha, meaning 'woman'. Actress Aishwarya Rai Bachchan is one of the most recognisable Bollywood stars.

Aislinn
(alt. Aislin, Aisling, Aislyn, Alene, Allene)

Irish Gaelic, meaning 'dream'.

Aiyanna
(alt. Aiyana)

Native American, meaning 'forever flowering'.

Aja

Hindi, meaning 'goat'. Also Scandinavian.

Aka
(alt. Akah, Akkah)

Maori, meaning 'loving one' or 'affectionate'.

Akela
(alt. Akilah)

Hawaiian, meaning 'noble'. Usually associated with the character of Akela in Rudyard Kipling's The Jungle Book.

Akilina

Greek or Russian, meaning 'eagle'.

Akiva

Hebrew, meaning 'protect and shelter'.

Alaina
(alt. Alane, Alani, Alayna, Aleena)

Feminine of Alan, from the Gaelic for 'rock'. Also used as a spelling alternative to Eleanor.

Alana
(alt. Alanna, Alannah)

Gaelic, meaning 'beauty'. In Hawaiian it means 'beautiful offering', and in Old German it means 'precious'.

Alanis
(alt. Alarice)

Variant of Alaina, meaning 'rock'. Canadian-American Alanis Morissette is a multi-award-winning singer.

Alba

Latin, meaning 'white'. Also the Gaelic word for Scotland. Name of the central character in the novel The Time Traveller's Wife.

Alberta
(alt. Albertha, Albertine)

Feminine of Albert, from the Old German for 'noble, bright, famous'. Also the name of a province in Canada.

Albina

Latin, meaning 'white' or 'fair'. Also the name of an Etruscan goddess of the dawn.

Alda

German, meaning 'old' or 'prosperous'. St Alda was an Italian mystic in the eleventh century, who took care of the sick.

Aldis

English, meaning 'battle-seasoned'. Used most commonly for boys but also for girls.

Aleah

Arabic, meaning 'high'; also Persian, meaning 'one of God's beings'. Often used as a spelling alternative for Aliyah.

Alesha
(alt. Alisha, Alysha)

Variant of Alice, meaning 'nobility'. Alesha Dixon is a British singer, dancer, model and TV presenter.

Aleta
(alt. Aletha)

Greek, meaning 'footloose'. Usually associated with the character of Queen Aleta Ellis in the comic strip The Legend of Prince Valiant.

Alethea
(alt. Aletheia)

Greek, meaning 'truth'. The first use of this name was in the seventeenth century.

Alexandra

(alt. Alejandra, Alejhandra, Aleksandra, Alessandra, Alexandria; abbrev. Alex, Alexi, Alexia, Alexina)

Feminine of Alexander, meaning 'defender of mankind'. Also one of the names of the ancient Greek goddess Hera.

Alexis

(alt. Alexus, Alexys)

Greek, meaning 'helper'. Alexis was also an ancient Greek comic poet and an ancient Greek sculptor.

Aleydis

Variant of Alice, meaning 'noble' or 'nobility'. Also an alternative name for St Alice of Scharbeek, patron saint of the blind and paralysed.

Alfreda

(alt. Alfre)

Old English, meaning 'elf' or 'magical counsel'. The female version of Alfred. Alfreda Benge is a lyricist and illustrator and Alfreda Hodgson is a singer.

Ali

(alt. Allie, Ally)

Shortened version of Alexandra, Aliyah, Alison or Alice, as well as a name in its own right.

Alibeth

Variant of Elizabeth, meaning 'consecrated to God'. More commonly used in the Middle Ages.

Alice

(alt. Alicia, Alize, Alyce, Alys, Alyse)

English, meaning 'noble' or 'nobility'. Usually associated with *Alice in Wonderland* by Lewis Carroll. Famous Alicias include singer Alicia Keys and actress Alicia Silverstone. Also the birth name of actress Jodie Foster.

Alida

(alt. Aleida)

Latin, meaning 'small winged one'. More commonly used in Dutch-speaking communities.

Alienor

(alt. Aliana)

Variant of Eleanor, from the Greek for 'light'. Also a spelling variation used by Queen Eleanor of Aquitaine in the twelfth century.

Aliki

(alt. Alika)

Variant of Alice, meaning 'noble' or 'nobility'. Actress Aliki Vougiouklaki was considered to be one of Greece's greatest actresses of the twentieth century.

Alima

Arabic, meaning 'cultured'.

Alina

(alt. Alena)

Variation of Helen, meaning 'light'. More commonly used in Brazil, France, Italy, and Spain.

Alison

(alt. Allison, Allisyn, Allyson, Alyson)

Variant of Alice, meaning 'noble' or 'nobility'. Originally the name was Alis in the Middle Ages, with the suffix 'on', which means 'little'.

Alivia

Variant of Olivia, meaning 'olive tree'. More commonly used in the USA.

Aliya

(alt. Aaliyah, Aleah, Alia, Aliah, Aliyah)

Arabic, meaning 'exalted' or 'sublime'.

Alla

Variant of Ella or Alexandra.

Allegra

Italian, meaning 'joyous'. Allegra Byron was the lovechild of the poet Lord Byron. Allegra Versace is the heiress to the Versace fashion empire.

Allura

French, from the word for entice, meaning 'the power of attraction'.

Allyn

Feminine of Alan, meaning 'rock'.

Alma

Three possible origins: Latin for 'giving nurture', Italian for 'soul' and Arabic for 'learned'.

Almeda

(alt. Almeta)

Latin, meaning 'ambitious'. Also the name of a district in Barcelona, Spain.

Almera

(alt. Almira)

Feminine of Elmer, from the Arabic for 'aristocratic' and the Old English meaning 'noble'.

Alohi

Variant of the Hawaiian greeting Aloha, meaning 'love and affection'. More commonly used in the USA.

Alona

(alt. Alora)

Hebrew, meaning 'oak tree'. Alona is the first name of a Ukrainian tennis player and of an Israeli actress.

Alpha

The first letter of the Greek alphabet, usually given to a firstborn daughter.

Alta

Latin, meaning 'elevated'. Also the name of many towns throughout Europe and the USA.

Altagracia

Spanish, meaning 'grace'. Alta Gracia is also the name of a city in Argentina.

Althaea

(alt. Altea, Altha, Althea)

Greek, meaning 'healing power'. Althaea was a prominent character in Greek mythology.

Alva

Spanish, meaning 'blonde' or 'fair skinned'. In Norway and Sweden it is considered the female version of Alf, which means 'elf'.

Alvena
(alt. Alvina)

Old English, meaning 'elf friend'. In Old German, it is considered the female version of Adelwin, which means 'noble friend'.

Alvia
(alt. Alyvia)

Variant of Olivia, meaning 'olive tree'; or Elvira, from the ancient Spanish city.

Alyssa
(alt. Alisa, Alissa, Allyssa, Alysa)

Greek, meaning 'rational'. Usually associated with the flower alyssum.

Amabel

Variant of Annabel, meaning 'grace and beauty'.

Amadea

Feminine of Amadeus, meaning 'love God'. More commonly used in German-speaking communities.

Amalia

Hebrew, meaning 'labour of love'. Also German, meaning 'work'.

Amana

Hebrew, meaning 'loyal and true'. Also the name of a type of tulip.

Amanda
(alt. Amandine)

Latin, meaning 'much loved'. Famous Amandas include presenter and actress Amanda Holden, and actresses Amanda Bynes and Amanda Seyfried.

Amara
(alt. Amani)

Greek, meaning 'lovely forever'. Actress Amara Miller is known for her role in *The Descendants*.

Amarantha

Contraction of Amanda and Samantha, meaning 'much loved listener'. Also associated with the amaranth plant.

Amari
(alt. Amaris, Amasa, Amata, Amaya)

Hebrew, meaning 'pledged by God'. Also the name of a province in Greece.

Amaryllis
(alt. Ameris)

Greek, meaning 'fresh'. Usually associated with the flowering plant.

Amber

French, from the word for the semi-precious stone of the same name. Famous Ambers include actresses Amber Heard and Amber Benson.

Amberly

Contraction of Amber and Leigh, meaning 'stone' and 'meadow'.

Amboree
(alt. Amber, Ambree)

American, meaning 'precocious'. More commonly used in the USA.

Amelia

(alt. Aemilia, Amalie, Amelie)
Greek, meaning 'industrious'.
Famous Amelias include flying legend Amelia Earhart, and two Princess Amelias of Great Britain during the eighteenth century.

America

From the country of the same name. Actress America Ferrera is known for her roles in *Ugly Betty* and *How to Train Your Dragon*.

Amethyst

Greek, from the word for the purple precious stone of the same name.

Amina

(alt. Aamina)
Arabic, meaning 'honest and trustworthy'. Also the name of an influential Nigerian princess in the seventeenth century. Aamina Sheik is a Pakistani American actress and model.

Amira

(alt. Amiya, Amiyah)
Arabic, meaning 'a high-born girl'. In Hebrew, the name also means 'rich princess'.

Amity

Latin, meaning 'friendship and harmony'. Also a name of a faction in the novel *Divergent*.

Amory

Variant of the Spanish name Amor, meaning 'love'. Also used as a boys' (more commonly) and girls' name in America during late 1800s to early 1900s, probably then derived from the French Ameury.

Amy

(alt. Aimee, Amee, Ami, Amie, Ammie, Amya)
Latin, meaning 'beloved'. Famous Amys include actress Amy Adams, Winter Olympic skeleton gold medallist Amy Williams and singer Amy Winehouse.

Anafa

Hebrew, meaning 'heron'.

Anaïs

Persian, meaning 'love'.

Ananda

Hindi, meaning 'bliss'. Also the name of one of the Buddha's disciples.

Anastasia

(alt. Athanasia)
Greek, meaning 'resurrection'. Usually associated with the Grand Duchess Anastasia of Russia, who was a member of the Russian royal family at the time of the Revolution of 1917.

Anat

Jewish, meaning 'water spring'. Name of a Semitic goddess.

Anatolia

Greek, meaning 'east sunrise'. The name of a large area within Turkey. Also a Christian saint.

Andrea

(alt. Andreia, Andria, Andrina)

Feminine of Andrew, from the Greek term for 'a man's woman'. Famous Andreas include singer Andrea Corr and writers Andrea Levy and Andrea Dworkin. Andrina is a Disney character who first appeared in *The Little Mermaid*. Andrina Carroll is a British actress.

Andromeda

Greek, meaning 'leader of men'. From the heroine of an ancient Greek legend.

Anemone

Greek, meaning 'breath'. Also the name of a type of flowering plant.

Angela

(alt. Angel, Angeles, Angelia, Angelle; abrrev. Angie)

Greek, meaning 'messenger from God' or 'angel'. Famous Angelas include actress Angela Lansbury and German Chancellor Angela Merkel.

Angelica

(alt. Angelina, Angeline, Angelique, Angelise, Angelita, Anjelica, Anjelina)

Latin, meaning 'angelic'. Famous Angelicas include actress Anjelica Huston and *Rugrats* cartoon character Angelica Pickle.

Angelina

(alt. Anjelina)

Derived from Angela, meaning 'messenger from God' or 'angel'. Famous Angelinas include actress Angelina Jolie and book and TV mouse Angelina Ballerina.

Anise

(alt. Anisa, Anissa)

French, from the liquorice-flavoured plant of the same name. Female form of Anis, a boys' name common in Tunisia and Morocco.

Anita

(alt. Anitra)

Variant of Ann, meaning 'grace'. Famous Anitas include actress Anita Dobson, *Body Shop* founder Anita Roddick and singer Anita Baker.

Anna

(alt. Ana, Anne)

Derived from Hannah, meaning 'grace'. Taken from the name of Anna the prophetess in the Bible. Anna Maxwell Martin is a BAFTA award-winning English actress.

Annabel

(alt. Anabel, Anabelle, Annabell, Annabella, Annabelle)

Contraction of Anna and Belle, meaning 'grace' and 'beauty'. Annabel Croft is known for her careers as a tennis pro and TV presenter.

Annalise

(alt. Annalee, Annaliese, Annalisa, Anneli, Annelie, Annelies, Annelise)

Combination of Anna and Lise, meaning 'grace' and 'pledged to God'. More commonly used in the USA and parts of Scandinavia.

Anne
(alt. Ann, Annie)

Derived from Hannah, meaning 'grace'. Famous Annes include actresses Anne Hathaway and wives of Henry VIII Anne Boleyn and Anne of Cleeves.

Annemarie
(alt. Annamae, Annamarie, Annelle, Annmarie, Anne-Marie)

Combination of Anne and Mary, meaning 'grace' and 'star of the sea'. Anne-Marie Duff is known for her roles in *Shameless* and *The Virgin Queen*.

Annette
(alt. Annetta)

Derived from Hannah, Hebrew, meaning 'grace'. Famous Annettes include actresses Annette Bening, Annette Crosby and Annette Funicello.

Annis

Greek, meaning 'finished or completed'. May also be a variant of Agnes. In English mythology the Black Annis is a blue-faced witch who eats children.

Annora

Latin, meaning 'honour'. More commonly used in Eastern European communities.

Anoushka
(alt. Anousha, Anushka)

Variant of Anne, meaning 'grace'. Most popular in Russia, Greece and India.

Anthea
(alt. Anthi)

Greek, meaning 'flowerlike'. Famous Antheas include presenters Anthea Turner and Anthea Redfern, and director Anthea Benton.

Antigone

In ancient Greek mythology, Antigone was the daughter of Oedipus.

Antoinette
(alt. Antonetta, Antonette, Antonietta)

Both a variation of Ann and the feminine of Anthony, meaning 'invaluable grace'. Usually associated with eighteenth-century French queen consort Marie Antoinette. Often shortened to Toni.

Antonia
(alt. Antonella, Antonina)

Latin, meaning 'invaluable'. Also the name of dozens of influential ancient Roman women.

Anwen

Welsh, meaning 'very fair'. Usually associated with the character of Anwen Williams in *Torchwood*.

Anya
(alt. Aanya, Aniya, Aniyah, Aniylah, Anja)

Russian, meaning 'favour' or 'grace'; or Sanskrit, meaning 'the inexhaustible'. Anya Hindmarch is known for her designs for fashion accessories.

Aoife

Gaelic, meaning 'beautiful joy'.
Usually associated with the goddess
Esuvia.

Apollonia

Feminine of Apollo, the Greek god
of the sun. St Apollonia was a virgin
martyr in the third century and is the
patron saint of dentistry.

Apple

From the name of the fruit. Famous
Apples include the technology
company Apple Inc, and the name of
Gwyneth Paltrow's daughter.

April

(alt. Avril)

Latin, meaning 'opening up'. Also
the name of the month, which has
associations with the goddess Venus.

Aquilina

(alt. Aqua, Aquila)

Spanish, meaning 'like an eagle'. St
Aquilina was a child martyr in the
third century.

Ara

Arabic, meaning 'brings rain'. Also
the name of a star constellation. Used
as both a girls' and a boys' name.

Arabella

Latin, meaning 'answered prayer'.
Also the name of an opera by
Richard Strauss.

Araceli

(alt. Aracely)

Spanish, meaning 'altar of Heaven'.

Araminta

(abbrev. Minnie, Minty)

Hebrew, meaning 'lofty'.

Araylia

(alt. Araelea)

Latin, meaning 'golden'. Associated
with aralia, a genus of trees and
shrubs.

Arcadia

Greek, meaning 'paradise'. Also the
name of a daughter of the ancient
Roman Emperor Arcadius.

Ardelle

(alt. Ardell, Ardella)

Latin, meaning 'burning with
enthusiasm'. Ardelle Kloss was
an early leading American ice
skater.

Arden

(alt. Ardis, Ardith)

Latin, meaning 'burning with
enthusiasm'.

Arella

(alt. Areli, Arely)

Hebrew, meaning 'angel'. More
commonly used in the USA.

Aretha

Greek, meaning 'woman of
virtue'. Aretha Franklin is a soul
singer.

Aria

(alt. Ariah)

Hebrew, meaning 'lioness', and
Italian, meaning 'melody'. It is used
as both a girls' and boys' name.

Ariadne

Greek and Latin, meaning 'the very holy one'. In ancient Greek mythology, Ariadne was the daughter of King Minos.

Ariana

(alt. Aaryanna, Ariane, Arianna, Arianne, Arienne)

Derived from Welsh word for 'silver'. Also the name of a large geographical area in ancient Greek times, covering most of modern-day Afghanistan.

Ariel

(alt. Ariela, Ariella, Arielle)

Hebrew, meaning 'lioness of God'. Character in Disney's *The Little Mermaid*.

Arlene

(alt. Arleen, Arlie, Arline, Arly)

Gaelic, meaning 'pledge'. Arlene Phillips is known for her appearances on *Strictly Come Dancing* and *So You Think You Can Dance*, as well as her work as a choreographer.

Armida

Latin, meaning 'little armed one'. Taken from the character of Armida in the epic poem *La Gerusalemme liberata*.

Artemisia

(alt. Artemis; abbrev. Artie, Arti)

Greek and Spanish, meaning 'perfect'. Also the name of a legendary female naval commander in Persia during the fifth century.

Arwen

Welsh, meaning 'fair' or 'fine'. Also an Elven character in J.R.R. Tolkien's *Lord of the Rings* trilogy.

Arya

Fictional brave tomboy character from George R. R. Martin's 'A Song of Ice and Fire' series.

Ashanti

From the geographical area in Ghana, Africa. Singer Ashanti Shequoiya Douglas is better known as just 'Ashanti'.

Ashby

English, meaning 'ash tree farm'.

Ashley

(alt. Ashely, Ashlee, Ashleigh, Ashli, Ashlie, Ashly)

English, meaning 'ash tree meadow'. Also a boys' name. Famous female Ashleys include actresses Ashley Jensen and Ashley Judd, and singer Ashley Roberts.

Ashlynn

(alt. Ashlyn)

Irish Gaelic, meaning 'dream'. Also a spelling variation for Aislinn.

Ashton

(alt. Ashtyn)

Old English, meaning 'ash tree town'. Used as a girls' and boys' name, but most commonly for boys.

Asia

From the name of the continent. Also a name for an Oceanid in ancient Greek mythology.

Asma

(alt. Aasmah, Asmara)

Arabic, meaning 'high-standing'. Aasmah Mir is a BBC TV presenter and radio journalist. Asmara is the capital city of Eritrea.

Aspen

(alt. Aspynn)

From the name of the tree. Also name of a city in the US state of Colorado.

Assumpta

(alt. Asumpta, Assunta)

Irish, meaning 'assumption', and Italian, meaning 'raised up'. Assumpta Serna is a Spanish actress, and several Irish actresses have this given name.

Asta

(alt. Asteria, Astor, Astoria)

Greek or Latin, meaning 'star-like'. Also the name of a type of moth.

Astrid

Old Norse, meaning 'beautiful like a God'. Author Astrid Lundgren is known for her children's novels such as *Pippi Longstocking*.

Atara

Hebrew, meaning 'diadem' or 'crown'. Also the name of a type of butterfly.

Athena

(alt. Athenais)

Greek, meaning 'wise'. From the ancient Greek goddess of wisdom, mathematics and arts and crafts.

Aubrey

(alt. Aubree, Aubriana, Aubrie)

French, meaning 'elf ruler'. Originally a name for boys, although it is now far more common for girls.

Audrey

(alt. Audra, Audrie, Audry, Autry, Audrina)

English, meaning 'noble strength'. St Etheldreda was known as St Audrey, and was an English princess in the seventh century. Famous Audreys include actress Audrey Hepburn and actress Audrey Tautou.

Augusta

(alt. August, Augustine)

Latin, meaning 'venerated'. The female version of the ancient Roman name Augustus.

Aura

(alt. Aurea)

Greek or Latin, meaning either 'soft breeze' or 'gold'.

Aurelia

(alt. Aurelie)

Latin, meaning 'gold'. The name of various ancient Roman women, including Julius Caesar's mother.

Aurora
(alt. Aurore)
Latin, meaning 'dawn'. In ancient Roman mythology, Aurora was the goddess of sunrise.

Austine
(alt. Austen, Austin)
Latin, meaning 'venerated'. Feminine version of Austin.

Autumn
Latin, from the name of the harvest season. Canadian-born Autumn Phillips is granddaughter-in-law to Queen Elizabeth II.

Ava
(alt. Avia, Avie)
Latin, meaning 'like a bird'. Ava Gardner was an iconic American actress during the 1950s–1970s.

Avalon
(alt. Avalyn, Aveline)
Celtic, meaning 'island of apples'. The name comes from a mythological island in the legend of King Arthur.

Axelle
Greek, meaning 'father of peace'. More commonly used in French- and Flemish-speaking communities.

Aya
(alt. Ayah)
Hebrew, meaning 'bird'.

Ayanna
(alt. Ayana)
Nigerian, meaning 'beautiful flower'.

Azalea
(alt. Azalia)
Latin, meaning 'dry earth'. Also the name of a type of flowering shrub.

Aziza
Hebrew, meaning 'mighty', or Arabic, meaning 'precious'.

Azure
(alt. Azaria)
French, meaning 'sky-blue'.

B Girls' names

Babette

French version of Barbara, from the Greek word meaning 'foreign'. Babette Cole is an author of children's books.

Badia

(alt. Badiyn, Badea)

Arabic, meaning 'elegant'.

Bailey

(alt. Baeli, Bailee)

English, meaning 'law enforcer'. Used as a girls' and boys' name, much more commonly for boys in recent years.

Bambi

Shortened version of the Italian Bambina, meaning 'child'. Usually associated with the cartoon Disney character.

Barbara

(alt. Barbra; abbrev. Barb, Barbie)

Greek, meaning 'foreign'. Famous Barbaras include actress Barbara Windsor, singer Barbra Streisand and Barbara McClintock, who won a Nobel Prize for genetics.

Basma

Arabic, meaning 'smile'.

Bathsheba

Hebrew, meaning 'daughter of the oath'. Usually associated with the story of Bathsheba and King David in the Bible. Also a character in the novel *Far From the Madding Crowd*.

Bay

(alt. Baya, Bae)

From the bay tree, with edible leaves used in cooking, or the indentation in a coastline (e.g. Byron Bay). Used as a boys' name most commonly, but also for girls.

Beata

Latin, meaning 'blessed'. Can be used as a shortened form of Beatrice or as a name in its own right.

Beatrice

(alt. Beatrix, Beatriz, Bellatrix, Betrys)

Latin, meaning 'blessed' or 'voyager'. A recent rapid riser in names for girls in the UK. Famous Beatrices include children's book author Beatrix Potter and Princess Beatrice, granddaughter of Queen Elizabeth II.

Becky

(alt. Becca, Beccie, Beccy, Beckie)

Shortened form of Rebecca, meaning 'joined', used as a name in its own right.

Belinda

(alt. Belen, Belina)

Contraction of Belle and Linda, meaning 'beautiful'. Famous Belindas include singer Belinda Carlisle and actress Belinda Stewart-Wilson.

Bell

Shortened form of Isabel, meaning 'pledged to God'.

Bella

(alt. Belle)

Latin, meaning 'beautiful'. Usually associated with the character of Isabella (Bella) Swan from the *Twilight* series or Belle from Disney's film *Beauty and the Beast*.

Belva

Latin, meaning 'beautiful view'. The inspiration for one of the characters in the musical *Chicago* was real-life murderer Belva Gaertner.

Bénédicta

(abbrev. Bennie, Benny)

Latin, the feminine of Benedict, meaning 'blessed'. Benedicta Henrietta of the Palatinate is a common ancestor of many present-day monarchs.

Benita

(alt. Bernita)

Spanish, meaning 'blessed'.

Berit

(alt. Beret)

Scandinavian, meaning 'splendid' or 'gorgeous'.

Bernadette

(alt. Bernadine; abbrev. Bernie)

French, meaning 'courageous'. St Bernadette was a known for her visions of the Virgin Mary.

Bernice

(alt. Berenice, Berniece, Burnice)

Greek, meaning 'she who brings victory'. The name of Herod's daughter in the Bible.

Bertha

(alt. Berta, Berthe, Bertie)

German, meaning 'bright'. There are four saints called Bertha, all from the early Middle Ages.

Beryl

Greek, meaning 'pale green gemstone'. Beryl Reid was a classic British actress and Beryl Cook an English artist.

Bess
(alt. Bessie)

Shortened form of Elizabeth, meaning 'consecrated to God'. Queen Elizabeth I has the nickname Good Queen Bess. Bessie Smith was a blues singer.

Beth

Hebrew, meaning 'house'. Also shortened form of Elizabeth, meaning 'consecrated to God', used in its own right.

Bethany
(alt. Bethan)

Hebrew, referring to a geographical location found in the Bible. The name has seen a return to popularity in recent years.

Bethel

Hebrew, meaning 'house of God'. Also the name of a city in the Bible.

Bettina

Spanish or German version of Elizabeth, meaning 'consecrated to God'.

Betty
(alt. Betsy, Bette, Bettie, Bettye)

Shortened version of Elizabeth, meaning 'consecrated to God', also used in its own right. Famous Bettys include cartoon character Betty Boop and actresses Betty White and Betty Grable.

Beulah

Hebrew, meaning 'married'. Also the name for a place that exists between Earth and Heaven.

Beverly
(alt. Beverlee, Beverley)

English, meaning 'beaver stream'. Beverley Knight is a British soul singer, actress and TV personality.

Bevin

Celtic, meaning 'fair lady'.

Beyoncé

Modern American, from the singer. Beyoncé's name was created by her parents as a tribute to her mother's maiden name, which was Beyince. However, some sources say the name is African, meaning 'beyond others'.

Bianca
(alt. Blanca)

Italian, meaning 'white'. Famous Biancas include activist Bianca Jagger, model Bianca Gascoigne, the character of Bianca from Shakespeare's *Othello* and the long-running *EastEnders* character of that name.

Bibiana

Greek, meaning 'alive'. St Bibiana was a Roman virgin and martyr during the fourth century.

Bijou

French, meaning 'jewel'.

Billie
(alt. Bill, Billy, Billye)

Shortened version of Wilhelmina, meaning 'determined' as well as a name in its own right. Billie Holiday was an iconic jazz singer. Billie Piper is a singer turned actress.

Bina

Hebrew, meaning 'knowledge'.

Birgit

(alt. Birgitta)

German, meaning 'power and strength'. Used as a variation of Bridget.

Blaer

Icelandic, meaning 'light breeze'.

Blair

Scottish Gaelic, meaning 'flat, plain area'. Blair Waldorf is the main character in *Gossip Girl*, the novel series, TV and film.

Blaise

French, meaning 'lisp' or 'stutter'. Also common as a boys' name.

Blake

(alt. Blakely, Blakelyn)

English, meaning either 'pale-skinned' or 'dark'. Used as a girls' and a boys' name, but most commonly male.

Blanche

(alt. Blanch)

French, meaning 'white or pale'. Extremely common in the Middle Ages, Blanche saw an increase in popularity before World War II, but hasn't been widely used since then.

Blodwen

Welsh, meaning 'white flower'.

Blossom

English, meaning 'flowerlike'.

Blythe

(alt. Blithe, Bly)

English, meaning 'happy and carefree'. Actress Blythe Danner is known for her roles in *Will & Grace*, *Meet the Parents*, and for being the mother of Gwyneth Paltrow.

Bobbi

(alt. Bobbie, Bobby)

Shortened version of Roberta, meaning 'bright fame', as well as a name in its own right. Usually associated with the cosmetics brand Bobbi Brown.

Bonamy

(alt. Bomani, Bonamia, Bonamea)

Derived from French, meaning 'close friend'.

Bonita

Spanish, meaning 'pretty'. Often associated with the song 'La Isla Bonita' by Madonna.

Bonnie

(alt. Bonny)

Scottish, meaning 'fair of face'. Actress Bonnie Langford was a child star who grew up to appear in West End musicals and *Dr Who*.

Brandy

(alt. Brandee, Brandi, Brandie)

From the name of the liquor created by distilling wine. Singer Brandy is known for her various pop songs as well as her role in *Moesha*.

Branwen

Welsh, meaning 'a white crow'.

Brea

(alt. Bree, Bria)

Shortened form of Brianna, meaning 'strong', but used in its own right. Also the name of a god in ancient Irish mythology.

Brenda

Old Norse, meaning 'sword'. Can also be used as a female variation of Brendan.

Brianna

(alt. Breana, Breanna, Breanne)

Irish Gaelic, meaning 'strong'. More commonly used in the USA.

Bridget

(alt. Bridgett, Bridgette, Brigette, Brigid, Brigitta, Brigitte)

Irish Gaelic, meaning 'strength and power'. Famous Bridgets include actress Bridget Fonda, Brigitte Bardot and the protagonist in the novel *Bridget Jones's Diary* by Helen Fielding.

Brier

(alt. Briar)

French, meaning 'heather'.

Brit

(alt. Britt, Britta)

Celtic, meaning 'spotted' or 'freckled'. Usually a shortened form of Brittany, though it can be used in its own right. Actresses Britt Ekland and Britt Robertson are both Brittanys.

Britannia

Latin, meaning 'Britain'. Britannia is the female personification of Great Britain.

Brittany

(alt. Britany, Britney, Britni, Brittani, Brittanie, Brittney, Brittni, Brittny)

Latin, meaning 'from England', though the name also refers to a region of France. Famous Brittanys include actress Brittany Murphy and singer Britney Spears.

Bronwen

(alt. Bronwyn)

Welsh, meaning 'fair breast'. In Wales it is more common to give the spelling Bronwen to girls and Bronwyn to boys, although the rest of the world doesn't follow the same pattern.

Brooke

(alt. Brook)

English, meaning 'small stream'. Brooke Shields is an American actress and model and Brooke Vincent a British TV actress.

Brooklyn

(alt. Brooklynn)

From the name of a New York borough. Used as a girls' name rarely, more commonly a boys' name.

Brunhilda

(alt. Brunhilde, Brynhildr)

German, meaning 'armour-wearing fighting maid'. Brynhildr, from which Brunhilda and Brunhilde orginated, was an important character in Old German mythology.

Bryn
(alt. Brynn)
Welsh, meaning 'mount' or 'hill'. Used as a boys' name and, less commonly, a girls' name.

Bryony
(alt. Briony)
English, from the name of bryonia, a European vine. Bryony Hannah is an Olivier-nominated British actress and star of *Call the Midwife*.

Buffy
A shortened form of Elizabeth, meaning 'consecrated to God'. Usually associated with the protagonist of the sci-fi series *Buffy the Vampire Slayer*.

Names of poets

Amy (Lowell)

Anne (Sexton)

Carol Ann (Duffy)

Charlotte (Smith)

Emily (Dickinson)

Fleur (Adcock)

Gwyneth (Lewis)

Pam (Ayres)

Ruth (Padel)

Sylvia (Plath)

Wendy (Cope)

Girls' names

Cadence

Latin, meaning 'with rhythm'. Used as feminine form of Caden.

Cadew

Derived from French, meaning 'gift'. English, meaning 'coarse woollen fabric'.

Cai

Vietnamese, meaning 'feminine'.

Caitlin

(alt. Cadyn, Caitlann, Caitlyn, Caitlynn, Katelin, Katelyn, Katelynn, Katlin, Katlyn)

Greek, meaning 'pure'. Caitlin Moran is a British broadcaster, newspaper columnist and author.

Calandra

Greek, meaning 'lark'. The calandra lark is a small bird found in Mediterranean countries. It is also the name of an asteroid belt.

Calantha

(alt. Calanthe)

Greek, meaning 'lovely flower'. Also refers to dozens of flowering shrubs.

Caledonia

Latin, meaning 'from Scotland'. Also an old name for Scotland.

Calia

American, meaning 'renowned beauty'. Also refers to several species of shrubs and trees.

Calista

(alt. Callista, Callisto, Kallista)

Greek, meaning 'most beautiful'. Actress Calista Flockhart is known for her roles in *Ally McBeal* and *Brothers and Sisters*.

Calla

Greek, meaning 'beautiful'. Also refers to a type of white-flowered plant.

Callie
(alt. Caleigh, Cali, Calleigh, Cally)
Greek, meaning 'beauty'.
Screenwriter Callie Khouri is known
for her work on *Thelma & Louise* and
Nashville.

Calliope
Greek, meaning 'beautiful voice'.
From the muse of epic poetry in
ancient Greek mythology.

Camas
Native American, from the root and
bulb of the same name.

Cambria
Welsh, from the alternative name for
Wales.

Camden
(alt. Camdin, Camdyn)
English, meaning 'winding valley'.
Usually a boys' name but can be
used for girls.

Cameo
Italian, meaning 'skin'. A cameo in
the acting world usually refers to a
small part played by a big star.

Cameron
(alt. Camryn)
Scottish Gaelic, meaning 'bent nose'.
Used as a boys' name but also for
girls, as with actress Cameron Diaz.

Camilla
*(alt. Camille, Camelia, Camellia,
Camila, Camillia)*
Latin, meaning 'spiritual serving
girl'. Camilla, Duchess of Cornwall,
is married to Prince Charles. The
French form, Camille, is often also
used for boys.

Candace
*(alt. Candice, Candis, Kandice;
abbrev. Candy, Candi, Kandy,
Kandi)*
Latin, meaning 'brilliant white'. In
the African ancient kingdom
of Kush, Candace was the title
given to queens and queen
mothers.

Candida
Latin, meaning 'white', associated
with purity and salvation.
Unfortunately, also the name of a
fungal infection.

Candra
Latin, meaning 'glowing'. The Candra
family dynasty ruled eastern Bengal
in the tenth century. Also the name
of an immmortal villainess in Marvel
comics.

Canei
Greek, meaning 'pure'. Also refers to
a type of shrub.

Caoimhe
Celtic, meaning 'gentle' or 'precious'.
Can be pronounced as 'kyva' or
'keeva', depending on where in
Ireland it is used.

Caprice
Italian, meaning 'ruled by whim'.
Caprice Bourret is a model best
known simply as 'Caprice'.

Cara

Latin, meaning 'darling'. Cara Delevingne is a top model.

Caren
(alt. Carin, Caron, Caryn)

Greek, meaning 'pure'. Comedian Whoopi Goldberg's real name is Caryn Elaine Johnson.

Carey
(alt. Cari, Carie, Carrey, Carri, Carrie, Cary)

Gaelic, meaning 'love'. Carey Mulligan is an English actress. Can also be used for boys.

Carina
(alt. Corina)

Italian, meaning 'dearest little one'. Also the name of a star constellation.

Carissa
(alt. Carisa)

Greek, meaning 'grace'. Also the name of a type of shrub.

Carla
(alt. Charla)

Feminine of the Old Norse Carl, meaning 'free man'. Singer Carla Bruni-Sarkozy is married to the former president of France Nicolas Sarkozy.

Carlin
(alt. Carleen, Carlene)

Gaelic, meaning 'little champion'.

Carlotta
(alt. Carlota)

Italian form of Charlotte, meaning 'little and feminine'. Also the name of a character in The Phantom of the Opera.

Carly
(alt. Carlee, Carley, Carli, Carlie)

Feminine of the German Charles, meaning 'free man'. Famous Carlys include singers Carly Simon and Carly Rae Jepson, and model Karlie Kloss.

Carmel
(alt. Carmela, Carmelita, Carmella)

Hebrew, meaning 'God's vineyard'. Mount Carmel is a place mentioned in the Bible.

Carmen
(alt. Carma, Carmina)

Latin, meaning 'song'. Usually associated with the opera Carmen by Georges Bizet.

Carol
(alt. Carole, Carrol, Carroll, Caryl)

Shortened form of Caroline, commonly used in its own right. Famous Carols include actress Carol Burnett, poet laureate Carol Ann Duffy and TV personality Carol Vorderman.

Caroline
(alt. Carolann, Carolina, Carolyn, Carolynn)

German, meaning 'man'. Famous Carolines include writer, actress and comedienne Caroline Aherne and Caroline Herschel, the astronomer.

Carrington

English, meaning 'Charles's town'.

Carys

(alt. Cerys)

Welsh, meaning 'love'. Singer Cerys Matthews was a founder member of the band Catatonia.

Casey

(alt. Kacey, Kaci, Kacie, Kacy, Kasey, Kasie, Kassie)

Irish Gaelic, meaning 'watchful'. Used especially in the USA and for both girls and boys.

Cassandra

(alt. Casandra, Cassandre, Kassandra)

Greek, meaning 'one who prophesies doom' or 'entangler of men'. Usually associated with the seer in ancient Greek mythology and sister of Helen of Troy. Cassandra Clare is the pen name of bestselling author Judith Rumelt

'. Cassia

er' or 'curly-
Wolf is an American teen beauty queen.

Cassiopeia

(alt. Cassiopia, Cassiopea)

Greek, from the constellation and the ancient Greek myth about a vain queen.

Catalina

(alt. Catarina, Caterina)

Spanish version of Catherine, meaning 'pure'.

Catherine

(alt. Catharine, Cathrine, Cathryn)

Greek, meaning 'pure'. Famous Catherines include Catherine, Duchess of Cambridge, actress Catherine Zeta Jones and two wives of King Henry VIII.

Cathleen

Irish version of Catherine, meaning 'pure'. Actress Cathleen Nesbitt was known for her roles in dozens of West End and Broadway productions.

Cathy

(alt. Cathey, Cathi, Cathie, Caty, Cato, Caitia, Kathie, Kathy)

Shortened form of Catherine, meaning 'pure'. Can be used in its own right. Author Cathy Cassidy is known for her young adult fiction.

Catrina

(alt. Caitrina, Caitriona)

Greek, meaning 'pure'.

Cayley

(alt. Cayla, Caylee, Caylen)

American, meaning 'pure'.

Cecilia

(alt. Cecile, Cecelia, Cecily, Cicely, Cicily)

Latin, meaning 'blind one'. Associated with the song 'Cecilia' by Simon and Garfunkel.

Celena

Greek, meaning 'goddess of the moon'. A spelling alternative to the Spanish name Selena.

Celeste

(alt. Celestina, Celestine)

Latin, meaning 'heavenly'. American Celeste Holm was an Oscar-winning actress in films and on Broadway.

Celine

(alt. Celia, Celina)

French version of Celeste, meaning 'heavenly'. Canadian Celine Dion is one of the most enduringly successful singers in pop music history.

Cerise

French, meaning 'cherry'. The colour cerise is a deep, pinky red.

Chanah

(alt. Chana)

Hebrew, meaning 'grace'. Usually used as a spelling alternative to Hannah.

Chandler

(alt. Chandell)

English, meaning 'candle maker'. Most commonly used as a boys' name.

Chandra

(alt. Chanda, Chandry)

Sanskrit, meaning 'like the moon'. Chandra is a god of the moon in Hinduism.

Chanel

(alt. Chanelle)

French, meaning 'pipe'. Usually associated with the designer and fashion brand Coco Chanel.

Chantal

(alt. Chantel, Chantelle, Chantilly)

French, meaning 'stony spot'. Chantelle Houghton was the first non-celebrity to win Celebrity Big Brother and is now a TV personality and columnist.

Chardonnay

French, from the wine variety of the same name.

Charis

(alt. Charissa, Charisse)

Greek, meaning 'grace'. Charis is one of the Graces in ancient Greek mythology.

Charity

Latin, meaning 'brotherly love'. Of the classic trio of names, Faith, Hope and Charity, this has been the least used, with a high point in the USA in the 1970s.

Charlene

(alt. Charleen, Charline)

German, meaning 'man'. Famous Charlenes include actress Charlene McKenna and the character Charlene in Aussie soap Neighbours, played by Kylie Minogue.

Charlotte
(alt. Charnette, Charolette, Charlize; abbrev. Charlie, Charly)

French, meaning 'little and feminine'. Famous Charlottes include author Charlotte Brontë, singer Charlotte Church and Princess Charlotte, born May 2015.

Charmaine
Latin, meaning 'clan'. The name possibly comes from Charmian, who was a favourite servant of Cleopatra.

Charnelle
(alt. Charnell, Charnel, Charnele)

American, meaning 'sparkles'. The spelling Charnel refers to a building that houses human remains, often located near a church.

Chastity
Latin, meaning 'purity'.

Chava
(alt. Chaya)

Hebrew, meaning 'beloved'.

Chelsea
(alt. Chelsee, Chelsey, Chelsi, Chelsie, Chelsy)

English, meaning 'port or landing place'. Chelsy Davy is a Zimbawean famous for being the on-off girlfriend of Prince Harry for many years.

Cher
French, meaning 'beloved'. Cher is an American singer and actress, originally part of the duo Sonny and Cher (with husband Sonny Bono) and later a hugely successful solo artist.

Cherie
(alt. Cheri, Cherise)

French, meaning 'dear'. Cherie Blair is a barrister and wife of former British prime minister Tony Blair.

Cherish
(alt. Cherith)

English, meaning 'to treasure'.

Chermona
Hebrew, meaning 'sacred mountain'. Sometimes used as a female spelling alternative for Sherman.

Cherry
(alt. Cherri)

English, meaning 'cherry fruit'.

Cheryl
(alt. Cheryle)

English, meaning 'little and womanly'. Singer Cheryl Cole found fame with girl group Girls Aloud and has been a judge on The X Factor.

Chesney
English, meaning 'place to camp'. Used as both a girls' and a boys' name.

Cheyenne
(alt. Cheyanne)

Native American, from the tribe of the same name from the state of Wyoming in the USA.

Chiara
(alt. Ceara, Chiarina)

Italian, meaning 'light'. Usually used as a spelling alternative to Ciara.

China

From the Asian country of the same name.

Chiquita

Spanish, meaning 'little one'.

Chloe

(alt. Cloe)

Greek, meaning 'pale green shoot'. Sometimes spelled with an accent on the 'e'. Famous Chloes include the fashion house Chloé, actresses Chloë Moretz and Chloë Sevigny and author Toni Morrison – whose birth name was Chloe Wofford.

Chloris

Greek, meaning 'pale'. Chloris was a nymph in ancient Greek mythology.

Christabel

Latin and French, meaning 'fair Christian'. The title of a poem by Samuel Taylor Coleridge.

Christina

(alt. Christine, Christiana, Cristina; abbrev. Chris, Chrissy, Christa, Christie, Christy, Crissy, Cristy)

Greek, meaning 'anointed Christian'. The female version of Christian, the name was originally constructed as a tribute to Jesus Christ. Christina Aguilera is a world famous pop singer. Christine Bleakley is a TV presenter, originally from Northern Ireland.

Chuma

Aramaic, meaning 'warmth'.

Ciara

Irish, meaning 'dark beauty'. Ciara Princess Harris, known simply as Ciara, is an American singer, dancer, actress and model.

Cierra

(alt. Ciera)

Irish, meaning 'black'. Usually used as a spelling alternative to Sierra.

Cinderella

French, meaning 'little ash-girl'. Most often associated with the fairy tale.

Cinnamon

Greek, from the exotic spice of the same name.

Citlali

(alt. Citlalli)

Nahuatl, meaning 'star'. An ancient Aztec name.

Citrine

Latin, from the gemstone of the same name.

Claire

(alt. Clare, Clara, Claira)

Latin, meaning 'bright'. A very popular name, especially in 1960s and 1970s Britain. Famous Claires include actress Claire Danes, agony aunt Claire Rayner, and sports presenter Clare Balding.

Clarabelle
(alt. Clarabella, Claribel)
Contraction of Clara and Isobel, meaning 'bright' and 'consecrated to God'. Clarabelle is a Disney cow character and Clarabella is the title of a Beatles song.

Clarissa
(alt. Clarice, Clarisse)
Variation of Claire, meaning 'bright'. One of the longest novels in English is the eighteenth-century *Clarissa, or, The History of a Young Lady*, by Samuel Richardson.

Clarity
Latin, meaning 'lucid'.

Claudette
Latin, meaning 'lame'. The first female prime minister of Haiti was Claudette Werleigh. Claudette Colvin is a pioneer of the American civil rights movement.

Claudia
(alt. Claudie, Claudine)
Latin, meaning 'lame'. TV presenter and film critic Claudia Winkleman co-presents *Strictly Come Dancing* and German Claudia Schiffer is a supermodel.

Clematis
Greek, meaning 'vine'. Also the name of a type of flowering plant.

Clementine
(alt. Clemency, Clementina, Clemmie)
Latin, meaning 'mild and merciful'. Also the name of the sweet orange fruit.

Cleopatra
Greek, meaning 'her father's renown'. Cleopatra was the last acting Pharaoh of ancient Egypt.

Clio
(alt. Cleo, Cliona)
Greek, from the ancient Greek muse of history of the same name. Clio Higgins is an English singer, who appeared on *The Voice*.

Clodagh
Irish, meaning 'river'.

Clotilda
(alt. Clothilda, Clothilde, Clotilde)
German, meaning 'renowned battle'. St Clotilde was known for her works of charity in the fifth century.

Clover
English, from the flower of the same name.

Coco
Spanish, meaning 'help'. Usually associated with the fashion designer Coco Chanel.

Cody
English, meaning 'pillow'. Used as a name for girls and, more commonly, boys.

Colleen
(alt. Coleen)
Irish Gaelic, meaning 'girl'. Colleen Nolan is the youngest of the singing sisters The Nolans, now a TV presenter.

Collette
(alt. Colette)

Greek and French, meaning 'people of victory'. Author Sidonie-Gabrielle Colette is known for her novel *Gigi*.

Connie
(alt. Konnie)

Latin, meaning 'steadfast'. Also used as a shortened version of Constance. Kanak Asha Huq, better known as Konnie, is the longest-serving female presenter of *Blue Peter*.

Constance
(alt. Constanza)

Latin, meaning 'steadfast'. Oscar Wilde's wife was called Constance Lloyd.

Consuelo
(alt. Consuela)

Spanish, meaning 'comfort'. The name originated from a Spanish name for the Virgin Mary, Our Lady of Consolation.

Cora

Greek, meaning 'maiden'.

Coral
(alt. Coralie, Coraline, Corelia, Corene)

Latin, from the marine life of the same name.

Corazon

Spanish, meaning 'heart'. Also a slang term in Spanish meaning 'darling'.

Cordelia
(alt. Cordia, Cordie)

Latin, meaning 'heart'. Also the name of a tragic character in Shakespeare's play *King Lear*.

Corey
(alt. Cori, Corrie, Cory)

Irish Gaelic, meaning 'the hollow'. Used for girls and, more commonly, for boys.

Corin
(alt. Corine, Corinne)

Latin, meaning 'spear'. More commonly used as a boys' name but can be used for girls.

Corinne
(alt. Corinna, Corrine)

French version of Cora, meaning 'maiden'. Famous Corinnes include Corinne Bailey Rae, the British singer-songwriter, and Corinne Day, the fashion photographer.

Corliss

English, meaning 'cheery'.

Cornelia

Latin, meaning 'like a horn'. Also the name of several important women in the ancient Roman empire.

Cosette

French, meaning 'people of victory'. Also the heroine in *Les Misérables*.

Cosima
(alt. Cosmina)

Greek, meaning 'order'. Cosima is the feminine version of Cosmo, who is one of the patron saints of medical doctors. Cosima Lawson is the daughter of celebrity chef Nigella Lawson.

Courtney
(alt. Cortney)

English, meaning 'court-dweller'. Actress Courtney Cox is known for her roles in *Friends* and *Cougar Town*.

Creola

French, meaning 'American-born, English descent'. Usually associated with the Creole people and language.

Crescent

French, meaning 'increasing'. Usually associated with the shape of the same name.

Cressida

From the Trojan heroine in Greek mythology.

Crystal
(alt. Christal, Chrystal, Cristal, Kristal, Kristel)

Greek, meaning 'ice'. Can also be spelled using a K in all forms. Very popular in the USA for many years, only gradually dropping off in popularity.

Csilla

Hungarian, meaning 'defences'. More commonly used in Eastern European countries.

Cyd

Shortened form of Sidney, meaning 'wide island'. Dancer and actress Cyd Charisse was known for her roles in *Singin' in the Rain*, *The Band Wagon* and *Silk Stockings*.

Cynara

Greek, meaning 'thistly plant'. Also the name of a type of thistle plant.

Cynthia
(abbrev. Cinda, Cindi, Cyndi, Cindy)

Greek, meaning 'goddess from the mountain'. Also the name of an ancient Greek goddess of the moon. Lady Cynthia Mosley was a British politican and Cynthia Nixon the American actress who played Miranda in *Sex in the City*. Famous Cindys include Cindy Crawford, one of the original supermodels, and Cyndi Lauper the singer, songwriter and actress.

Cyra

Persian, meaning 'sun'. Also the name of a type of ladybird.

Cyrilla

Latin, meaning 'lordly'. Also the name of a type of flowering plant.

Girls' names

Dacey
Irish Gaelic, meaning 'from the south'.

Dada
Nigerian, meaning 'curly haired'.

Daelan
English, meaning 'aware'. Used most commonly as a boys' name but can also be used for girls.

Dagmar
German, meaning 'day's glory'. Dagmar was the stage name of the first real television star, Virginia Egnor.

Dagny
Nordic, meaning 'new day'.

Dahlia
Scandinavian, from the flowering plant of the same name.

Dai
Welsh, meaning 'darling'. Also Japanese for 'large, great'. Used in Wales for boys as a shortened form of Daffyd (David). Used rarely for girls.

Daisy
(alt. Dasia)
English, meaning 'eye of the day'. Also the common flower. Daisy has seen a rise in popularity in recent years.

Dakota
Native American, meaning 'allies'. There are two American states named after the Dakota people. Actress Dakota Johnson stars in the film version of *50 Shades of Grey*.

Dalia
(alt. Dalila)
Hebrew, meaning 'delicate branch'. Also the name of a goddess of property in ancient Lithuanian mythology.

Dallas
Scottish Gaelic, from the village of the same name. Also the name of a city in Texas, USA.

Damaris

Greek, meaning 'calf'. Found in the Bible.

Damica

(alt. Damika)

French, meaning 'friendly'. Often used as a spelling alternative to Danica.

Damita

Spanish, meaning 'little noblewoman'.

Dana

(alt. Dania, Danna, Dayna)

English, meaning 'from Denmark'. In Persian, the name also means 'a perfect and valuable pearl'. Actress Dana Delany played one of the *Desperate Housewives*.

Danae

Greek, from the ancient Greek mythological heroine of the same name.

Danica

(alt. Danika)

Latin, meaning 'from Denmark'. Danica Patrick made waves as the most successful female racing driver in history.

Danielle

(alt. Danelle, Daniela, Daniella, Danila, Danyelle; abbrev. Dani, Danii)

The feminine form of the Hebrew Daniel, meaning 'God is my judge'. Model Danielle O'Hara is known for her glamour modelling and *Big Brother* career.

Danita

English, meaning 'God will judge'. More commonly used in the USA.

Daphne

(alt. Dafne, Daphna)

Greek, meaning 'laurel tree'. Daphne was a water nymph in ancient Greek mythology.

Dara

Hebrew and Persian, meaning 'wisdom'. Found in the Bible. Used for both girls and boys.

Darby

(alt. Darbi, Darbie)

Irish, meaning 'a park with deer'.

Darcy

(alt. Darcey, Darci, Darcie,)

Irish Gaelic, meaning 'dark'. Ballerina Darcey Bussell is one of the reasons behind the recent rise in popularity of the name in the UK.

Daria

Greek, meaning 'rich'. Usually associated with the teenage cartoon character Daria.

Darla

English, meaning 'darling'. Actress Darla Hood was known for her roles as a child star in the 1930s and 1940s.

Darlene
(alt. Darleen, Darline)

American, meaning 'darling'. Actress Darlene Gillespie was one of the original *Mickey Mouse Club* members.

Darva
Slavic, meaning 'honeybee'. Also the name of several locations in Iran.

Daryl
(alt. Darrell, Darryl)

English, originally used as a surname. Famous Daryls include actress Daryl Hannah. Darrell Rivers was the central character in Enid Blyton's classic *Malory Towers* books.

Davina
Hebrew, meaning 'loved one'. English TV presenter Davina McCall is the best-known owner of the name.

Dawn
(alt. Dawna)

English, meaning 'to become day'. Dawn French is one of the most successful comedy actresses and writers of recent decades.

Daya
Hebrew, meaning 'bird of prey'. Also the term used for a form of teaching in the Sikh religion.

Deanna
(alt. Dayana, Deana, Deanna, Deanne)

English, meaning 'girl from the valley'. Singer and actress Deanna Durbin was a Hollywood star in the 1930s and 1940s. Deanna Troi was a central female character in *Star Trek*.

Deborah
(alt. Debbra, Debora, Debra, Debrah, Dvora; abbrev. Debbi, Debbie, Debby)

Hebrew, meaning 'bee'. Also the name of a prophetess in the Bible. Among the many famous Deborahs are actress Deborah Kerr and entrepreneur Deborah Meaden, star of *Dragons' Den*.

December
Latin, meaning 'tenth month'.

Decima
(alt. Decia)

Latin, meaning 'tenth'. Also the name of a goddess in ancient Roman mythology.

Dee
Welsh, meaning 'swarthy'.

Deidre
(alt. Deidra, Deirdre)

Irish, meaning 'raging woman'. Deirdre Barlow was one of *Coronation Street*'s longest-running characters.

Deja
(alt. Dejah)

French, meaning 'already'. The commonly used French phrase déjà vu means 'already seen'.

Delaney

Irish Gaelic, meaning 'offspring of the challenger'.

Delia

Greek, meaning 'from Delos'. Delia Smith is one of the most enduringly successful stars of cookery TV programmes and books.

Delilah
(alt. Delina)

Hebrew, meaning 'seductive'. Famous Delilahs include the lover of Samson in the Bible, and the song 'Delilah' by Tom Jones.

Della
(alt. Dell)

Shortened form of Adele, meaning 'noble'. Used as a name in its own right. Donald Duck's twin sister is called Della Duck.

Delores
(alt. Deloris, Dolores, Doloris)

Spanish, meaning 'sorrows'. In Spanish, the shortened form of Delores is Lolita or Lola.

Delphine
(alt. Delpha, Delphia, Delphina, Delphinia)

Greek, meaning 'dolphin'. More commonly used in French-speaking communities.

Delta

Greek, meaning 'fourth child'. Also the name of the fourth letter of the Greek alphabet.

Demetria
(alt. Demetrice, Dimitria)

Greek, from the ancient Greek mythological heroine of the same name.

Demi

French, meaning 'half'. American actress Demi Moore is a star of Hollywood films across several decades.

Dena
(alt. Deena)

English, meaning 'from the valley'. Also the name of a mountain range in Iran.

Denise
(alt. Denice, Denisa, Denisse)

French, meaning 'devoted to Bacchus'. Denise is the French female form of Dionysius, the ancient Greek god of wine.

Derora

Hebrew, meaning 'stream'. Also the name of a clan in India.

Desdemona

Greek, meaning 'wretchedness'. A character in Shakespeare's play Othello.

Desiree
(alt. Desirae, Des'ree)

French, meaning 'much desired'. Singer Des'ree adapted her name from Desiree, her given name.

Desma

Greek, meaning 'blinding oath'. More commonly used as a shortened version of Desdemona.

Destiny

(alt. Destany, Destinee, Destiney, Destini)
French, meaning 'fate'.

Deva

Hindi, meaning 'God-like'. Deva is also a name for several Buddhist, Hindu and New Age spiritual entities or people.

Devin

(alt. Devinne)
Irish Gaelic, meaning 'poet'. Used for boys most commonly but can be used for girls, often using the feminine form Devinne.

Devon

English, from the southern English county of the same name.

Diamond

English, meaning 'brilliant'.

Diana

(alt. Dian, Diane, Dianna, Dianne)
Roman, meaning 'divine'. Famous Dianas include Princess Diana, singing legend Diana Ross and Diana the Roman goddess of hunting.

Diandra

Greek, meaning 'two males'.

Dilys

Welsh, meaning 'reliable'. Famous Dilyses include actress Dilys Watling and actress and screenwriter Dilys Laye.

Dimona

Hebrew, meaning 'south'. Also the name of a town in the Bible, now situated in modern Israel.

Dinah

(alt. Dina)
Hebrew, meaning 'justified'.

Dionne

Greek, from the mythological heroine of the same name. Famous Dionnes include singers Dionne Warwick and Dionne Bromfield.

Divine

Italian, meaning 'heavenly'.

Dixie

French, meaning 'tenth'. Usually used as a term for the South of the USA.

Dodie

Hebrew, meaning 'well-loved'. Author Dodie Smith is best known for her children's novel *101 Dalmations*.

Dolly
(alt. Dollie)

Shortened form of Dorothy, meaning 'gift of God'. Can be used in its own right. Dolly Parton is the world-famous country and western singer. Reality TV star Chantelle Houghton named her daughter Dolly, perhaps signifying a name revival.

Dominique
(alt. Domenica, Dominica, Domonique)

Latin, meaning 'Lord'. Usually associated with the song 'Dominique' by Soeur Sourire, a singing nun.

Donata
(alt. Donatella)

Latin, meaning 'given', also Italian for 'gift'. Donatella Versace is a leading Italian fashion designer and vice president of the Versace empire.

Donna
(alt. Dona, Donnie)

Italian, meaning 'lady'. Actress and presenter Donna Air started out as a child star in *Byker Grove*.

Dora

Greek, meaning 'gift'. Usually associated with the cartoon character Dora the Explorer.

Dorcas

Greek, meaning 'gazelle'. Also the name of a character in the Bible.

Doreen
(alt. Doren, Dorene, Dorine)

Greek, meaning 'gift'. In Irish Gaelic, the suffix 'een' indicates that a child has the same name as a parent.

Doria

Greek, meaning 'of the sea'. Also the name of an influential Genoese family in the twelfth century.

Doris
(alt. Dorris)

Greek, from the region of the same name. Actress and singer Doris Day was a big star in the 1940s and 1950s, and is also a leading animal rights campaigner.

Dorothy
(alt. Dorathy, Doretha, Dorotha, Dorothea, Dorthy; abbrev. Dot, Dottie, Dotty)

Greek, meaning 'gift of God'. Famous Dorothys include the central character in *The Wizard of Oz* and Dorothy Hodgkin, who won a Nobel Prize for chemistry.

Dorrit
(alt. Dorit)

Greek, meaning 'gift of God'. Usually associated with the novel *Little Dorrit* by Charles Dickens.

Dory
(alt. Dori)

French, meaning 'gilded'. Usually associated with the character from Disney's film *Finding Nemo* and *Finding Dory*.

Dove
(alt. Dovie)

English, from the bird of the same name. Often used as a symbol for peace.

Drew

Greek, meaning 'masculine'. Actress Drew Barrymore became a child star when she appeared in *E.T.*

Drusilla
(alt. Drucilla)

Latin, meaning 'of the Drusus clan'. Found in the Bible.

Dulcie
(alt. Dulce, Dulcia)

Latin, meaning 'sweet'. Actress Dulcie Gray was known for her roles on stage and screen in the mid-twentieth century.

Dusty
(alt. Dusti)

Old German, meaning 'brave warrior'. Singer Dusty Springfield was a 1960s star.

Less common three-syllable names

Cassandra	Jessamy
Dolores	Julia
Gloria	Marilyn
Harriet	Miranda
Imogen	Nigella

E Girls' names

Eadlin
(alt. Eadlinn, Eadlyn, Eadlen, Edlin)
Anglo-Saxon, meaning 'royalty'. Can also be a nickname for Adeline.

Earla
English, meaning 'leader'. Also a variation of the German name Herlinde, meaning 'shield'.

Eartha
English, meaning 'earth'. Singer Eartha Kitt was best known for her hit 'Santa Baby'.

Easter
From the festival of the same name.

Ebba
English, meaning 'fortress of riches'. One of the Top 10 names for baby girls in Sweden.

Ebony
(alt. Eboni)
Latin, meaning 'deep black wood'.

Echo
Greek, meaning 'reflected sound'. From the mythological nymph of the same name.

Eda
(alt. Edda)
English, meaning 'wealthy and happy'. An ancient goddess of time and wealth.

Edelmira
Spanish, meaning 'admired for nobility'. Feminine form of Edelmiro.

Eden
Hebrew, meaning 'pleasure'. In the Bible, the Garden of Eden was humankind's first home on Earth.

Edina
Scottish, meaning 'from Edinburgh'. Jennifer Saunders's character in TV hit *Absolutely Fabulous* was named Edina Monsoon.

Edith

(alt. Edyth; abbrev. Edie)

English, meaning 'prosperity through battle'. Pulitzer Prize-winner Edith Wharton is the author of *The Age of Innocence*. Actress Edie Falco starred in *The Sopranos*.

Edna

Hebrew, meaning 'enjoyment'. Australian comedian Barry Humphries is best known for his alter ego Dame Edna Everage.

Edrea

English, meaning 'wealthy and powerful'. Edrea Vorsal was a soprano opera singer.

Edris

(alt. Edriss, Edrys)

Anglo-Saxon, meaning 'prosperous ruler'. Sometimes used as a female form of Idris.

Edwina

English, meaning 'wealthy friend'. Edwina Currie was a controversial British politician.

Effie

Greek, meaning 'pleasant speech'. Effie Trinket is a key character in the 'Hunger Games' trilogy, known for her outrageous fashion sense.

Eglantine

French, from the shrub of the same name covered in tiny roses.

Eibhlín

Irish Gaelic, meaning 'shining and brilliant'. Eibhlín Dubh Ní Chonaill was an Irish poet and noblewoman.

Eileen

Irish, meaning 'shining and brilliant'. English version of Eibhlín, and often associated with the song 'Come on Eileen' by Dexys Midnight Runners.

Ekaterina

(alt. Ekaterini)

Slavic, meaning 'pure'.

Elaine

(alt. Elaina, Elayne)

French, meaning 'bright, shining light'. Singer and performer Elaine Paige is a star of West End musical theatre.

Elba

Italian, from the island of the same name.

Elberta

English, meaning 'highborn'.

Eldora

Spanish, meaning 'covered with gold'. Eldora is also the name of a small 'ghost' town in Florida, USA, which has remained uninhabited for over 100 years.

Eldoris

(alt. Eldoriss, Eldorys)

Greek, meaning 'woman of the sea'. Usually found as a variation of Doris.

Eleanor

(alt. Elana, Elena, Elanor, Eleanora)

Greek, meaning 'light'. Queen Eleanor of Aquitaine was married to England's King Henry II, and one of the most influential, wealthy and powerful women of medieval times.

Electra

(alt. Elektra)

Greek, meaning 'shining'. Also a character from an ancient Greek myth. In psychology, Electra is the female counterpart of Oedipus.

Elfrida

(alt. Elfrieda)

English, meaning 'elf power'. Elfrida Andrée was a nineteenth-century composer and conductor, and the first female organist to be recognised in Sweden.

Eliana

(alt. Eliane)

Hebrew, meaning 'Jehovah is God'. Becoming increasingly popular in the UK and elsewhere, thanks to the growing trend for names for girls ending in -a.

Elise

(alt. Elisa, Elissa)

French, meaning 'my vow to God'. Commonly associated with Beethoven's 'Für Elise', a piano solo.

Elizabeth

(alt. Elisabet, Elisabeth, Elizabella, Elizabelle, Elsbeth, Elspeth, Elisha; abbrev. Beth, Eliza, Libby, Liz, Lizzie, Lizzy)

Hebrew, meaning 'consecrated to God'. Two queens of England have been named this: Queen Elizabeth I ruled England from 1558 to 1603, and Queen Elizabeth II has been on the throne since 1952. Enduringly popular, especially with its many variant and shortened forms including Beth, Lizzie and Libby.

Elke

German, meaning 'nobility'. A reasonably popular name in Germany.

Ella

German, meaning 'completely'. Now becoming a name in its own right, Ella is traditionally a shortened version of Eleanor, Elizabeth and Ellen.

Elle

French, meaning 'she'. Elle Macpherson was one of the original supermodels in the 1980s, and known as 'The Body'.

Ellema

(alt. Ellemah, Elema, Ellemma, Elemah)

African, meaning 'dairy farmer' or 'milking a cow'.

Ellen

(alt. Elin, Eline, Ellyn)

Greek, meaning 'shining'. Ellen DeGeneres is a popular actress and TV host.

Ellice

(alt. Elyse)

Greek, meaning 'the Lord is God'.

Ellie
(alt. Elie)

Shortened form of Eleanor which can be used in its own right. A popular shortened form for many years. Singer and Brit Award winner Ellie Goulding is actually an Elena.

Elma
(alt. Elna)

Latin, meaning 'soul'. Elma Napier was the first woman to be elected to any Caribbean parliament, in 1940.

Elmira
(alt. Elmyra)

Arabic, meaning 'aristocratic lady'. Elmyra Duff is one of a host of characters on the cartoon *Tiny Toons*.

Elodie

French, meaning 'marsh flower'. Élodie Bouchez-Bangalter is a French actress.

Eloise
(alt. Elois, Eloisa, Elouise)

French, meaning 'renowned in battle'. Also a shortened version and English spelling of French name Héloïse.

Elsa
(alt. Else, Elsie)

Hebrew, meaning 'consecrated to God'. Elsa the Snow Queen is one of the lead characters in Disney's *Frozen*.

Elva

Irish, meaning 'noble'. Also the name of a British sports car manufacturer.

Elvina

English, meaning 'noble friend'. Also an ancient place name.

Elvira
(alt. Elvera)

Spanish, from the ancient city of the same name. Commonly associated with the 1980s film *Elvira, Mistress of the Dark*.

Ember
(alt. Embry)

English, meaning 'spark'. Sometimes used as a shortened version of, or instead of, the name September.

Emerald

English, meaning 'green gemstone'.

Emery
(alt. Emory)

German, meaning 'ruler of work'.

Emiko
(alt. Emuko)

Japanese, meaning 'pretty child'. Popular name for girls in Japan.

Emilia

Latin, meaning 'rival, eager'. British actress Emilia Clarke plays lead character Daenerys Targaryen in *Game of Thrones*.

Emily
(alt. Emalee, Emelie, Emely, Emilee, Emilie, Emlyn)

Latin, meaning 'rival, eager'. Emily Dickinson is one of the most well-known poets of the nineteenth century. A very popular name choice in recent years.

Emma

German, meaning 'embraces everything'. The title character of Jane Austen's novel. Actress Emma Watson starred as Hermione in the 'Harry Potter' films and has been linked with fair trade fashion.

Emmanuelle

Hebrew, meaning 'God is with us'. Female form of Emanuel.

Emmeline

(alt. Emmelina; abbrev. Emmy, Emmie, Emi)

German, meaning 'embraces everything' or 'industrious'. Emmeline Pankhurst was the leader of the Suffragettes, a political activist group in the UK that campaigned in the early twentieth century for women's right to vote.

Ena

Shortened form of Georgina, meaning 'farmer'. Ena Sharples was one of the original cast of characters on Coronation Street.

Enid

(alt. Eneida)

Welsh, meaning 'life spirit'. Enid Blyton was a hugely popular children's author, known for the Noddy, Famous Five and Malory Towers series, amongst others.

Enola

Native American, meaning 'solitary'.

Enya

Irish Gaelic, meaning 'fire'. Enya is an Irish singer and songwriter.

Eowyn

Fictional character from J.R.R. Tolkien's Lord of the Rings trilogy. Eowyn was a noblewoman who disguised herself as a man in order to fight in a major battle.

Eranthe

Greek, meaning 'delicate like the spring'.

Erica

(alt. Ericka, Erika)

Scandinavian, meaning 'ruler forever'. Also a flowering plant similar to heather.

Erin

(alt. Eryn)

Irish Gaelic, meaning 'from the isle to the west'. Used to be a romanticised name for Ireland. Erin Brockovich is an American housewife turned environmental activist, played by Julia Roberts in the film of the same name.

Eris

Greek, from the mythological goddess. Eris is responsible for chaos, strife and discord.

Erlinda

Hebrew, meaning 'spirited'. Erlinda Cortes was a popular actress after World War II.

Erma

German, meaning 'universal'. Erma Franklin, the sister of soul legend Aretha Franklin, was an American gospel singer.

Ermine

French, meaning 'weasel'. The white winter fur of a stoat is known as ermine.

Erna

English, meaning 'sincere'. Erna was a character in Norse mythology.

Ernestine
(alt. Ernestina)

English, meaning 'sincere'. Ernestine Gilbreth Carey was the co-author of *Cheaper by the Dozen*, the novel upon which the popular films of the same name were based.

Esme

French, meaning 'esteemed'. Esme Cullen is a key character in the *Twilight* series.

Esmeralda

Spanish, meaning 'emerald'. Esmeralda is the female protagonist in *The Hunchback of Notre Dame*.

Esperanza

Spanish, meaning 'hope'. Popular name for girls in Spain.

Estelle
(alt. Estela, Estell, Estella)

French, meaning 'star'. British R&B singer Estelle is known by her first name only.

Esther
(alt. Esta, Ester, Etha, Ethna, Ethne)

Persian, meaning 'star'. Esther is a Jewish and Persian queen mentioned in the Bible.

Eternity

Latin, meaning 'forever'.

Ethel
(alt. Ethyl)

English, meaning 'noble'. Ethel Merman was an enormously popular American actress and singer, a star of musical theatre.

Etinia
(alt. Eteniah, Etene, Eteniya)

Native American, meaning 'prosperous'.

Etta
(alt. Etter, Ettie)

Shortened form of Henrietta, meaning 'ruler of the house'. Etta James was a singer-songwriter known for her blues and soul records.

Eudora

Greek, meaning 'generous gift'. Princess Tiana's mother is called Eudora in Disney's *Princess and the Frog*.

Eugenia
(alt. Eugenie)

Greek, meaning 'well born'. Also a type of flowering plant. Princess Eugenie is a granddaughter of Queen Elizabeth II.

Eulalia
(alt. Eula, Eulah, Eulalie)

Greek, meaning 'sweet-speaking'. St Eulalia was a Spanish virgin who was martyred for her faith.

Eunice

Greek, meaning 'victorious'.
Eunice Kennedy Shriver was John F.
Kennedy's sister and the founder of
the Special Olympics.

Euphemia

Greek, meaning 'favourable speech'.
Great Martyr Euphemia was killed for
her Christian faith.

Eva

Hebrew, meaning 'life'. Eva Perón,
the First Lady of Argentina from 1946
to 1952, was the inspiration for the
musical *Evita*.

Evadne

Greek, meaning 'pleasing one'.
Found frequently in Greek
mythology.

Evangeline

(alt. Evangelina)

Greek, meaning 'good news'. The
very first 'musical comedy' was
called *Evangeline*, and it premiered
in 1874.

Evanthe

Greek, meaning 'good flower'.
Occasionally used as an alternative to
names Eve, Eva and Evelyn.

Eve

(alt. Evie)

Hebrew, meaning 'life'. Found in the
Bible.

Evelina

(alt. Evelia)

German, meaning 'hazelnut'. Its
popularity was at its peak in the late
eighteenth century, after a novel
called *Evelina* by Fanny Burney was
published in 1778.

Evelyn

(alt. Evalyn, Evelin, Eveline, Evelyne)

German, meaning 'hazelnut'.
Used as a name for girls and boys
equally. Dame Evelyn Glennie is
a multi-award winning Scottish
virtuoso percussionist, despite being
profoundly deaf.

Everly

(alt. Everleigh, Everley)

English, meaning 'grazing meadow'.

Evette

French, meaning 'yew wood'.
Often used as a spelling variation of
Yvette.

Evonne

(alt. Evon)

French, meaning 'yew wood'.
Evonne Goolagong was a women's
tennis legend in the 1970s.

Girls' names

Fabia

(alt. Fabiana, Fabienne, Fabiola, Fabriana)
Latin, meaning 'one who grows beans'. Originally an old Roman name.

Fabrizia

Italian, meaning 'works with her hands'. Also the name of an Italian town.

Fahari

Swahili, meaning 'splendour'. Can also mean 'magnificent'.

Faith

English, meaning 'loyalty'. Famous Faiths include singers Faith Hill and Faith Evans.

Faiza

Arabic, meaning 'victorious'. The first ever British Muslim superhero to be created by Marvel comics was Faiza Hussain, codenamed Excalibur.

Fallon

Irish Gaelic, meaning 'descended from a ruler'.

Fanny

(alt. Fannie)
Latin, meaning 'from France'. Extremely popular name in the eighteenth and nineteenth centuries. The protagonist of Jane Austen's *Mansfield Park* was Fanny Price.

Farica

German, meaning 'peaceful ruler'. A female form of Frederick.

Farrah

English, meaning 'fair haired', and Arabic, meaning 'joy'. American actress Farrah Fawcett was one of TV's original *Charlie's Angels*.

Fatima

Arabic, meaning 'baby's nurse'. Popular choice for girls in Muslim communities.

Faustine

Latin, meaning 'fortunate'. Female form of Faustinus.

Fawn

French, meaning 'young deer'.

Fay

(alt. Fae, Faye)

French, meaning 'fairy'. Bestselling author Fay Weldon has written more than 30 books.

Fayola

(alt. Fayolah, Fayeena)

Nigerian, meaning 'walks with honour'. Can also mean 'lucky'.

Felicia

(alt. Felicity, Felecia, Felice, Felicita, Felisha)

Latin, meaning 'lucky and happy'. Actress Felicia Day starred in *Buffy the Vampire Slayer*. Felicity Kendall became a household name after her role in 1970s comedy series *The Good Life*.

Fenella

Irish Gaelic, meaning 'white shoulder'. Actress Fenella Fielding is known for her husky voice and sensual image.

Fenia

Scandinavian, from the mythological giantess of the same name.

Fennel

Latin, name of a herb. Also a boys' name.

Fern

(alt. Fearne, Ferne, Ferrin)

English, from the plant of the same name.

Fernanda

German, meaning 'peace and courage'. A popular name in Brazil and Mexico.

Ffion

(alt. Fion)

Irish Gaelic, meaning 'fair and pale'. Currently among the Top 20 names in Wales for baby girls.

Fia

Italian, meaning 'flame'. Also used as a nickname for Fiona.

Fifi

Hebrew, meaning 'Jehovah increases'. Famous Fifis include British children's TV character *Fifi and the Flowertots* and Fifi Trixibelle, eldest daughter of Bob Geldof and Paula Yates.

Filomena

Greek, meaning 'loved one'. Sometimes used as an alternative spelling to Philomena.

Finlay

(alt. Finley)

Irish Gaelic, meaning 'fair-haired courageous one'. More commonly used as a name for boys.

Finola
(alt. Fionnula)

Irish Gaelic, meaning 'white shoulder'. British actress Finola Hughes appears regularly on American TV, having featured in several soap operas.

Fiona

Scottish, meaning 'fair and pale'. The name was actually invented by poet James Macpherson in the eighteenth century. Famous Fionas include TV presenter Fiona Bruce and *Shrek* character Princess Fiona.

Fiora

Irish Gaelic, meaning 'fair and pale'. Sometimes used as an alternative to Fiona.

Fiorella

Italian, meaning 'little flower'. Feminine form of the Italian boys' name Fiorello.

Flanna
(alt. Flannery)

Irish Gaelic, meaning 'russet hair' or 'red hair'.

Flavia

Latin, meaning 'yellow hair'. Popular name in both ancient and modern literature, but rarely used for baby girls in the UK. Flavia Cacace is an Italian professional dancer on *Strictly Come Dancing*.

Fleur

French, meaning 'flower'. Fleur Delacour is a character in the 'Harry Potter' series.

Flora

Latin, meaning 'flower'. Flora was one of the fairy godmothers (the red one) in Disney's *Sleeping Beauty*.

Florence
(alt. Florencia, Florene, Florine; abbrev. Florrie, Flossie, Floy, Flo)

Latin, meaning 'in bloom'. Also an Italian city.

Florida

Latin, meaning 'flowery'. Also a state in the USA.

Frances
(alt. Francine, Francis; abbrev. Fran, Frankie, Frannie)

Latin, meaning 'from France'. Famous Franceses include actress Frances McDormand, author Frances Trollope and playwright Frances Hodgson Burnett.

Francesca
(alt. Franchesca, Francisca; abbrev. Fran, Frankie, Frannie)

Latin, meaning 'from France'. Francesca Simon is the author of the 'Horrid Henry' children's book series.

Freda
(alt. Freeda, Freida, Frida, Frieda)

German, meaning 'peaceful'. Frida Kahlo was a Mexican artist known for her self-portraits and heavy eyebrows.

Frederica

German, meaning 'peaceful ruler'. A popular name for European princesses, it has been used nearly 20 times since the seventeenth century.

Fuchsia

German, from the flower of the same name. Fuchsia Dunlop is a renowned British chef who specialises in Chinese food.

Fumiko

Japanese, meaning 'little friend' or 'beautiful child'.

Movie inspirations

Bella (*Twilight*)

Elsa (*Frozen*)

Fiona (*Shrek*)

Holly (*Breakfast at Tiffany's*)

Katniss (*The Hunger Games*)

Lara (*Tomb Raider*)

Maria (*The Sound of Music*)

Marla (*Fight Club*)

Mary (*Mary Poppins*)

Nina (*Black Swan*)

Pandora (*Avatar*)

Trinity (*The Matrix*)

Girls' names

Gabrielle
(alt. Gabriel, Gabriela, Gabriella; abbrev. Gabby, Gabbi)
Hebrew, meaning 'heroine of God'. Gabriella Wilde is a rising star British actress. Gabby Logan is a high-profile female TV sports presenter.

Gadara
Armenian, meaning 'mountain's peak'. The ancient town of Gadara is situated in northern Jordan.

Gaia
(alt. Gaea)
Greek, meaning 'the earth'. In ancient Greece, Gaia was the Greek Mother Goddess and the most important.

Gail
(alt. Gale, Gayla, Gayle)
Hebrew, meaning 'my father rejoices'. Badminton player Gail Emms represented England at international level for many years.

Gala
French, meaning 'festive merrymaking'. Used more commonly in Spanish-speaking communities.

Galiena
German, meaning 'high one'.

Galina
Russian, meaning 'shining brightly'. Feminine form of Galen.

Garnet
(alt. Garnett)
English, meaning 'red gemstone'.

Gay
(alt. Gaye)
French, meaning 'glad and lighthearted'. Rarely used in recent years.

Gaynor
Welsh, meaning 'white and smooth'.

Gemini

Greek, meaning 'twins'. One of the signs of the zodiac.

Gemma

Italian, meaning 'precious stone'. Bond girl Gemma Arterton was born in the 1980s, when Gemma was at its most popular.

Gene

Greek, meaning 'well born'. More commonly used for boys.

Genesis

Greek, meaning 'beginning'.

Geneva
(alt. Genevra)

French, meaning 'juniper tree'. Also the name of the Swiss city.

Genevieve
(abbrev. Genie)

German, meaning 'white wave'. St Genevieve is said to have saved Paris.

Georgette

French, meaning 'farmer'. Georgette Heyer was an author of historical romance novels.

Georgia
(alt. Georgiana, Georgianna, Georgie)

Greek, meaning 'farmer'. Also the name of the European country and a state in the USA.

Georgina
(alt. Georgene, Georgine, Giorgina)

Greek, meaning 'farmer'. The name's popularity was at its peak during the 1980s. Georgina was the spirited character in Enid Blyton's *Famous Five* books, who insisted on being referred to as George.

Geraldine
(abbrev. Geri, Gerri, Gerry)

German, meaning 'spear ruler'. Spice Girls singer Geri Halliwell's full name is Geraldine.

Gerda

Nordic, meaning 'shelter'. Gerda is the female protagonist in Hans Christian Andersen's *Snow Queen*.

Germaine

French, meaning 'from Germany'. Germaine Greer is the Australian author and activist who lives mostly in the UK.

Gertrude
(abbrev. Gertie)

German, meaning 'strength of a spear'. Gertrude Stein was an influential nineteenth-century American author. One of the earliest animated cartoon films was called *Gertie the Dinosaur*, made in 1914.

Ghislaine

French, meaning 'pledge'. Believed to have derived from Giselle.

Gia

(alt. Ghia)

Italian, meaning 'God is gracious'. Often used by itself, or as a shortened form of Gianna.

Gianina

(alt. Giana)

Hebrew, meaning 'God's graciousness'. Sometimes associated with the town of Ioannina in Greece.

Gigi

(alt. Giget)

Shortened form of Georgina, meaning 'farmer'. Also the name of a successful 1958 musical film.

Gilda

English, meaning 'gilded'. The name of Rigoletto's daughter in Verdi's opera *Rigoletto*.

Gilia

Hebrew, meaning 'joy of the Lord'. Also the name of a genus of flowering plants.

Gillian

(abbrev. Gill, Gilly, Gillie)

Latin, meaning 'youthful'. Famous Gillians include actress Gillian Anderson and children's author Gillian Cross.

Gina

(alt. Geena, Gena)

Shortened form of Regina, meaning 'queen', often used in its own right. Bestselling author Gina Ford has published nine books on the subject of babies and bringing up children.

Ginger

Latin, from the spicy root of the same name. Ginger Rogers was an Oscar-winning American singer, dancer and actress, best known for dancing with Fred Astaire. Her real first name was Virginia.

Ginny

Shortened form of Virginia, meaning 'virgin'. Made popular by the character of Ginny Weasley in the 'Harry Potter' series.

Giovanna

Italian, meaning 'God is gracious'. The English equivalent is Joanna or Jane.

Giselle

(alt. Gisela, Gisele, Giselle, Gisselle)

German, meaning 'pledge'. *Giselle* is the name of a romantic ballet. Gisele Bündchen is a Brazilian supermodel and actress.

Gita

(alt. Geeta)

Sanskrit, meaning 'song'. The *Bhagavad Gita* is a 700-verse Hindu scripture.

Giulia

(alt. Giuliana)

Italian, meaning 'youthful'. The Italian form of the name Julia.

Gladys

(alt. Gladyce)

Welsh, meaning 'lame'. Singer Gladys Knight is known as the 'Empress of Soul'.

Glenda

Welsh, meaning 'fair and good'. A variation of Glenna and Glynda. Glenda Jackson is a British actress turned politician.

Glenna

(alt. Glennie)

Irish Gaelic, meaning 'glen'. Feminine form of Glenn.

Gloria

(alt. Glory)

Latin, meaning 'glory'. There have been many famous Glorias including singers Gloria Estefan and Gloria Gaynor.

Glynda

(alt. Glinda)

Welsh, meaning 'fair'. The good witch in the *Wizard of Oz*.

Glynis

Welsh, meaning 'small glen'. The first Olympic gold medallist of the heptathlon was Australian athlete Glynis Nunn.

Golda

(alt. Goldia, Goldie)

English, meaning 'gold'. Golda Meir was the prime minister of Israel from 1969 to 1974.

Grace

(alt. Graça, Gracie, Gracin, Grayce)

Latin, meaning 'grace'. Film actress Grace Kelly became Princess Grace of Monaco. Grace Darling was an English lighthouse keeper's daughter, famous for her part in the rescue of survivors from a shipwreck.

Gráinne

(alt. Grania)

Irish Gaelic, meaning 'love'.

Gratia

(alt. Grasia)

Latin, meaning 'blessing'. Gratia was the ancient Greek goddess of charm, beauty and fertility, amongst other things.

Greer

(alt. Grier)

Latin, meaning 'alert and watchful'.

Gregoria

Latin, meaning 'alert'. Empress Gregoria was a key figure in the Byzantine empire.

Greta

(alt. Gretel)

Greek, meaning 'pearl'. Gretel is the name of the female protagonist in the fairy tale Hansel and Gretel. Greta also refers to a genus of butterfly.

Gretchen

German, meaning 'pearl'. Actress Gretchen Mol is known for her role in *Boardwalk Empire*.

Griselda

(alt. Griselle)

German, meaning 'grey fighting maid'. Nicknames include Zelda and Selda.

Grytha

English, meaning 'fiery'. Denmark's Queen Grytha ruled during the fifth century.

Gudrun

Scandinavian, meaning 'battle'. Key recurring figure in Norse and Germanic literature.

Guinevere

Welsh, meaning 'white and smooth'. The queen in Arthurian legend.

Gwen

Shortened form of Gwenda or Gwendolyn, as well as a name in its own right. Gwen Stefani is a singer-songwriter who recently became mother to Apollo, her third son.

Gwenda

Welsh, meaning 'fair and good'. As well as being a name in its own right, Gwenda can also be a shortened form of Gwendolyn or Gwyneth.

Gwendolyn

(alt. Gwendolen, Gwenel)

Welsh, meaning 'fair bow'. Gwendolyn Brooks was a Pulitzer Prize-winning poet.

Gwyneth

(alt. Gwynneth, Gwynyth; abbrev. Gwyn, Gwynn)

Welsh, meaning 'happiness'. Actress and author Gwyneth Paltrow is mum to Apple and Moses.

Gypsy

English, meaning 'of the Roma tribe'.

Girls' names

Habibah
(alt. Habiba)
Arabic, meaning 'beloved'.

Hadassah
Hebrew, meaning 'myrtle tree'. Usually associated with the character of Esther in the Bible, whose Hebrew name is Hadassah.

Hadley
English, meaning 'heather meadow'. Hadley Freeman is an author and journalist.

Hadria
Latin, meaning 'from Hadria'. Also the name of two ancient cities in Italy.

Hala
Arabic, meaning 'halo'. Also the name of a female weather demon in Serbian and Bulgarian mythology.

Halima
(alt. Halimah, Halina)
Arabic, meaning 'gentle'. The prophet Mohammad's foster mother was called Halimah.

Hallie
(alt. Halle, Halley)
German, meaning 'ruler of the home or estate'. Oscar-winning actress Halle Berry was originally given the name Maria Halle.

Hannah
(alt. Haana, Hana, Hanna)
Hebrew, meaning 'grace'. Famous Hannahs include Hannah Cockroft, the wheelchair athlete and world record holder, and Hannah Montana, of the musical comedy series.

Harika
Turkish, meaning 'superior one'. In India, the name is associated with Parvati, the Hindu goddess of power and creation.

Harley
(alt. Harlene)
English, meaning 'the long field'.

Harlow
English, meaning 'army hill'.

Harmony

Latin, meaning 'harmony'.

Harper

English, meaning 'minstrel'. Harper Lee is the author of classic novel *To Kill a Mockingbird*. Harper Seven is the name of David and Victoria Beckham's fourth child.

Harriet

(alt. Harriett, Harriette; abbrev. Hattie)

German, meaning 'ruler of the home or estate'. Famous Harriets include activist Harriet Tubman, author Harriet Beecher Stowe, and politician Harriet Harman.

Haven

English, meaning 'a place of sanctuary'.

Hayden

(alt. Haydn)

Old English, meaning 'hedged valley'. Used as a boys' name as well as a girls' name.

Hayley

(alt. Haelee, Haely, Hailee, Hailey, Hailie, Haleigh, Haley, Hali, Halie, Haylee, Hayleigh, Haylie)

English, meaning 'hay meadow'. The name became popular in the 1980s after the success of child actress Hayley Mills, but is less common now.

Hazel

(alt. Hazle)

English, from the tree of the same name. Famous Hazels include children's author Hazel Hutchins, singer Hazel O'Connor and politician Hazel Blears.

Heather

English, from the flower of the same name. Famous Heathers include actresses Heather Graham and Heather Locklear, and model Heather Mills.

Heaven

English, meaning 'everlasting bliss'.

Hedda

German, meaning 'warfare'. Also the name of the protagonist in the play *Hedda Gabler*, by Henrik Ibsen.

Hedwig

German, meaning 'warfare and strife'. Although the name stems from two different St Hedwigs, it is now most associated with Harry Potter's owl!

Heidi

(alt. Heidy)

German, meaning 'nobility'. One of the top-selling children's books of all time is the Swiss novel *Heidi*, by Johanna Spyri.

Helen

(alt. Halen, Helena, Helene, Hellen)

Greek, meaning 'light'. In ancient Greek mythology Helen of Troy was considered to be the most beautiful woman in the world.

Helga

German, meaning 'holy and sacred'. Extemely popular name in Germany and Norway.

Helia

Greek, meaning 'sun'.

Héloïse

French, meaning 'renowned in war'. Héloïse d'Argenteuil was a nun and writer known for having an affair with the theologian Peter Abelard in the twelfth century.

Henrietta
(alt. Henriette)

German, meaning 'ruler of the house'. Usually associated with Henrietta Maria of France, who was queen consort to Charles I.

Hephzibah
(alt. Hefzibah)

Hebrew, meaning 'my delight is in her'. Found in the Bible.

Hera

Greek, meaning 'queen'. Hera is the Queen of the Gods, and the goddess of marriage, women and birth in ancient Greek mythology.

Hermia
(alt. Hermina, Hermine, Herminia)

Greek, meaning 'messenger'. Also the name of a character in Shakespeare's play A Midsummer Night's Dream.

Hermione

Greek, meaning 'earthly'. Now inseparable from the main female character in the 'Harry Potter' series.

Hero

Greek, meaning 'brave one of the people'.

Hertha

English, meaning 'earth'. Also another name for Nerthus, the goddess of fertility in ancient German mythology.

Hesper
(alt. Hesperia)

Greek, meaning 'evening star'.

Hester
(alt. Hestia)

Greek, meaning 'star'. Also the name of the protagonist in The Scarlet Letter by Nathaniel Hawthorne.

Hettie

Shortened form of Hester or Henrietta, also used as a name in its own right.

Hilary
(alt. Hillary)

Greek, meaning 'cheerful and happy'. Also a boys' name. Famous Hilarys include politician Hillary Rodham Clinton and actress Hilary Swank.

Hilda
(alt. Hildur)

German, meaning 'battle woman'. Famous Hildas include the first female pilot to hold a licence, Hilda Hewlett, the Coronation Street character Hilda Ogden and author Hilda Doolittle – known as H.D.

Hildegarde
(alt. Hildegard)

German, meaning 'battle stronghold'.

Hildred

German, meaning 'battle counsellor'. More commonly used as a name for boys.

Hilma

German variant of Wilhelmina, meaning 'helmet'. The female equivalent of Hilmar or Hilmer.

Hirkani

Indian, meaning 'like a diamond'.

Hollis

English, meaning 'near the holly bushes'.

Holly
(alt. Holli, Hollie)

English, from the tree of the same name. Famous Hollys include TV presenter Holly Willoughby, actress Holly Hunter and singer Holly Valance.

Honey

English, from the word 'honey'.

Honor
(alt. Honour, Honora, Honoria)

Latin, meaning 'woman of honour'. Actress Honor Blackman played the Bond girl Pussy Galore.

Hope

English, meaning 'desire and expectation'. One of three virtues in most religions: faith, hope and charity. Hope Powell represented England in football for many years before becoming the England Women's coach for more than a decade.

Hortense
(alt. Hortencia, Hortensia)

Latin, meaning 'of the garden'. Also the name of one of Napoleon Bonaparte's stepdaughters, and a character in Charles Dickens's novel *Bleak House*.

Hudson

English, meaning 'adventurous'.

Hulda

German, meaning 'loved one'. Also the name of a prophetess in the Bible.

Hyacinth

Greek, from the flower of the same name. Hyacinth was also a hero in ancient Greek mythology.

Girls' names

Ianthe
(alt. Iantha)
Greek, meaning 'purple flower'. Also the name of a character in ancient Greek mythology.

Ichigo
Japanese, meaning 'strawberry'.

Ida
English, meaning 'prosperous'. Also the name of several characters in both ancient Greek mythology and the Hindu religion.

Idella
(alt. Idell)
English, meaning 'prosperous'. Idella Purnell was an academic and author of children's books, best known in the 1930s and 1940s.

Idona
Nordic, meaning 'renewal'.

Ignacia
(alt. Iggy)
Latin, meaning 'ardent' or 'burning'. The female vartiation of Ignatius.

Ila
French, meaning 'island'. In Hindu mythology Ila is a character able to change sex at will.

Ilana
Hebrew, meaning 'tree'. Ilana Vered is a classical pianist known for her work with dozens of major international orchestras.

Ilaria
Italian, meaning 'cheerful'. Ilaria has featured as a Top 10 name for girls in Italy in recent years. The English equivalent is Hilary.

Ilene
American, meaning 'light'. Ilene Woods was a voice actor known for being the voice of Cinderella in Disney's film of the same name.

Iliana
(alt. Ileana)

Greek, meaning 'Trojan'. Actress Ileana D'Cruz is a star in Bollywood films.

Ilona

Hungarian, meaning 'light'. Also the name of the Queen of the Fairies in Magyar mythology.

Ilsa

German, meaning 'pledged to God'. Also the name of Ingrid Bergman's character in the film *Casablanca*.

Ima

German, meaning 'embraces everything'. Ima Hogg was an influential philanthropist in the early twentieth century.

Iman

Arabic, meaning 'faith'. The Somali supermodel known simply as Iman is also an entrepreneur and is married to David Bowie.

Imara

Hungarian, meaning 'great ruler'. Also the name of a genus of moths.

Imelda

German, meaning 'all-consuming fight'. Famous Imeldas include actress Imelda Staunton, politician Imelda Marcos and actress Anne Crawford, whose real name was Imelda.

Imogen
(alt. Imogene)

Latin, meaning 'last-born'. Famous Imogens include actresses Imogen Stubbs and Imogen Hassall and singer-songwriter Imogen Heap.

Ina

Latin, meaning 'to make feminine'. Famous Inas include author and presenter Ina Garten and childbirth pioneer Ina May Gaskin.

Inaya

Arabic, meaning 'taking care'. Singer Inaya Day's voice features on many dancefloor house music classics.

India
(alt. Indie)

Hindi, from the country of the same name. India Knight is a British journalist and author.

Indiana

Latin, meaning 'from India'. Also the name of a state in the USA.

Indigo

Greek, meaning 'deep blue dye'. Also the name of one of the seven colours of the rainbow.

Indira
(alt. Inira)

Sanskrit, meaning 'beauty'. Indira Gandhi was the first and to date only female prime minister of India.

Inez
(alt. Ines)

Spanish, meaning 'pure'. Also a spelling variation of Agnes.

Inga
(alt. Inge, Ingeborg, Inger)
Scandinavian, meaning 'guarded by Ing'. Also the name of a type of tropical shrubs and trees.

Ingrid
Scandinavian, meaning 'beautiful'. Actress Ingrid Bergman was known for her roles in *Casablanca*, *Notorious* and *Gaslight*.

Io
(alt. Eyo)
Greek, from the mythological priestess and heroine of the same name in ancient Greek mythology.

Ioanna
Greek, meaning 'grace'. Usually used as a spelling alternative to Joanna.

Iola
(alt. Iole)
Greek, meaning 'cloud of dawn'. The novel *Iola Leroy*, by Frances Harper, was one of the first novels published by a black female author.

Iolanthe
Greek, meaning 'violet flower'. Usually associated with the opera *Iolanthe* by Gilbert and Sullivan.

Iona
Greek, from the island of the same name. Also the name of a small island off the coast of Scotland.

Ione
Greek, meaning 'violet'. Also the name of a type of orchid.

Iorwen
Welsh, meaning 'fair'.

Iphigenia
Greek, meaning 'sacrifice'. Iphigenia was an ancient Greek victim of slaughter whose name became synonymous with strength and being the mother of strong children.

Ira
(alt. Iva)
Hebrew, meaning 'watchful'. More commonly used as a name for boys.

Irene
(alt. Irelyn, Irena, Irina, Irini)
Greek, meaning 'peace'.

Iris
Greek, meaning 'rainbow'. Also from the flower of the same name.

Irma
German, meaning 'universal'. Often associated with Irma Bunt, a Bond villainess.

Isabel
(alt. Isabela, Isabell, Isabella, Isabelle, Isabeth, Isobel, Izabella, Izabelle)
Spanish, meaning 'pledged to God'. Dozens of royals have been called Isabel or Isabella over the centuries, including Queen Isabella I of Spain, who financed Christopher Columbus' voyage to North America.

Isadora

Latin, meaning 'gift of Isis'. Isadora Duncan was a famed dancer at the turn of the twentieth century, whose life was made into the film *Isadora*.

Ishana

Sanskrit, meaning 'desire'. One of the names for Shiva in the Hindu faith.

Isis

From the ancient Egyptian goddess of motherhood, magic and fertility.

Isla

(alt. Isa, Isela, Isley)

Scottish Gaelic, meaning 'river'. Actress Isla Fischer was born in Oman to Scottish parents and was raised in Australia.

Isolde

Welsh, meaning 'fair lady'. Usually associated with the opera *Tristan und Isolde* by Richard Wagner.

Istas

Native American, meaning 'snow'. In Latin, istas also refers to the feminine form of 'that person'.

Ivana

Slavic, meaning 'Jehovah is gracious'. Model Ivana Trump is known for her marriage to businessman Donald Trump.

Ivette

Variation of Yvette, meaning 'yew wood'. This spelling is more commonly used in Spanish-speaking communities.

Ivonne

Variation of Yvonne, meaning 'yew wood'. This spelling is more commonly used in Spanish-speaking communities.

Ivory

Latin, meaning 'white as elephant tusks'.

Ivy

English, from the plant of the same name. Famous Ivys include elderly internet sensation Ivy Bean, the first British female lawyer, Ivy Williams, and children's author Ivy Wallace.

Ixia

South African, from the flower of the same name.

J

Girls' names

Jaamini

Hindi, meaning 'evening'.

Jacinda

(alt. Jacinta)

Spanish, meaning 'hyacinth'. Jacinda Barrett is an Australian-American model turned actress.

Jacqueline

(alt. Jacalyn, Jacklyn, Jaclyn, Jacquelin, Jacquelyn, Jacquline, Jaqlyn, Jaquelin, Jaqueline; abbrev. Jack, Jacky, Jackie, Jacque, Jacqui)

French, meaning 'he who supplants'. Famous Jacquelines include children's author Jacqueline Wilson, actress Jacqueline Bisset and cellist Jacqueline du Pré.

Jade

(alt. Jada, Jaida, Jayda, Jayde)

Spanish, meaning 'green stone'. Famous Jades include former reality TV star Jade Goody, athletes Jade Jones and Jade Johnson and designer Jade Jagger.

Jaden

(alt. Jadyn, Jaiden, Jaidyn, Jayden)

Hebrew, meaning 'Jehovah has heard'. More commonly used as a name for boys.

Jael

Hebrew, meaning 'mountain goat'. Also the name of a character in the Bible.

Jaime

(alt. Jaima, Jaimie, Jami, Jamie)

Spanish, meaning 'he who supplants'. Jamie is a common short form of James, more commonly used for boys.

Jamila

Arabic, meaning 'lovely'. Author Jamila Gavin is known for her children's books, most of which have an Indian influence.

Jan

(alt. Jana, Jann, Janna, Janae)

Hebrew, meaning 'the Lord is gracious'. In Arabic, the name Jan also means 'dear', and in Persian it means 'life'.

Jane

(alt. Jayne, Janie)

Feminine form of the Hebrew John, meaning 'the Lord is gracious'. A very popular name in the 1960s and 1970s but much less common now. Famous Janes include Tarzan's friend Jane and Henry VIII's third wife, Jane Seymour.

Janelle

(alt. Janel, Janell, Jenelle)

American, meaning 'the Lord is gracious'. A very popular name in the 1970s and 1980s in both America and Australia but less common now.

Janet

(alt. Janette)

Scottish, meaning 'the Lord is gracious'. Singer Janet Jackson is known for being part of the musical Jackson family, as well as a performer in her own right.

Janice

(alt. Janis)

American, meaning 'the Lord is gracious'. Famous Janices include rower Janice Meek, former supermodel Janice Dickinson and the character of Janice Battersby in Coronation Street.

Janine

(alt. Janeen)

English, meaning 'the Lord is gracious'. Famous Janines include the character of Janine Butcher in EastEnders, the character of Janine in Friends and actress Janine Turner.

Janoah

(alt. Janiya, Janiyah)

Hebrew, meaning 'quiet and calm'. Also used as a spelling alternative for Genoa.

January

Latin, meaning 'the first month'. Actress January Jones is known for her roles in Mad Men, Unknown and X-Men: First Class.

Jarita

Hindi-Sanskrit, meaning 'famous bird'. Usually associated with the bird character in the Hindu Mahabharata.

Jasmine

(alt. Jasmin, Jazim, Jazmine)

Persian, meaning 'jasmine flower'.

Jay

Latin, meaning 'jaybird'. Jays are colourful birds from the crow family, found throughout the world.

Jayna

Sanskrit, meaning 'bringer of victory'. More commonly used in Indian communitites.

Jean
(alt. Jeane, Jeanne)

Scottish, meaning 'the Lord is gracious'. Famous Jeans include actresses Jean Harlow and Jean Marsh and author Jean Auel.

Jeana
(alt. Jeanna)

Latin, meaning 'queen'.

Jeanette
(alt. Jeannette, Janette; abbrev. Jeannie, Jeanie) .

French, meaning 'the Lord is gracious'. Jeanette Winterson is a BAFTA-winning British author and journalist. The shortened form is commonly associated with the sitcom *I Dream of Jeannie*.

Jeanine
(alt. Jeannine)

Latin, meaning 'the Lord is gracious'. Jeanine Tesori is known for her musical theatre arrangements and compositions.

Jemima

Hebrew, meaning 'dove'. Jemima Khan is a writer and campaigner.

Jemma

English variant of Gemma, meaning 'precious stone'. Actress Jemma Redgrave is a fourth-generation member of the Redgrave acting dynasty.

Jena

Arabic, meaning 'little bird'. Actress Jena Malone starred in *Donnie Darko*, *Pride and Prejudice* and *The Hunger Games: Catching Fire*.

Jenna

Shortened form of Jennifer, meaning 'white and smooth'. The name was very popular in the 1980s, especially in the USA, and there are many actresses of that era with the name.

Jennifer
(alt. Jenifer; abbrev. Jenny, Jennie, Jenni)

Cornish alternative to Guinevere, meaning 'white and smooth'. Famous Jennifers include actresses Jennifer Lawrence and Jennifer Aniston and singer Jennifer Hudson.

Jerri
(alt. Jeri, Jerrie, Jerrie, Jerry)

German, meaning 'spear ruler'. Famous Jerries include actress Jerri Manthey, model Jerry Hall and pioneering South Pole physician Dr Jerri Nielsen.

Jerusha

Hebrew, meaning 'married'. Jerusha Hess and husband Jared Hess are filmmakers whose films include *Napoleon Dynamite*.

Jeryl

English, meaning 'spear ruler'. Jeryl Prescott is an American actress.

Jessa

Shortened form of Jessica, meaning 'He sees'. Jessa Gamble is an English-Canadian author and scientific researcher and Jessa Johansson is a leading character in *Girls*.

Jessamy

(alt. Jessame, Jessamine, Jessamyn)

Persian, meaning 'jasmine flower'. Usually associated with the children's book *Jessamy* by Barbara Sleigh.

Jessica

(alt. Jesica, Jesika, Jessika; abbrev. Jess, Jessi, Jessie, Jessye)

Hebrew, meaning 'He sees'. A popular name over several decades. Famous Jessicas include actresses Jessica Alba and Jessica Lange and athlete Jessica Ennis. Famous Jessies include singer Jessie J.

Jesusa

Spanish, meaning 'mother of the Lord'. Also a shortened form of Jerusalem.

Jethetha

Hebrew, meaning 'princess'.

Jette

(alt. Jetta, Jettie)

Danish, meaning 'black as coal'. Also the name of a town in Belgium.

Jewel

(alt. Jewell)

French, meaning 'delight'. Singer-songwriter, producer and actress Jewel is professionally known just by her first name.

Jezebel

(alt. Jezabel, Jezabelle)

Hebrew, meaning 'pure and virginal'. Conversely, widely used as a term for 'bad women' after the misbehaving wife of a king in the Bible.

Jill

Latin, meaning 'youthful'. Famous Jills include actress Jill Clayburgh, presenter Jill Dando and children's author Jill Murphy.

Jillian

Latin, meaning 'youthful'. Often used as a spelling alternative to Gillian.

Jimena

Spanish, meaning 'heard'. Jimena Diaz was the ruler of Valencia in the twelfth century.

Jo

Shortened form of Joanna, meaning 'the Lord is gracious'. Famous Jos include supernanny Jo Frost, presenter Jo Coburn and athlete Jo Ankier.

Joan

Hebrew, meaning 'the Lord is gracious'. Famous Joans include St Joan of Arc, actress Joan Collins and comedienne Joan Rivers.

Joanna

(alt. Joana, Joanie, Joann, Joanne, Johanna, Joni)

Hebrew, meaning 'the Lord is gracious'. Famous Joannas include author J.K. Rowling (real name Joanne) and actresses Joanna Lumley and Joanna Page.

Jocasta

Italian, meaning 'lighthearted'.
Jocasta was an influential character in
ancient Greek mythology.

Jocelyn

(alt. Jauslyn, Jocelyne, Joscelin, Joslyn)
German, meaning 'cheerful'.

Jody

(alt. Jodee, Jodi, Jodie)
Shortened form of Judith, meaning
'Jewish'. Famous Jodys include
actresses Jodie Foster and Jody
Lawrance and singer Jody Watley.

Joelle

(alt. Joela)
Hebrew, meaning 'Jehovah is the
Lord'. Famous Joelles include teen
singer Joelle and actress Joelle Carter.

Joie

French, meaning 'joy'.

Jolene

Contraction of Joanna and Darlene,
meaning 'gracious darling'. Usually
associated with the song 'Jolene' by
Dolly Parton.

Jolie

(alt. Joely)
French, meaning 'pretty'.

Jordan

(alt. Jordana, Jordin, Jordyn)
Hebrew, meaning 'down-flowing'.
Model and reality television star Katie
Price is known by her professional
name Jordan. Also used for boys.

Josephine

*(alt. Josefina, Josephina; abbrev. Jo,
Joss, Josie)*
Hebrew, meaning 'Jehovah
increases'. Famous Josephines
include the first Empress of France,
wife of Napoleon, pioneering actress
Josephine Baker and mystery author
Josephine Bell.

Jovita

(alt. Jovie)
Latin, meaning 'made glad'. St
Jovita was a Christian martyr with
her brother St Faustinus during the
second century.

Joy

Latin, meaning 'joy'. Famous Joys
include comedienne Joy Behar,
actress Joy Lauren and poet Joy
Harjo.

Joyce

Latin, meaning 'joyous'. Famous
Joyces include author Joyce Carol
Oates and actresses Joyce Blair and
Joyce DeWitt.

Juanita

(alt. Juana)
Spanish, meaning 'the Lord is
gracious'.

Jubilee

Hebrew, meaning 'horn of a
ram'. Usually associated with the
celebration of an anniversary, such as
the Queen's Diamond Jubilee.

Judith

(alt. Judit; abbrev. Judi, Judie, Judy)

Hebrew, meaning 'Jewish'. Found in the Bible. Very popular in the 1940s and 1950s. Actress Judy Garland was the star of *The Wizard of Oz*.

Jules

French, meaning 'Jove's child'. Sometimes used as a variant of Julie or Julia but more commonly used as a name for boys.

Julia

(alt. Julie, Juli)

Latin, meaning 'youthful'. Famous Julias include actresses Julia Roberts and Julia Sawalha and TV chef Julia Child, while famous Julies include three Golden Globe and BAFTA-winning actresses: Julie Andrews, Julie Christie and Julie Walters.

Julianne

(alt. Juliana, Juliann, Julianne)

Latin, meaning 'youthful'. Oscar-nominated British-American actress Julianne Moore has starred in a string of blockbuster films and is also a children's author.

Juliet

(alt. Joliet, Juliette)

Latin, meaning 'youthful'. Usually associated with the heroine of Shakespeare's play *Romeo and Juliet*.

June

(alt. Juna)

Latin, after the month of the same name. Famous Junes include actress June Bland, singer June Carter Cash and presenter June Sarpong.

Juniper

Dutch, from the shrub of the same name, used for distilling the spirit gin.

Juno

(alt. Juneau)

Latin, meaning 'queen of heaven'. Juno was an ancient Roman Queen of the Gods, and the goddess of marriage and Rome.

Justice

English, meaning 'to deliver what is just'.

Justine

(alt. Justina)

Latin, meaning 'fair and righteous'. Famous Justines include singer Justine Frischmann and actresses Justine Bateman and Justine Waddell.

Jørgina

Dutch, meaning 'farmer'. More commonly used as a spelling alternative for Georgina.

 Girls' names

K

Kadenza
(alt. Kadence)

Latin, meaning 'with rhythm'.
More commonly used as a spelling
alternative for Cadenza.

Kadisha

Hebrew, meaning 'religious one'.

Kaitlin
(alt. Kaitlyn)

Greek, meaning 'pure'. Variant of
Caitlin that became popular, especially
in the USA, after the 1970s. Kaitlin
Doubleday is a Hollywood actress.

Kala
(alt. Kaela, Kaiala, Kaila)

Sanskrit, meaning 'black one'. Also
known for being the great ape that
saved Tarzan as a baby.

Kali
*(alt. Kailee, Kailey, Kaleigh, Kaley,
Kalie, Kalli, Kally, Kaylee, Kayleigh)*

Sanskrit, meaning 'black one'. Also
known in Hinduism as the Goddess
of Time and Change.

Kalila

Arabic, meaning 'beloved'.

Kalina

Slavic, meaning 'flower'.

Kalliope
(alt. Calliope)

Greek, meaning 'beautiful voice'.
From the muse of the same
name.

Kama

Sanskrit, meaning 'love'. Known in
Hinduism as one of the four goals
of life, kama refers to intellectual
fulfilment.

Kami

Japanese, meaning 'lord'.

Kamilla
(alt. Kamilah)

Slavic, meaning 'serving girl'. A
spelling alternative for Camilla.

Kana

Hawaiian, from the demi-god of the same name. In Hawaiian mythology Kana could take the form of a rope that could stretch from the island of Molokai to Hawaii.

Kanika

African, meaning 'black cloth'. The stage name of Indian actress Divya Venkatasubramaniam.

Kara

Latin, meaning 'dear one'.

Karen

(alt. Karan, Karalyn, Karin, Karina, Karon, Karren; abbrev. Kari, Karrie)

Greek, meaning 'pure'. Very popular during the 1960s and 1970s in England. Famous Karens include comedienne Karen Taylor, actress Karen Walker and musician Karen Carpenter. Kari is one of Saturn's moons.

Karimah

Arabic, meaning 'giving'. A spelling variation of Karima.

Karishma

(alt. Karisma)

Sanskrit, meaning 'miracle'. Both Karisma and Karishma are popular names in India, reflected in the number of Indian actresses with the name.

Karla

German, meaning 'man'. A spelling variation for Carla.

Karly

(alt. Karlee, Karley, Karli)

German, meaning 'free man'. Has become popular in Scotland especially, including Karly Robertson the ice skater and Karly Ashworth from Big Brother.

Karlyn

German, meaning 'man'. Also a spelling variation of Carlin.

Karma

Hindi, meaning 'destiny'. Known as a principle of Buddhism where good deeds lead to a positive influence on a person's future and bad deeds lead to a bad influence.

Karol

(alt. Karolina, Karolyn)

Slavic, meaning 'little and womanly'. A spelling variation of Carol.

Kasumi

Japanese, meaning 'of the mist'.

Katarina

(alt. Katarine, Katerina, Katharina)

Greek, meaning 'pure'. Katarina was one of the first companions of Doctor Who.

Kate

(alt. Kat, Katie, Kathi, Kathie, Kathy, Kati, Katy)

Shortened form of Katherine, meaning 'pure'. Famous Kates include actress Kate Winslet, actress Kate Hudson and the current Duchess of Cambridge.

Katherine
(alt. Katharine, Katheryn, Kathrine, Kathryn; abbrev. Kathie, Kathy)

Greek, meaning 'pure'. A spelling variation for Catherine that became very popular earlier than some of the other K-variation spelling names.

Kathleen
(alt. Kathlyn)

Greek, meaning 'pure'. Very popular in the 1960s and so shared by many actresses, politicans and scientists.

Katrina
(alt. Katina)

Greek, meaning 'pure'. More commonly used as a shortened version of Katherine.

Kaveri

Indian, meaning 'sacred river'. Known for the large river that flows across India.

Kay
(alt. Kaye)

Shortened form of Katherine, meaning 'pure'. A popular name in both Kay and Kaye forms, in North America, Australia and England.

Kaya

Sanskrit, meaning 'nature', or Turkish, meaning 'rock'. Kaya also refers to a sweet coconut jam popular in Asia.

Kayla
(alt. Kaylah)

Greek, meaning 'pure'. Kayla Harrison won a gold medal in judo at the 2012 London Olympics.

Kayley
(alt. Kayley, Kayli)

American, meaning 'pure'. Also know as one of the main characters in *The Magic Sword: Quest for Camelot*.

Kaylin

American, meaning 'pure'. A spelling variation for Caylin.

Keary

Gaelic, meaning 'black-haired'. Also a boys' name.

Keeley
(alt. Keely)

Irish, meaning 'battle maid'. Actress Keeley Hawes is a popular star of British TV drama.

Keila

Hebrew, meaning 'citadel'.

Keira

Irish Gaelic, meaning 'dark'. A rise in popularity of the name followed the success of actress Keira Knightley.

Keisha
(alt. Keesha)

Arabic, meaning 'woman'. Keisha Castle-Hughs is an Australian actress.

Kelis

American, meaning 'beautiful'. Award-winning singer Kelis is known widely by her first name only.

Kelly

(alt. Keli, Kelley, Kelli, Kellie)

Irish Gaelic, meaning 'battle maid'. Famous Kellys include singer Kelly Clarkson, TV personality Kelly Osbourne and Olympic winning athlete Kelly Holmes.

Kelsey

(alt. Kelcee, Kelcie, Kelsea, Kelsi, Kelsie)

Old English, meaning 'victorious ship'. More popular in the USA, where it is the name of several cities and is used for both girls and boys.

Kendall

(alt. Kendal)

English, meaning 'the valley of the River Kent'. Also a place in Cumbria.

Kendra

English, meaning 'knowing'. Name of a character in Buffy The Vampire Slayer. Kendra Wilkinson is an American TV personality.

Kenna

Irish Gaelic, meaning 'handsome'.

Kennedy

(alt. Kenadee, Kennedi)

Irish Gaelic, meaning 'helmet head'. Also used as a boys' name.

Kenzie

Shortened form of McKenzie, meaning 'son of the wise ruler'. Also commonly used as a boys' name.

Kerensa

Cornish, meaning 'love'. Also a variation on the name Karen.

Kerrigan

Irish, meaning 'black haired'.

Kerry

(alt. Keri, Kerri, Kerrie)

Irish, from the county of the same name. Used for both girls and boys.

Khadijah

(alt. Khadejah)

Arabic, meaning 'premature baby'. Khadija bint Khuwaylid was the first wife of Muhammad and is known as the 'Mother of Islam'.

Kiana

(alt. Kia, Kiana)

American, meaning 'fibre'. Kiana is an American TV personality known for her physical fitness and physical training videos.

Kiara

Irish, meaning 'dark'. Also Latin, meaning 'light'. It is possible that the name could come from two sources – Irish 'ciar' meaning 'dark' or 'dark haired', or the Latin 'chiara', meaning 'light'.

Kiki

Spanish, meaning 'home ruler'. Also an American slang term for a party centred around gossip and laughter.

Kimana

Native American, meaning 'butterfly'.

Kimberly
(alt. Kimberleigh, Kimberley; abbrev. Kim)

Old English, meaning 'royal forest'. Famous Kimberlys include singers Kimberly Wyatt and Kimberley Walsh and rapper Kimberly 'Lil' Kim' Denise Jones. Famous Kims include TV personality Kim Kardashian, actress Kim Basinger and singer Kim Wilde.

Kingsley
(alt. Kinsley)

English, meaning 'king's meadow'. More commonly used as a boys' name.

Kinsey
English, meaning 'king's victory'.

Kira
Greek, meaning 'lady'.

Kiri
Maori, meaning 'tree bark'. Dame Kiri Te Kanawa is known for her opera singing career spanning over 40 years.

Kirsten
(alt. Kirstin; abbrev. Kirstie, Kirsty)

Scandinavian, meaning 'Christian'. Kirsten Dunst is a German-American actress, singer and model. Famous Kirsties include TV presenters Kirsty Young and Kirstie Allsopp and American actress Kirstie Alley.

Kitty
(alt. Kittie)

Shortened form of Katherine, meaning 'pure'. Can be used in its own right.

Kizzy
Hebrew, meaning the plant 'cassia'. Singer Kizzy Crawford sings in both English and Welsh.

Klara
Hungarian, meaning 'bright'. Commonly used in German-speaking communities.

Komal
Hindi, meaning 'soft and tender'. Most commonly used as a name for Indian boys.

Konstantina
Latin, meaning 'steadfast'. The female version of the male name Constantine.

Kora
(alt. Kori)

Greek, meaning 'maiden'. A spelling variation for Cora.

Kristen
(alt. Kristan, Kristin, Kristine, Krysten; abbrev. Kris, Krista, Kristi, Kristie, Kristy)

Greek, meaning 'Christian'. Actress Kristen Stewart is known for her roles in the *Twilight* films.

Kwanza
(alt. Kwanzaa)

African, meaning 'beginning'. Also known for the week-long celebration of African–American culture near Christmas time.

Kyla
(alt. Kya, Kylah, Kyle)
Scottish, meaning 'narrow spit of land'.

Kylie
(alt. Kiley, Kylee)
Irish Gaelic, meaning 'graceful'. The rise in popularity of this name is likely to be linked to the career of Kylie Minogue, developing from Australian soap star to international queen of pop.

Kyoko
Japanese, meaning 'girl who sees her own true image'.

Kyra
Greek, meaning 'lady'. Also known as a village in Cyprus.

Kyrie
Greek, meaning 'the Lord'. Also a prayer sung at the beginning of the Christian mass.

TV personality names

Alesha (Dixon)

Alex (Jones)

Caroline (Flack)

Cherry (Healey)

Christine (Bleakley)

Davina (McCall)

Emma (Willis)

Fearne (Cotton)

Holly (Willoughby)

Kirstie (Allsopp)

Lauren (Laverne)

Myleene (Klass)

Tess (Daly)

L Girls' names

Lacey
(alt. Laci, Lacie, Lacy)

French, from a nobleman's surname. Most popular in North America, but English Lacey Turner is an actress and *EastEnders* star.

Ladonna
Italian, meaning 'lady'. Usually used as a spelling alternative to Madonna.

Lady
English, meaning 'bread kneader' and an aristocratic title for a woman. Usually associated with the character of Lady from Disney's *Lady and the Tramp*.

Laidh
Scottish meaning 'a ship's course'. Also a spelling alternative to Lady.

Laila
(alt. Laelia, Layla, Leila, Lejla, Lela, Lelah, Lelia)

Arabic, meaning 'night'. Famous Lailas include boxer Laila Ali and the song 'Layla' by Eric Clapton. Has become popular in recent years.

Lainey
(alt. Laine, Laney, Lany)

French, meaning 'bright light'. In Poland, the most common spelling is Lany, whereas in other countries it can be Lainey or Laney.

Lakeisha
(alt. Lakeshia)

American, meaning 'woman'. Its origins seem to be a combination of La and Keisha.

Lakshmi
(alt. Laxmi)

Sanskrit, meaning 'good omen'. Also the Hindu goddess of wealth.

Lana

Greek, meaning 'light'. Famous Lanas include singer Lana Del Rey, actress Lana Turner and the language-communication chimpanzee Lana.

Lani
(alt. Lanie)

Hawaiian, meaning 'heaven and sky'.

Lara

Latin, meaning 'famous'. Famous Laras include actress Lara Flynn Boyle, *Tomb Raider* protagonist Lara Croft and the ancient Roman nymph of the same name.

Larissa
(alt. Larisa)

Greek, meaning 'lighthearted'. Larissa was a nymph in ancient Greek mythology.

Lark
(alt. Larkin)

English, meaning 'playful songbird'.

Larsen
(alt. Larsen)

Scandinavian, meaning 'son of Lars'.

Latifa
(alt. Latifah)

Arabic, meaning 'gentle and pleasant'. Queen Latifah is the stage name of the singer and pioneer of female hip hop.

Latika
(alt. Lotika)

Hindi, meaning 'a plant'. Usually associated with the character of Latika from *Slumdog Millionaire*.

Latisha

Latin, meaning 'happiness'. More commonly used in the USA.

Latona
(alt. Latonia)

Roman, from the ancient Roman mythological heroine of the same name who had twin sons with the god Zeus.

Latoya

Spanish, meaning 'victorious one'. Singer LaToya Jackson is known for being a member of the musical Jackson family.

Latrice
(alt. Latricia)

Latin, meaning 'noble'. More commonly used in the USA.

Laura
(alt. Lora)

Latin, meaning 'laurel'. Famous Lauras include designer Laura Ashley, author Laura Ingalls Wilder and actress Laura Dern.

Laurel

Latin, meaning 'laurel tree'. A Laurel is also a term used for young women in the Mormon Church.

Lauren
(alt. Lauran, Loren)
Latin, meaning 'laurel'. Famous Laurens include actresses Lauren Bacall and Lauren Crace and DJ Lauren Laverne.

Laveda
(alt. Lavada)
Latin, meaning 'cleansed'.

Lavender
Latin, from the flowering plant of the same name.

Laverne
(alt. Lavern, Laverna)
Latin, from the goddess of the same name. Famous Lavernes include the Andrews Sisters member Laverne Andrews, and US sitcom *Laverne & Shirley*.

Lavinia
(alt. Lavina)
Latin, meaning 'woman of Rome'. Lavinia was an ancient Roman character whose hair caught fire during sacrifices to the gods.

Lavita
American, meaning 'charming'. The original 'la vita' means 'life' in Latin.

Lavonne
(alt. Lavon)
French, meaning 'yew wood'. More commonly used in the USA.

Leah
(alt. Lea, Leia)
Hebrew, meaning 'weary'.

Leandra
Greek, meaning 'lion man'. In the novel *Don Quixote* by Miguel de Cervantes, Leandra is a beautiful woman whose many suitors withdraw to the mountains to write about how beautiful she is.

Leanne
(alt. Leann, Leanna, Leeann, Lee Ann)
Contraction of Lee and Ann, meaning 'meadow grace'. Famous Leannes include singers LeAnn Rimes and Lee Ann Womack and actress Leanne Wilson.

Leda
Greek, meaning 'gladness'. Leda was an ancient Greek character who was seduced by the god Zeus in the form of a white swan, and whose children included Helen of Troy.

Lee
(alt. Leigh)
English, meaning 'pasture or meadow'. Used equally for girls and boys.

Leilani
Hawaiian, meaning 'flower from heaven'. Actress Leilani Jones is known for her roles in *Little Shop of Horrors* and various voice acting roles.

Leith
Scottish Gaelic, meaning 'broad river'.

Lena
(alt. Leena, Lina)
Latin, meaning 'light'. Famous Lenas include actresses Lena Dunham, Lena Headey and Lena Ashwell.

Lenna
(alt. Lennie)
German, meaning 'lion's strength'.

Lenore
(alt. Lenora, Leonora, Leonor, Leonore)
Greek, meaning 'light'. Usually associated with the poem *Lenore* by Edgar Allan Poe.

Léonie
(alt. Leona, Leone)
Latin, meaning 'lioness'. Poet Leonie Adams wrote during the mid-twentieth century.

Leora
(alt. Liora)
Hebrew, meaning 'light'. The male version of Leora is Leor.

Lerola
Latin, meaning 'like a blackbird'.

Lesley
(alt. Leslee, Lesli)
Scottish Gaelic, from the name of the prominent clan. Also meaning 'holly garden'. The boys' variation is usually spelt Leslie.

Leta
Latin, meaning 'glad and joyful'. Leta Hollingworth was an influential child psychologist in the twentieth century.

Letha
Greek, meaning 'forgetfulness'. Also the name of a type of butterfly.

Lefitia
(alt. Leticia, Lettice, Lettie)
Latin, meaning 'joy and gladness'. St Leticia was a Spanish virgin martyr.

Lexia
(alt. Lexi, Lexie)
Greek, meaning 'defender of mankind'. Also the name of a type of butterfly.

Lia
Italian, meaning 'bringer of the gospel'. Actress Lia Williams is known for her roles in both theatre and film.

Liana
French, meaning 'to twine around'. Also the name of a type of vine.

Libby
(alt. Libbie)
Shortened form of Elizabeth, meaning 'consecrated to God'. Famous Libbys include journalist Libby Purves, *EastEnders* character Libby Fox and singer Libby Holman.

Liberty
English, meaning 'freedom'.

Lida
Slavic, meaning 'loved by the people'.

Liese
(alt. Liesel, Liesl)
German, meaning 'pledged to God'. Also used as a shortened form of Elizabeth.

Lila
(alt. Lilah)
Arabic, meaning 'night'. In the Hindu faith, Lila refers to playtime or pastimes.

Lilac
Latin, from the flower of the same name. Also associated with the pale purple colour.

Lilia
(alt. Lilias)
Scottish, meaning 'lily'. More commonly used in Russian and Ukrainian communities.

Lilith
Arabic, meaning 'ghost'. Also the name of a female demon in Hebrew mythology.

Lillian
(alt. Lilian, Liliana, Lilla, Lillianna)
Latin, meaning 'lily'. Famous Lillians include actress Lillian Gish, playwright Lillian Hellman and pioneering nurse Lillian Wald.

Lily
(alt. Lili, Lillie, Lilly)
Latin, from the flower of the same name. Famous Lilys include singer Lily Allen, actress Lily Collins and model Lily Cole.

Linda
(alt. Lynda)
Spanish, meaning 'pretty'. Famous Lindas include presenter Linda Barker, actress Linda Blair and singer Linda Ronstadt.

Linden
(alt. Lindie, Lindy)
From the tree of the same name. Used more commonly for boys.

Lindsay
(alt. Lindsey, Linsey)
English, meaning 'island of linden trees'. Famous Lindsays include actresses Lindsay Lohan, Lindsay Sloane and Lindsay Wagner.

Linette
Welsh, meaning 'idol'.

Linnea
(alt. Linnae, Linny)
Scandinavian, meaning 'lime or linden tree'.

Lirit
Hebrew, meaning 'musically talented'.

Lisa
(alt. Leesa, Lise, Liza)
Hebrew, meaning 'pledged to God'. Famous Lisas include singer Lisa Bonet, *Friends* actress Lisa Kudrow and *The Simpsons* character Lisa Simpson.

Lissa
Greek, meaning 'bee'. Also used as a shortened form of Melissa.

Lissandra
(alt. Lisandra)
Greek, meaning 'man's defender'.

Liv
Nordic, meaning 'defence'. Actress Liv Tyler appeared in the *Lord of the Rings* trilogy.

Livia
Latin, meaning 'olive'. Livia Drusilla was a prominent ancient Roman woman, wife of the Emperor Augustus.

Liz
(alt. Lizzie, Lizzy)
Shortened form of Elizabeth, meaning 'consecrated to God'. Many Elizabeths go by Liz, including actress Liz Taylor.

Logan
Irish Gaelic, meaning 'small hollow'. More commonly used as a name for boys.

Lois
German, meaning 'renowned in battle'. Usually associated with the character of Lois Lane from the Superman comic series.

Lola
Spanish, meaning 'sorrows'. Also used as a shortened form of Delores.

Lolita
(alt. Lollie)
Spanish, meaning 'sorrows'. Usually associated with the character of Lolita in Vladimir Nabokov's novel *Lolita*.

Lona
Latin, meaning 'lion'. Lona is a moon deity in Hawaiian mythology.

Lora
Latin, meaning 'laurel'. Sometimes used as a spelling alternative to Laura.

Lorelei
(alt. Loralai, Loralie)
German, meaning 'dangerous rock'. Ancient German mythology tells of a maiden who lives on the Lorelei Rock in the river Rhine and lures sailors to their deaths.

Lorenza
Latin, meaning 'from Laurentium'.

Loretta
(alt. Loreto)
Latin, meaning 'laurel'. Mostly used in the USA, where actresses with this name include Loretta Devine and Loretta Swit.

Lori
(alt. Laurie, Lorie, Lorri)
Latin, meaning 'laurel'. Actress Lori Petty is known for her roles in *Point Break*, *A League of Their Own* and *Tank Girl*.

Lorna
Scottish, from the town of Lorne. Usually associated with the protagonist in R.D. Blackmore's novel *Lorna Doone*.

Lorraine
(alt. Laraine, Loraine)

French, meaning 'from Lorraine'. TV presenter Lorraine Kelly is best known for breakfast TV and chat show work.

Lottie
(alt. Lotta, Lotte)

French, meaning 'little and womanly'. Usually used as a shortened form of Charlotte.

Lotus

Greek, meaning 'lotus flower'.

Louise
(alt. Louisa, Luisa; abbrev. Lou, Louie)

German, meaning 'renowned in battle'. Very popular as a name in 1970s England in particular.

Lourdes

French, from the town of the same name. Madonna famously chose this name for her daughter in 1996.

Love

English, from the word 'love'.

Lowri

Welsh, meaning 'crowned with laurels'. Lowri Turner is a TV presenter.

Luanne
(alt. Luann, Luanna)

German, meaning 'renowned in battle'. In Hawaiian, the name also means 'enjoyment'.

Luba

Hebrew, meaning 'dearly loved'.

Lucia
(alt. Luciana)

Italian, meaning 'light'. The female version of the ancient Roman name Lucius.

Lucille
(alt. Lucile, Lucilla)

French, meaning 'light'. American Lucille Ball was the star of *I Love Lucy*.

Lucinda

English, meaning 'light'. Lucinda Green (Lucinda Prior-Palmer) was a world champion equestrian who won Badminton six times.

Lucretia
(alt. Lucrece)

Spanish, meaning 'light'. Also an important character in ancient Roman mythology.

Lucy
(alt. Lucie)

Latin, meaning 'light'. St Lucy was a martyr in the fourth century.

Ludmilla

Slavic, meaning 'beloved of the people'.

Luella
(alt. Lue)

English, meaning 'renowned in battle'. Designer Luella Bartley is known for her fashion brands and journalism for various fashion magazines.

Lulu
(alt. Lula)

German, meaning 'renowned in battle'. Singer Lulu became a star of the 1960s and is a successful model still today.

Luna

Latin, meaning 'moon'. Luna was the personification of the moon in ancient Roman mythology.

Lupita

Spanish, short form of Guadelupe. Actress Lupita Nyong'o is known for her role in *12 Years a Slave*.

Luz

Spanish, meaning 'light'. Also the name of an ancient city in the Bible.

Lydia
(alt. Lidia)

Greek, meaning 'from Lydia'. Famous Lydias include activist Lydia Becker, ballerina Lydia Lopokova and the character of Lydia Bennet in *Pride and Prejudice*.

Lynn
(alt. Lyn, Lynne)

Spanish, meaning 'pretty'; English, meaning 'waterfall'. Actress Lynn Redgrave is part of the Redgrave acting dynasty.

Lynton

English, meaning 'town of lime trees'. Also the name of a town in Devon. Most commonly used for boys.

Lyra

Latin, meaning 'lyre'. The central character in Philip Pullman's 'His Dark Materials' trilogy.

Girls' names

Mab

Irish Gaelic, meaning 'joy'. Queen Mab is a character in Shakespeare's play *Romeo and Juliet*.

Mabel

(alt. Mabelle, Mable)

Latin, meaning 'loveable'. Although the name Mabel is very old and dates from the fifth century, it did not become popular until the nineteenth century, when the novel *The Heir of Redclyffe* was published.

Macaria

Spanish, meaning 'blessed'.

Machiko

Japanese, meaning 'knowledgeable child'. Machiko Kawana is a Japanese voice artist.

Macy

(alt. Macey, Maci, Macie)

French, meaning 'weapon'. Macy Gray is the stage name of the award winning R&B singer-songwriter and actress Natalie McIntyre.

Mada

English, meaning 'from Magdala'. In Hindu mythology, Mada also refers to an enormous monster who is able to swallow the entire universe.

Madaio

Hawaiian, meaning 'gift from God'.

Madden

(alt. Maddyn)

Irish, meaning 'little dog'.

Madeline

(alt. Madaline, Madalyn, Madeleine, Madelyn, Madelynn, Madilyn; abbrev. Maddy, Maddi, Maddie, Madie)

Greek, meaning 'from Magdala'. Madeleine Albright was the first female Secretary of State in the US. Maddy Prior is one of the best-known English folk singers.

Madge

Greek, meaning 'pearl'. Also a shortened form of several names including Margaret, Madeline and Marjorie. Madge was especially common around 1880–1900, being the name of several actresses of that time. More recently, it's the nickname of pop icon Madonna.

Madhuri

Hindi, meaning 'sweet girl'. Madhuri Dixit is one of Bollywood's most well-known and popular actresses, appearing in dozens of Hindi films.

Madison

(alt. Maddison, Madisen, Madisyn, Madyson)

English, meaning 'son of the mighty warrior'. The sudden increase in the popularity of Madison can be traced back to the mermaid character of Madison in the film Splash, played by Daryl Hannah.

Madonna

Latin, meaning 'my lady'. Usually associated with the pop singer legend Madonna, or as one of the Virgin Mary's many names.

Maeve

Irish Gaelic, meaning 'intoxicating'. Famous Maeves include Queen Maeve from Irish mythology, author Maeve Binchy and writer Maeve Brennan.

Mafalda

Spanish, meaning 'battle-mighty'. The character of Mafalda Hopkirk appears in the 'Harry Potter' series.

Magali

Greek, meaning 'pearl'. More commonly used in French- or Portuguese-speaking communities.

Magdalene

(alt. Magdalen, Magdalena)

Greek, meaning 'from Magdala'. Mary Magdalene was one of Jesus's disciples in the Bible.

Magnolia

Latin, from the flowering plant of the same name.

Mahala

(alt. Mahalia)

Hebrew, meaning 'tender affection'.

Maia

(alt. Maja, Maya)

Greek, meaning 'mother'. Also an important character in ancient Greek mythology.

Maida

English, meaning 'maiden'.

Maisie

(alt. Maisey, Maisy, Maizie, Masie, Mazie)

Greek, meaning 'pearl'. Famous Maisies include children's book character Maisey Mouse and Maisie Williams, child star of Game of Thrones.

Malin

Hebrew and English, meaning 'of Magdala'. Malin is most common in Sweden.

Maliya
(alt. Malia, Maliyah)

Hawaiian, meaning 'beloved'.
Malia Obama is the daughter of the
president of the USA, Barack Obama.

Malka
Hebrew, meaning 'queen'.

Mallory
(alt. Malorie)

French, meaning 'unhappy'. Author
Malorie Blackman is known for her
children's literature.

Malvina
Gaelic, meaning 'smooth brow'. The
name was invented by poet James
Macpherson in the eighteenth century.

Mamie
(alt. Maimie, Mammie)

Shortened form of Margaret,
meaning 'pearl'. Famous Mamies
include former US first lady Mamie
Eisenhower, wife of President Dwight
Eisenhower.

Mandy
(alt. Mandie)

Shortened form of Amanda, meaning
'much loved'. Famous Mandys
include actress Mandy Moore and
the song *Mandy* by Barry Manilow.

Manisha
Sanskrit, meaning 'desire'. Manisha is
the goddess of wisdom in the Hindu
faith.

Mansi
Hopi, meaning 'plucked flower'. Also
the name of an indigenous group of
people in Russia.

Manuela
Spanish, meaning 'the Lord is
among us'. More commonly used in
German-speaking communities.

Mara
Hebrew, meaning 'bitter'. Famous
Maras include actress Mara Wilson
and children's author Mara Bergman.

Marcela
(alt. Marceline, Marcella, Marcelle)

Latin, meaning 'war-like'.

Marcia
(alt. Marcy, Marci, Marcie)

Latin, meaning 'war-like'. Famous
Marcias include legendary British
leader Queen Marcia, actress Marcia
Cross and voice actress Marcia
Wallace.

Margaret
*(alt. Margarete, Margaretta,
Margarette, Margret; abbrev. Maggie)*

Greek, meaning 'pearl'. Famous
Margarets include former prime
minister Margaret Thatcher, author
Margaret Atwood and actress
Margaret Rutherford. Famous Maggies
include actresses Maggie Gyllenhaal
and Maggie Grace, and the song
'Maggie May' by Rod Stewart.

Margery
*(alt. Marge, Margie, Margit, Margy,
Marjorie)*

French, meaning 'pearl'. Author
Margery Kempe wrote the first English-
language autobiography, *The Book
of Margery Kempe*, in the fifteenth
century. Marjorie Bruce was daughter
of Robert the Bruce of Scotland.

Margot
(alt. Margo)

French, meaning 'pearl'. Famous Margots include ballerina Margot Fonteyn, actress Margot Kidder and the sister of Anne Frank, Margot Frank.

Marguerite
(alt. Margarita)

French, meaning 'pearl'. Marguerite de Valois was Queen of France during the sixteenth century.

Maria
(alt. Mariah)

Latin, meaning 'bitter'. Famous Marias include tennis pro Maria Sharapova, performer Maria von Trapp and the character of Maria from the musical West Side Story.

Marian
(alt. Mariam, Mariana, Mariann, Marianne, Maryann, Maryanne, Marion)

French, meaning 'bitter grace'. Usually associated with the character of Maid Marian from the legend of Robin Hood. Marianne Faithfull is an English singer and songwriter who began her career in the 1960s in 'swinging London'.

Maribel
Hebrew, meaning 'bitter'. Also used as a contraction of Maria and Isabel.

Marie
French, meaning 'bitter'. Famous Maries include French Queen Marie Antoinette, physicist Marie Curie, and singer Marie Osmond.

Mariel
(alt. Mariela, Mariella)

Dutch, meaning 'bitter'. Also the name of a city in Cuba.

Marietta
(alt. Marieta)

French, meaning 'bitter'. Activist Marietta Stow was an influential campaigner for women's suffrage during the nineteenth century.

Marigold
English, from the flowering plant of the same name.

Marika
Dutch, meaning 'bitter'. More commonly used in Greek-speaking communities.

Marilyn
(alt. Marilee, Marilene, Marilynn)

English, meaning 'bitter'. Marilyn Monroe starred in films such as Gentlemen Prefer Blondes, The Seven Year Itch and Some Like It Hot.

Marina
(alt. Marine)

Latin, meaning 'from the sea'. Marina is a truly global name, with famous Marinas of many nationalities and backgrounds. Marina Hyde is one of few Brits with the name – she's a journalist and newspaper columnist for the Guardian.

Mariposa
Spanish, meaning 'butterfly'. Also the name of a group of lilies.

Marisa

(alt. Maris, Marissa)

Latin, meaning 'of the sea'. Famous Marisas include actress Marisa Tomei, a character from 'His Dark Materials' trilogy and the notorious Yahoo! business executive Marissa Mayer.

Marisol

Spanish, meaning 'bitter sun'. Also a contraction of Maria de la Soledad, which is another title for the Virgin Mary in Spain.

Marjolaine

French, meaning 'marjoram'.

Marlene

(alt. Marlen, Marlena; abbrev. Marla)

Hebrew, meaning 'bitter'. Actress Marlene Dietrich was German born but became an American in 1939 and was a front-line entertainer for the troops during World War II. The character of Marla Singe from the film *Fight Club*, was played by Helena Bonham Carter.

Marley

(alt. Marlee)

American, meaning 'bitter'.

Marlo

(alt. Marlowe)

American, meaning 'bitter'. More commonly used as a name for boys.

Marnie

(alt. Marney)

Scottish, meaning 'from the sea'. Famous Marnies include the character of Marnie from *Girls* and the film *Marnie* by Alfred Hitchcock. It was also the birth name of ballerina Darcey Bussell.

Marseille

French, from the city of the same name in France.

Marsha

English, meaning 'war-like'. Famous Marshas include actress Marsha Thomason, singer Marsha Hunt and playwright Marsha Norman.

Martha

(alt. Marta)

Aramaic, meaning 'lady'. Found in the Bible. Martha Lane Fox was a leading dotcom entrepreneur in the 2000s, later becoming the youngest female member of the House of Lords.

Martina

Latin, meaning 'war-like'. Famous Martinas include tennis pros Martina Hingis and Martina Navratilova and Martina, Empress of the Byzantine empire.

Marvel

French, meaning 'something to marvel at'. Usually associated with the comic book brand.

Mary

Hebrew, meaning 'bitter'. Famous Marys include the Virgin Mary from the Bible, author Mary Shelley and morality campaigner Mary Whitehouse.

Masada

Hebrew, meaning 'foundation'. Also the name of an ancient Jewish fortification in Israel.

Matilda
(alt. Mathilda, Mathilde, Matilde)

German, meaning 'battle-mighty'. Famous Matildas include the lead character from the novel *Matilda* by Roald Dahl, Queen consort of England Matilda of Flanders, and twelfth-century Queen Matilda of England.

Mattea

Hebrew, meaning 'gift of God'.

Maude
(alt. Maud)

German, meaning 'battle-mighty'. Usually associated with the character of Maude Flanders from *The Simpsons* or the film *Harold and Maude*.

Maura

Irish, meaning 'bitter'. Also the name of a French saint of the fourth century.

Maureen
(alt. Maurine)

Irish, meaning 'bitter'. Famous Maureens include actresses Maureen Lipman, Maureen McCormick and Maureen O'Hara.

Mavis

French, meaning 'thrush'. The name originated in the nineteenth century after the publication of the novel *The Sorrows of Satan*.

Maxine
(alt. Maxie)

Latin, meaning 'greatest'. Famous Maxines include the Andrews Sisters member Maxine Andrews, actress Maxine Audley and the character of Maxine Peacock from *Coronation Street*.

May
(alt. Mae, Maye,)

Hebrew, meaning 'gift of God'. Also the name of the fifth month.

Maya
(alt. Mya, Myah)

Greek, meaning 'mother'. Famous Mayas include author Maya Angelou, comedian Maya Rudolph and the Mayan people of Central America.

Mckenna
(alt. Mackenna)

Irish Gaelic, meaning 'son of the handsome one'.

Mckenzie
(alt. Mackenzie, Mckenzy, Mikenzi)

Irish Gaelic, meaning 'son of the wise ruler'. More commonly used as a boys' name.

Meara

Gaelic, meaning 'filled with happiness'.

Medea
(alt. Meda)

Greek, meaning 'ruling'. Also the name of a prominent figure in ancient Greek mythology.

Meg

Shortened form of Margaret, meaning 'pearl'. Famous Megs include actress Meg Ryan and the character of Meg from Disney's *Hercules*.

Megan
(alt. Meagan, Meghan, Meghann)

Welsh, meaning 'pearl'. Famous Megans include actresses Megan Fox and Megan Mullally and tennis pro Meghann Shaughnessy.

Mehri

Persian, meaning 'kind'. Also the name of a group of people and a language spoken in southern Arabia.

Meiwei

Chinese, meaning 'forever enchanting'.

Melanie
(alt. Melania, Melany, Melonie; abbrev. Mel)

Greek, meaning 'dark-skinned'. Famous Melanies include singers Melanie Brown and Melanie Chisholm of the Spice Girls and actress Melanie Griffith.

Melba

Australian, meaning 'from Melbourne'.

Melia
(alt. Meliah)

German, meaning 'industrious'.

Melina

Greek, meaning 'honey'. Actress Melina Kanakaredes has appeared in several US-based crime dramas, including *CSI:NY*.

Melinda

Latin, meaning 'honey'. Famous Melindas include TV presenter and model Melinda Messenger, philanthropist Melinda Gates and actress Melinda Clarke.

Melisande

French, meaning 'bee'. Melisandre is a character from George R.R. Martin's 'A Song of Ice and Fire' series.

Melissa
(alt. Melisa, Mellissa)

Greek, meaning 'bee'. Famous Melissas include singer Melissa Etheridge and actresses Melissa Joan Hart and Melissa George.

Melody
(alt. Melodie)

Greek, meaning 'song'. Aptly, there are a number of Melodys who have gone on to be singers as well as actresses. Melody is also a character in Disney's *The Little Mermaid*.

Melvina

Celtic, meaning 'chieftain'.

Menora
(alt. Menorah)
Hebrew, meaning 'candlestick'.

Mercedes
Spanish, meaning 'mercies'. Usually associated with the luxury car manufacturer Mercedes-Benz.

Mercy
English, meaning 'mercy'.

Meredith
(alt. Meridith)
Welsh, meaning 'great ruler'. Not common outside of Wales, the name is used equally for girls and boys.

Merle
French, meaning 'blackbird'. Used equally for girls and boys, though not a common name anywhere.

Merry
English, meaning 'lighthearted'.

Meryl
(alt. Merrill)
Irish Gaelic, meaning 'sea-bright'. Actress Meryl Streep has made a string of top film appearances including Kramer vs. Kramer, Sophie's Choice and The Iron Lady.

Meta
German, meaning 'pearl'. Also a Greek term for 'after or beyond'.

Mia
Italian, meaning 'mine'. Famous Mias include actresses Mia Wasikowska and Mia Farrow and singer M.I.A.

Michaela
(alt. Makaela, Makaila, Micaela, Mikaila, Mikayla)
Hebrew, meaning 'resembles God'. Famous Michaelas include presenter Michaela Strachan, actress Michaela Conlin, and gymnast McKayla Maroney.

Michelle
(alt. Machelle, Mechelle, Michaele, Michal, Michele, Michen; abbrev. Mickey, Mickie)
French, meaning 'resembles God'. Famous Michelles include singers Michelle Gayle and Michelle McManus, actress Michelle Rodriguez and current first lady of the USA, Michelle Obama.

Mieko
(alt. Meiko)
Japanese, meaning 'born into wealth'.

Migdalia
Greek, meaning 'from Magdala'.

Mignon
French, meaning 'sweet'.

Mika
(alt. Micah)
Hebrew, meaning 'resembles God'.

Milada
Czech, meaning 'my love'. More commonly used in Slavic and Czech communities.

Milagros
Spanish, meaning 'miracles'. Also a term used for folk charms with healing properties in Mexico.

Milan

Italian, from the city of the same name in Italy.

Mildred

English, meaning 'gentle strength'. Famous Mildreds include the character of Mildred Hubble from the *Worst Witch* series, author Mildred B. Davies and actress Mildred Dunnock.

Milena

Czech, meaning 'love and warmth'.

Miley

American, meaning 'smiley'. Made popular by singer and actress Miley Cyrus.

Millicent

(alt. Milicent; abbrev. Millie, Milly)

German, meaning 'high-born power'. Famous Millicents include suffragist Millicent Fawcett, British spy Milicent Bagot and the character of Millicent Bulstrode in the 'Harry Potter' seies.

Mimi

Italian, meaning 'bitter'. Also the name of the female protagonist in the opera *La bohème*, by Giacomo Puccini.

Mina

(alt. Mena)

German, meaning 'love'. In Persian, the name also means 'coloured glass'.

Mindy

(alt. Mindi)

Latin, meaning 'honey'. Used as a shortened form of Melinda as well as a name in its own right. Most commonly used in the USA.

Minerva

Latin, from the goddess of the same name. Minerva was the goddess of wisdom, the arts and defence, in ancient Roman mythology.

Ming

Chinese, meaning 'bright'. Usually associated with the Ming Dynasty, which ruled China from the fourteenth to the seventeenth century.

Minnie

(alt. Minna)

German, meaning 'helmet'. Usually associated with the Disney character Minnie Mouse.

Mira

(alt. Meera)

Latin, meaning 'admirable'. Also the name of a giant red star.

Mirabel

(alt. Mirabella, Mirabelle)

Latin, meaning 'wonderful'. Also the name of a type of plum.

Miranda

(alt. Meranda; abbrev. Randi, Randy)

Latin, meaning 'admirable'. Famous Mirandas include actresses Miranda Richardson and Miranda Hart and model Miranda Kerr.

Mirella
(alt. Mireille, Mirela)

Latin, meaning 'admirable'. Opera singer Mirella Freni is known in Italy as being one of the finest in her art.

Miriam

Hebrew, meaning 'bitter'. Also the name of a prophetess in the Bible. Miriam Margolyes is a popular British BAFTA-winning character actress. She appeared in the 'Harry Potter' films as Professor Sprout.

Mirta

Spanish, meaning 'crown of thorns'.

Missy

Shortened form of Melissa, meaning 'bee'. Famous Missys include musician Missy Elliot, singer Missy Higgins, and performer Missy Malone.

Misty
(alt. Misti)

English, meaning 'mist'. A character in the Pokémon series.

Mitzi

German, meaning 'bitter'. Actress Mitzi Gaynor appeared in South Pacific.

Miu

Japanese, meaning 'beautiful feather'. Also the name of an endangered language spoken in Papua New Guinea.

Moira
(alt. Maira)

Irish, meaning 'bitter'. Famous Moiras include actress Moira Brooker, ballet dancer Moira Shearer and news presenter Moira Stuart.

Molly
(alt. Mollie)

American, meaning 'bitter'. Famous Mollys include actresses Mollie Sugden, Molly Ringwald and Molly Sims.

Mona

Irish Gaelic, meaning 'aristocratic'. A character from the children's television programme Mona the Vampire.

Monica
(alt. Monika, Monique)

Latin, meaning 'adviser'. Famous Monicas include singer Monica, infamous White House intern Monica Lewinsky and tennis pro Monica Seles.

Monroe

Gaelic, meaning 'mouth of the river Rotha'. Usually associated with Marilyn Monroe.

Montserrat
(alt. Monserrate)

Spanish, from the town of the same name. Opera singer Montserrat Caballe is known for her work in the bel canto technique, and for the song 'Barcelona' with Freddie Mercury.

Morag

Scottish, meaning 'star of the sea'. Also the pet name of a monster that supposedly inhabits Loch Morar in Scotland.

Morgan
(alt. Morgann)

Welsh, meaning 'great and bright'. Used for both girls and, more commonly, boys.

Moriah

Hebrew, meaning 'the Lord is my teacher'. Also the name of a mountain mentioned in the Bible.

Morwenna
(alt. Modwenna)

Welsh, meaning 'maiden'. Morwenna Banks is a British comedy actress, writer and producer. She is known to toddlers everywhere as the voice of Mummy Pig in *Peppa Pig*.

Moselle
(alt. Mozell, Mozella, Mozelle)

Hebrew, meaning 'saviour'. Also the name of a river and a German wine.

Mulan

Chinese, meaning 'wood orchid'. Usually associated with the protagonist from the Disney film *Mulan*.

Munin

Scandinavian, meaning 'good memory'.

Muriel

Irish Gaelic, meaning 'sea-bright'. Author Muriel Spark was known for her novel *The Prime of Miss Jean Brodie*.

Myfanwy

Welsh, meaning 'my little lovely one'. The name originally appeared in a song called 'Myfanwy' by Joseph Parry.

Myra

Latin, meaning 'scented oil'. Famous Myras include pioneering lawyer Myra Bradwell and pianist Myra Hess, and also Moors murderer Myra Hindley.

Myrna
(alt. Mirna)

Irish Gaelic, meaning 'tender and beloved'. Actress Myrna Fahey appeared in Walt Disney's *Zorro*.

Myrtle

Irish, from the flowering shrub of the same name. Usually associated with the character of Myrtle Wilson from F. Scott Fitzgerald's novel *The Great Gatsby*.

Girls' names

Nadia
(alt. Nadya)

Russian, meaning 'hope'. Romanian Nadia Elena Comăneci is the first female Olympic gymnast to be awarded a perfect score of 10, and has three gold medals. Nadia Petrova is a tennis pro and Nadia Sawalha is a TV presenter and actress.

Nadine
French, meaning 'hope'. It is the title of a Chuck Berry song, released after he left prison. Nadine Gordimer is a South African writer and activist who won the Nobel Prize for literature.

Nahara
Aramaic, meaning 'light'.

Naima
Arabic, meaning 'water nymph'. Naima Belkhiata is a singer with the group Honeyz.

Nakia
Egyptian, meaning 'pure'.

Nalani
Hawaiian, meaning 'serenity of the skies'.

Nan
(alt. Nanna, Nannie)

Hebrew, meaning 'grace'. A character in Louisa May Alcott's *Little Women*.

Nancy
(alt. Nanci, Nancie)

Hebrew, meaning 'grace'. Nancy Reagan is a former first lady of the USA and anti-drug advocate who began her career as a film actress.

Nanette
(alt. Nannette)

French, meaning 'grace'. *No, No Nanette* is a musical comedy from the 1920s. Nanette Lepor is an American fashion designer and Nanette Newman is a British actress.

Naomi

(alt. Naoma, Noemi)

Hebrew, meaning 'pleasant'. A character in the Bible. Naomi Campbell is one of the original five 'supermodels'.

Narcissa

Greek, meaning 'daffodil'. Narcissa Whitman, a missionary, became one of the most famous women of the early American West.

Nastasia

Greek, meaning 'resurrection'. Can also mean 'born on Christmas Day'.

Natalie

(alt. Natalee, Natalia, Natalya, Nathalie)

Latin, meaning 'birth day'. From the late Latin name Natalia, meaning 'Christmas Day'. Its popularity increased in the USA after the 1940s due to actress Natalie Wood, who was the daughter of Russian immigrants.

Natasha

(alt. Natasa)

Russian, meaning 'birth day'. A character in Leo Tolstoy's *War and Peace*. Used in the English-speaking world only since the twentieth century.

Natividad

Spanish, meaning 'Christmas'.

Neda

English, meaning 'wealthy'. Neda was also an Arcadian nymph who nursed the infant Zeus.

Nedra

English, meaning 'underground'.

Neema

Swahili, meaning 'born of prosperity'.

Neka

Native American, meaning 'goose'.

Nell

(alt. Nelda, Nell, Nella, Nellie, Nelly)

Shortened form of Eleanor, meaning 'light'. May have roots in old German *nelle*, meaning 'crown of the head', perhaps suggesting an obstinate person.

Nemi

Italian, from the lake of the same name.

Neoma

Greek, meaning 'new moon'.

Nereida

Spanish, meaning 'sea nymph'. A mermaid in Greek mythology.

Nerissa

Greek, meaning 'sea nymph'. The name of Portia's waiting woman in Shakespeare's *The Merchant of Venice*.

Nettie
(alt. Neta)

Shortened form of Henrietta, meaning 'ruler of the house'.

Neva

Spanish, meaning 'snowy'.

Nevaeh

American, meaning 'heaven'. The name Nevaeh is the word 'Heaven' spelled backwards. May also be linked with Spanish 'snowy'.

Nhung

Vietnamese, meaning 'velvet'.

Niamh
(alt. Neave, Neve)

Gaelic, meaning 'brightness'. In Irish mythology, Niamh was a goddess, the daughter of the god of the sea and a queen of the land of eternal youth. Now finding increasing popularity outside of Ireland.

Nicola
(alt. Nichola, Nichole, Nicole, Nicolette, Nicolle, Nikole; abbrev. Nicky, Nicki, Nikki)

Greek, meaning 'victory of the people'. Nicola is a boys' name in Italy, but became widely used in England and Germany as a girls' name, perhaps due to the -a ending of the name. As a girls' name in England it was especially popular around the 1960s–1970s. Nicole Kidman is an Oscar-winning Australian actress. Nicole Farhi is a French fashion designer and sculptor.

Nidia

Spanish, meaning 'graceful'.

Nigella

Irish Gaelic, meaning 'champion'. Nigella Lawson is a TV chef and author, famous for her sensual style of cookery.

Nikita

Greek, meaning 'unconquered'. Popular in Russia. Also the one-word title of a song by Elton John, a film and a recent US TV series.

Nila

Egyptian, meaning 'Nile'.

Nilda

German, meaning 'battle woman'.

Nimra

Arabic, meaning 'number'. Also a name of Punjabi origin, meaning 'humble'.

Nina

Spanish, meaning 'girl'. One of the three ships used by Christopher Columbus on his first voyage. Nina Conti is a comedienne and ventriloquist and Nina Simone was a jazz singing legend and civil rights campaigner.

Nissa

Hebrew, meaning 'sign'.

Nita

Spanish, meaning 'gracious'.

Nixie

German, meaning 'water sprite'.

Noel
(alt. Noelle)

French, meaning 'Christmas'. Noel is used most commonly for boys. Noelle is a feminine variant.

Nola

Irish Gaelic, meaning 'white shoulder'. Also a city and area in Italy.

Nona

Latin, meaning 'ninth'.

Nora
(alt. Norah)

Shortened form of Eleanor, meaning 'light', used in its own right. Nora Roberts is an American author who has written over 200 romance novels, some under pseudonyms.

Noreen
(alt. Norine)

Irish, meaning 'light'. Professor Noreen Murray was a very highly regarded molecular geneticist who helped develop a vaccine against hepatitis B.

Norma

Latin, meaning 'pattern'. In Bellini's tragic opera of the same name, Norma is a druidess at the time of the Roman occupation of England.

Normandie
(alt. Normandy)

French, from the province of the same name.

Novia

Latin, meaning 'new'.

Nuala

Irish Gaelic, meaning 'white shoulder'. A popular name in Ireland, likely to follow the pattern of Irish names that have been emerging more in England.

Nydia

Latin, meaning 'nest'.

Nyimbo

Swahili, meaning 'song'.

Nysa
(alt. Nyssa)

Greek, meaning 'ambition'. A mountainous district in Greek mythology.

Girls' names

Oceana
(alt. Ocean, Océane, Ocie)
Greek, meaning 'ocean'.

Octavia
Latin, meaning 'eighth'. Sister to Caesar and wife to Antony in Shakespeare's *Antony and Cleopatra*.

Oda
(alt. Odie)
Shortened form of Odessa, meaning 'long voyage'. Also Germanic, meaning 'wealth' or 'inheritance'.

Odele
(alt. Odell)
English, meaning 'woad hill'. Woad is a plant used as a natural blue dye.

Odelia
Hebrew, meaning 'I will praise the Lord'. Also an eighth-century French saint.

Odessa
Greek, meaning 'long voyage'. A place in the Ukraine, known as the pearl of the Black Sea.

Odette
(alt. Odetta)
French, meaning 'wealthy'. In the famous ballet *Swan Lake*, Odette is the good swan.

Odile
(alt. Odilia)
French, meaning 'prospers in battle'. The evil black swan in the famous ballet *Swan Lake*.

Odina
Feminine form of Odin, from the Nordic god of the same name, meaning 'creative inspiration'.

Odyssey
Greek, meaning 'long journey'.

Oksana

Russian, meaning 'praise to God'. Oksana Baiul is a Ukrainian Olympic figure-skating champion and Oksana Grigorieva is a Russian pianist and former wife of actor Mel Gibson.

Ola
(alt. Olie)

Greek, meaning 'man's defender'.

Olena
(alt. Olene)

Russian, meaning 'light'.

Olga

Russian, meaning 'holy'. The first Russian female ruler, later canonised as the first Russian saint of the Orthodox Church.

Oliana

American, meaning 'the Lord has answered'.

Olivia
(alt. Olive, Olivev, Oliviana, Olivié; abbrev. Ollie)

Latin, meaning 'olive'. Has featured in the Top 10 names for girls in England for several years now, including at number one.

Olwen

Welsh, meaning 'white footprint'. Olwen Hufton is a British historian of early modern Europe, women's history and social history.

Olympia
(alt. Olimpia)

Greek, meaning 'from Mount Olympus'. A sanctuary of ancient Greece, known as the site of the Olympic Games in classical times.

Oma
(alt. Omie)

Arabic, meaning 'leader'. In German, oma often refers to 'grandmother'.

Omyra

Latin, meaning 'scented oil'.

Ondine

French, meaning 'wave of water'. Also the name of a French play.

Oneida
(abbrev. Ona, Onnie)

Native American, meaning 'long awaited'. The Oneida Indians were believed to have emerged as a tribe in the fourteenth century.

Onyx

Latin, meaning 'veined gem'. A precious stone.

Oona
(alt. Oonagh)

Irish, meaning 'unity'.

Opal

Sanskrit, meaning 'gem'. A gemstone made of this mineral, noted for its rich iridescence.

Ophelia
(alt. Ofelia, Ophélie)
Greek, meaning 'help'. Lead character from Shakespeare's play *Hamlet*.

Oprah
Hebrew, meaning 'young deer'. Most often associated with Oprah Winfrey.

Ora
Latin, meaning 'prayer'.

Orabela
Latin, meaning 'prayer'.

Oralie
(alt. Oralia)
French, meaning 'golden'. Oralia Dominguez is a Mexican opera singer.

Orane
French, meaning 'rising'.

Orchid
Greek, from the flower of the same name.

Oriana
(alt. Oriane)
Latin, meaning 'dawning'. Oriana was the nickname for Queen Elizabeth I.

Orla
(alt. Orlaith, Orly)
Irish Gaelic, meaning 'golden lady'. Orla Kiely is an Irish fashion designer.

Orlean
French, meaning 'plum'. Orleans is a city in France.

Ornelia
Italian, meaning 'flowering ash tree'.

Orsa
(alt. Osia, Ossie)
Latin, meaning 'bear'.

Otthid
Greek, meaning 'prospers in battle'.

Ottilie
(alt. Ottie)
French, meaning 'prospers in battle'. Ottilie Metzger was a German opera singer well known in the early 1900s.

Ouida
French, meaning 'renowned in battle'. Pseudonym of the English novelist Maria Louise Ramé, known for her extravagant melodramatic romances.

Oyintsa
Native American, meaning 'white duck'.

Ozette
Native American, from the village of the same name.

Girls' names

Pacifica
(alt. Pacifika)

Spanish, meaning 'peaceful'. Pacifica Fernández was once Costa Rica's first lady, she also designed the Costa Rican flag.

Padma

Sanskrit, meaning 'lotus'. A major Buddhist symbol. Padma Lakshmi is an Indian-born American chef, cookbook author, model and TV presenter.

Paige
(alt. Page)

French, meaning 'serving boy'.

Paisley

Scottish, from the town of the same name.

Palma
(alt. Palmira)

Latin, meaning 'palm tree'.

Paloma

Spanish, meaning 'dove'. Paloma Picasso is the youngest daughter of artist Pablo Picasso. Singer Paloma Faith is known for her eccentric style.

Pamela
(alt. Pamala, Pamella, Pamla; abbrev. Pam)

Greek, meaning 'all honey'. Pamela Stephenson is an actress and comedienne turned clinical psychologist and author. Pamela (P.L.) Travers is the author of *Mary Poppins*.

Pandora

Greek, meaning 'all gifted'. Also from the Greek myth, Pandora was given a box containing all the evils of the world, not to be opened. Now also commonly associated with the jewellery company.

Pangiota

Greek, meaning 'all is holy'. Comes from a Greek epithet widely used in reference to the Virgin Mary.

Paniz

Persian, meaning 'candy'.

Pansy

French, from the flower of the same name. Pansy Potter is a strong girl character in comic *The Beano* and Pansy Parkinson a character in the 'Harry Potter' series.

Paprika

English, meaning 'spice'.

Paradisa
(alt. *Paradis*)

Greek, meaning 'garden orchard'.

Paris
(alt. *Parisa*)

Greek, from the mythological hero of the same name. Also from the city. Paris Hilton is the hotel heiress and socialite.

Parker

English, meaning 'park keeper'.

Parthenia

Greek, meaning 'virginal'.

Parthenope

Greek, from the mythological Siren of the same name. Parthenope Nightingale was the elder sister of Florence Nightingale.

Parvati

Sanskrit, meaning 'daughter of the mountain'. The Hindu goddess of love and devotion. Parvati Patil is a character in the 'Harry Potter' series.

Pascale

French, meaning 'Easter'.

Patience

French, meaning 'the state of being patient'. A Shakespearean name. Patience Wheatcroft was a respected journalist before joining the House of Lords.

Patricia
(alt. *Patrice;* abbrev. *Pat, Patsy, Patti, Pattie, Patty*)

Latin, meaning 'noble'. Patricia Routledge is an English character comedy actress and singer. Patricia Neal was an American actress whose birth name was Patsy Louise Neal.

Paula

Latin, meaning 'small'. Paula Radcliffe is a British long-distance runner, and current world record holder for the marathon.

Pauline
(alt. *Paulette, Paulina*)

Latin, meaning 'small'. The name of a British opera. A very popular name between the 1940s and the 1960s.

Paxton

Latin, meaning 'town of peace'.

Paz

Spanish, meaning 'peace'.

Pazia

Hebrew, meaning 'golden'.

Peace

English, meaning 'peace'.

Peaches

English, meaning 'peaches'. Rarely used. Peaches Geldof was the most famous bearer of the name.

Pearl

(alt. Pearle, Pearlie, Perla)

Latin, meaning 'pale gemstone'. Pearl Buck was an American author.

Peggy

(alt. Peggie)

Greek, meaning 'pearl'. Peggy Parish was the author of the children's story series Amelia Bedelia.

Pelia

Hebrew, meaning 'marvel of God'.

Penelope

(abbrev. Penny, Penni, Pennie)

Greek, meaning 'bobbin worker'. In Homer's Odyssey, Penelope is the faithful wife of Odysseus.

Peony

Greek, from the flower of the same name.

Perdita

Latin, meaning 'lost'. Perdita is one of the heroines of William Shakespeare's play The Winter's Tale.

Peri

(alt. Perri)

Hebrew, meaning 'outcome'. In Persian mythology, the Peri are spirits who have been denied paradise until they have done penance.

Perry

French, meaning 'pear tree'. Also an English alcoholic drink made from pears.

Persephone

Greek, meaning 'bringer of destruction'. In Greek mythology, Queen of the Underworld.

Petra

(alt. Petrina)

Greek, meaning 'rock'. City in Jordan dating back to the time of Jesus and the Apostles.

Petula

Latin, meaning 'to seek'. Petula Clark is an English singer, actress and composer.

Petunia

Greek, from the flower of the same name.

Phaedra

Greek, meaning 'bright'.

Philippa

(abbrev. Pippa, Pippie)

Greek, meaning 'lover of horses'. Philippa Foot was a twentieth-century philosopher and pioneer in the field of modern ethics. Philippa Gregory is an author of historical novels.

Philomena
(alt. Philoma)

Greek, meaning 'loved one'. Also a Catholic saint.

Phoebe

Greek, meaning 'shining and brilliant'. In Greek mythology, Phoebe was one of the original Titans and is associated with the moon.

Phoenix

Greek, meaning 'dark red'. In ancient Greek mythology, a phoenix is a bird that has the power to regenerate itself from its ashes.

Phyllida

Greek, meaning 'leafy bough'. Phyllida Lloyd is a British director, best known for her work in theatre and as the director of *Mamma Mia!* and *The Iron Lady*.

Phyllis
(alt. Phillia, Phylis)

Greek, meaning 'leafy bough'.

Pia

Latin, meaning 'pious'.

Piera

Italian, meaning 'rock'.

Pilar

Spanish, meaning 'pillar'. In Latin America, Nuestra Señora del Pilar (Our Lady of the Pillar), the name given to the Blessed Virgin Mary.

Piper

English, meaning 'pipe player'. Piper Laurie, an American actress, was born Rosetta Jacobs.

Plum

Latin, from the fruit of the same name.

Polly

Hebrew, meaning 'bitter'. A nickname for 'Mary'. Polly Dunbar is a British author-illustrator.

Pomona

Latin, meaning 'apple'. Pomona was a goddess of fruitful abundance in ancient Roman religion and myth.

Poppy

Latin, from the flower of the same name. Poppy Delevingne is a British socialite and model.

Portia
(alt. Porsha)

Latin, meaning 'from the Portia clan'. The heroine in Shakespeare's *The Merchant of Venice*.

Posy

English, meaning 'small flower'. Posy Hawthorne is a character in the 'Hunger Games' series.

Precious

Latin, meaning 'of great worth'.

Priela

Hebrew, meaning 'fruit of God'.

Primavera

Italian, meaning 'springtime'. Also the name of a painting by Botticelli.

Primrose

English, meaning 'first rose'.

Princess

English, meaning 'daughter of the monarch'.

Priscilla

(alt. Prisca, Priscila)

Latin, meaning 'ancient'. Priscilla Wakefield was an eighteenth-century Quaker educational writer and philanthropist.

Priya

Hindi, meaning 'loved one'.

Prudence

(abbrev. Pru, Prue, Prudie)

Latin, meaning 'caution'. Known as the mother of all virtues.

Prunella

Latin, meaning 'small plum'. Prunella Clough was a prominent British artist and Prunella Scales is an actress best known for playing Sybil in *Fawlty Towers*.

Psyche

Greek, meaning 'breath'. In Greek mythology, the wife of Eros. Also the name of an opera.

Q

Girls' names

Qiana
(alt. Qianah, Qiania, Qyana, Qianne)
American, meaning 'gracious'. Qiana
Chase is an American model.

Qiturah
Arabic, meaning 'incense'.

Queen
(alt. Queenie)
English, meaning 'queen'.

Quiana
American, meaning 'silky'. Quiana
Grant is an American model.

Quincy
(alt. Quincey)
French, meaning 'estate of the fifth
son'. Also used as a boys' name.

Quinn
Irish Gaelic, meaning 'counsel'.
Quinn Fabray is a character from the
American musical comedy-drama
series *Glee*.

Quintessa
Latin, meaning 'creative'.

R Girls' names

Rachel
(alt. Rachael, Rachelle)

Hebrew, meaning 'ewe'. Rachel is a figure in the Bible. A very popular name during the 1960s and 1970s, especially. Famous Rachels include actresses Rachel Weisz and Rachel Bilson and the characters of Rachel Berry from *Glee* and Rachel Green from *Friends*.

Radhika
(alt. Raadhika)

Sanskrit, meaning 'prosperous'. Raadhika Sarathkumar is one of Bollywood's most prolific actresses and producers.

Rae
(alt. Ray)

Shortened form of Rachel, meaning 'ewe'. Rae Armantrout is known for her poetry and academic writing.

Rafferty

Irish, meaning 'abundance'. More commonly found as a surname.

Rahima

Arabic, meaning 'compassionate'.

Raina
(alt. Rain, Raine, Rainey, Rayne)

Latin, meaning 'queen'.

Raisa
(alt. Raissa)

Yiddish, meaning 'rose'. Extremely popular name in Russia, particularly as Mikhail Gorbachev's wife was called Raisa.

Raleigh
(alt. Rayleigh)

Old English, meaning 'deer's meadow'.

Rama
(alt. Ramey, Ramya)

Hebrew, meaning 'exalted'. Also one of the god Vishnu's avatars in the Hindu faith.

Ramona
(alt. Romona)

Spanish, meaning 'wise guardian'. Also the *Ramona* children's novels and the film *Ramona and Beezus*, by Beverly Cleary.

Ramsey
(alt. Ramsay)

Old English, meaning 'wild garlic island'. Can be used for girls and boys.

Rana
(alt. Rania, Rayna)

Arabic, meaning 'beautiful thing'.

Rani

Sanskrit, meaning 'queen'. Also a character from *Doctor Who*.

Raphaela
(alt. Rafaela, Raffaella)

Spanish, meaning 'God has healed'. A feminine form of Raphael, name of the painter and artist.

Raquel
(alt. Racquel)

Hebrew, meaning 'ewe'. Famous Raquels include actress Racquel Welch and the character in *Only Fools and Horses*.

Rashida

Turkish, meaning 'righteous'. Rashida Jones is an actress.

Raven
(alt. Ravyn)

English, from the black bird of the same name. Raven-Symoné is an actress often known as just Raven.

Razia

Arabic, meaning 'contented'. Razia Sultan was the only female ruler of the Sultanate Delhi and of the Mughal period of Indian history, during the thirteenth century.

Reagan
(alt. Reagen, Regan)

Irish Gaelic, meaning 'descendant of Riagán'.

Reba

Shortened form of Rebecca, meaning 'joined'. Reba McEntire is an American country singer.

Rebecca
(alt. Rebekah)

Hebrew, meaning 'joined'. Rebecca is a figure in the Bible. Also a classic novel by Daphne Du Maurier. A popular name through several decades, with many abbreviated forms including Reb, Becca, Becky, Bex, Becs and more.

Reese

Welsh, meaning 'fiery and zealous'. Actress Reese Witherspoon starred in *Legally Blonde* and *Walk the Line*.

Regina

Latin, meaning 'queen'. Famous Reginas include actresses Regina King and Regina Hall and the character of Regina George in the film *Mean Girls*.

Reiko

Japanese, meaning 'thankful one'.

Reina
(alt. Reyna, Rheyna)
Spanish, meaning 'queen'.

Rena
(alt. Reena)
Hebrew, meaning 'serene'.

Renata
Latin, meaning 'reborn'. Renata Tebaldi was one of the best-loved post-war opera singers.

Rene
Greek, meaning 'peace'. Actress Rene Russo appeared in *Get Shorty*, *The Thomas Crown Affair* and the *Thor* series.

Renée
(alt. Renae, Renee)
French, meaning 'reborn'. Famous Renées include actresses Renée Zellweger and Renee Roberts, and one half of the singing duo Renée and Renato.

Renira
A rare name with no clear agreed origin. Used, but rarely, in a range of countries including England and Scotland, the USA, Germany, Brazil and Hungary.

Renita
Latin, meaning 'resistant'. Most commonly used in the USA.

Reshma
(alt. Resha)
Sanskrit, meaning 'silk'.

Reta
(alt. Retha, Retta)
Shortened form of Margaret, meaning 'pearl'. In Portuguese the name also means 'straight'.

Rhea
Greek, meaning 'earth'. Also the name of the mother of the gods in ancient Greek mythology.

Rheta
Greek, meaning 'eloquent speaker'.

Rhiannon
(alt. Reanna, Reanne, Rhian, Rhianna)
Welsh, meaning 'witch'. Also the name of the mother of Pryderi, King of Dyfed, in Welsh mythology.

Rhoda
Greek, meaning 'rose'. Found in the Bible.

Rhona
Nordic, meaning 'rough island'. Popular in Scotland. Rhona Martin represented Britain in curling at the 2002 Salt Lake City Olympics. Rhona Cameron is a comedienne.

Rhonda
(alt. Ronda)
Welsh, meaning 'noisy'.

Ria
(alt. Rie, Riya)
Shortened form of Victoria, meaning 'victor'.

Ricki
(alt. Rieko, Rika, Rikki)

Shortened form of Frederica, meaning 'peaceful ruler'. Actress and presenter Ricki Lake hosted a talk show bearing her name for a decade.

Riley

Irish Gaelic, meaning 'courageous'. Used as a boys' name and girls' name equally.

Rilla

German, meaning 'small brook'.

Rima

Arabic, meaning 'antelope'. Rima the Jungle Girl is the fictional heroine of novel *Green Mansions* and was briefly a comic book character also.

Riona

Irish Gaelic, meaning 'like a queen'. Sometimes used as a spelling alternative to Fiona.

Ripley

English, meaning 'shouting man's meadow'.

Risa

Latin, meaning 'laughter'. More commonly used in Japanese- and Spanish-speaking cultures.

Rita

Shortened form of Margaret, meaning 'pearl'. Famous Ritas include actresses Rita Hayworth and Rita Moreno and singer Rita Coolidge.

River
(alt. Riviera)

English, from 'river'. Used as both a boys' and a girls' name, sometimes in the plural.

Roberta
(abbrev. Robbie, Robi, Roby, Bobby, Bobbie)

English, meaning 'bright fame'. Singer Roberta Flack won Grammy Record of the Year for two consecutive years in the 1970s with 'The First Time Ever I Saw Your Face' and 'Killing Me Softly with His Song'.

Robin
(alt. Robbin, Robyn)

English, meaning 'bright fame'. Used slightly more often for boys than for girls. Famous Robins include actress Robin Wright Penn and singer Robyn.

Rochelle
(alt. Richelle, Rochel)

French, meaning 'little rock'. Singer Rochelle Humes featured in S Club 8 and The Saturdays.

Rogue

French, meaning 'beggar'. A character from the *X-Men* comic series. Extremely rare as a girls' name.

Rohina
(alt. Rohini)

Sanskrit, meaning 'sandalwood'.

Roisin

Irish Gaelic, meaning 'little rose'. Singer Roisin Murphy was one half of group Moloko before going solo.

Roja

Spanish, meaning 'red-haired lady'. The name also means 'rose' in Tamil.

Rolanda

German, meaning 'renowned land'.

Roma

Italian, meaning 'Rome'. Also the name of an ancient Roman deity, and of a group of nomadic European people.

Romaine
(alt. Romina)

French, meaning 'from Rome'.

Romola
(alt. Romilda, Romily)

Latin, meaning 'Roman woman'. Actress Romola Garai appeared in films including *Atonement* and *Emma*.

Romy

Shortened form of Rosemary, meaning 'dew of the sea', and often the German variation. Actress Romy Rosemont is known for her TV roles in *Prison Break*, *Grey's Anatomy* and *Glee*.

Rona
(alt. Ronia, Ronja, Ronna)

Nordic, meaning 'rough island'. Also the name of two Scottish islands, North Rona and South Rona.

Ronnie
(alt. Roni, Ronni)

English, meaning 'strong counsel'. Impressionist and actress Ronni Ancona has also appeared on TV panel shows.

Roro

Indonesian, meaning 'nobility'. Sometimes used as a nickname for Ro- names (Rosa, Rosalind, etc).

Rosa

Italian, meaning 'rose'. Activist Rosa Parks is credited with being the 'first lady of American civil rights' after she refused to give up her seat to a white passenger on a bus in 1955.

Rosabel
(alt. Rosabella)

Contraction of Rose and Belle, meaning 'beautiful rose'. Most commonly used in the USA.

Rosalie
(alt. Rosale, Rosalia, Rosalina)

French, meaning 'rose garden'. Actress Andie MacDowell's birth name is Rosalie.

Rosalind
(alt. Rosalinda)

Spanish, meaning 'pretty rose'. A character in Shakespeare's *As You Like It*.

Rosalyn
(alt. Rosaleen, Rosaline, Roselyn)

Contraction of Rose and Lynn, meaning 'pretty rose'. Also a song by the Pretty Things, which was later recorded by David Bowie.

Rosamund
(alt. Rosamond)

German, meaning 'renowned protector'. Famous Rosamunds include actress Rosamund Pike, author Rosamunde Pilcher and the long-time mistress of Henry II, Rosamund Clifford.

Rose

Latin, from the flower of the same name. Famous Roses include actresses Rose Byrne and Rose McGowan and the character of Rose DeWitt Bukater from the film *Titanic*.

Roseanne
(alt. Rosana, Rosann, Rosanna, Rosanne, Roseann, Roseanna)

Combination of Rose and Anne, meaning 'graceful rose'. Actress and comedienne Roseanne Barr is know for her stand-up work and sitcom *Roseanne*.

Rosemary
(alt. Rosemarie; abbrev. Ros, Rosy, Rosie, Romy)

Latin, meaning 'dew of the sea'. Rosemary has regularly been used over long periods. The name is also the title of several songs. Famous Rosies include actresses Rosie O'Donnell and Rosie Perez and supermodel Rosie Huntington-Whiteley.

Rosita

Spanish, meaning 'rose'. A character in *Sesame Street*.

Rowena
(alt. Rowan)

Welsh, meaning 'slender and fair'. In ancient British mythology, Rowena was a powerful and beautiful seductress.

Roxanne
(alt. Roxana, Roxane, Roxanna; abbrev. Roxie, Roxey, Roxy)

Persian, meaning 'dawn'. A song by The Police. Famous Roxies include the character of Roxie Hart from the musical *Chicago*, inventor Roxey Ann Caplin, and the band Roxy Music.

Rubina
(alt. Rubena)

Hebrew, meaning 'behold, a son'. Also a tropical plant.

Ruby
(alt. Rubi, Rubie)

English, meaning 'red gemstone'. Associated with the comedienne Ruby Wax, or the songs 'Ruby Tuesday' by The Rolling Stones and 'Ruby' by Kaiser Chiefs.

Rusty

American, meaning 'red-headed'. Use for girls and, more commonly, boys.

Ruth
(alt. Ruthe, Ruthie)

Hebrew, meaning 'friend and companion'. A prominent figure in the Bible.

Girls' names

Saba
(alt. Sabah)

Greek, meaning 'from Sheba'. Also the name of a small Caribbean island.

Sabina
(alt. Sabine)

Latin, meaning 'from the Sabine tribe'. Sabina was also the name given to certain women of political standing in ancient Rome.

Sabrina

Latin, meaning 'the River Severn'. Also a film starring Audrey Hepburn, and the title character of the sitcom *Sabrina, the Teenage Witch*.

Sadella

American, meaning 'fairytale princess'. More commonly used in the USA.

Sadie
(alt. Sade, Sadye)

Hebrew, meaning 'princess'. Famous Sadies include actress and business owner Sadie Frost, actress Sadie Miller and academic pioneer Sadie Tanner Mossell Alexander.

Saffron

English, from the reddish-yellow spice of the same name. Saffron is a character from *Absolutely Fabulous*, Edina's level-headed and long-suffering daughter.

Safiyya
(alt. Safiya)

Arabic, meaning 'sincere friend'. Also the name of one of Muhammad's wives.

Sage
(alt. Saga, Saige)

Latin, meaning 'wise and healthy'. Also the name of a herb.

Sahara

Arabic, meaning 'desert'.

Sakura

Japanese, meaning 'cherry blossom'.

Sally
(alt. Sallie)

Hebrew, meaning 'princess'. Famous Sallys include actresses Sally Field and Sally Whittaker and athlete Sally Gunnell.

Salma

Arabic, meaning 'peaceful'. Also Persian, meaning 'sweetheart'. Actress Salma Hayek is a Mexican-American.

Salome
(alt. Salma)

Hebrew, meaning 'peace'. Also the name of an influential character in the Bible thought to be associated with seductive dance.

Samantha
(abbrev. Sam, Sammie, Sammy)

Hebrew, meaning 'told by God'. Famous Samanthas include actresses Samantha Morton and Samantha Bond and the wife of the current British prime minister, Samantha Cameron.

Samara
(alt. Samaria, Samira)

Hebrew, meaning 'under God's rule'. Also the name of several places in Russia.

Sanaa

Arabic, meaning 'brilliance'. Also the capital of Yemen.

Sandra
(alt. Saundra; abbrev. Sandi, Sandy)

Shortened form of Alexandra, meaning 'defender of mankind'. Famous Sandras include actresses Sandra Bullock, Sandra Dee and Sandra Gough. Sandy is the main female character in the film *Grease*

Sangeetha

Hindi, meaning 'musical'. Actress Sangeetha Arvind Krish is known in the Bollywood film industry as simply Sangeetha.

Sanna
(alt. Saniya, Sanne, Sanni)

Hebrew, meaning 'lily'. Sometimes used as a shortened version of Susanna.

Santana
(alt. Santina)

Spanish, meaning 'holy'. Usually associated with the (male) guitar legend Carlos Santana.

Saoirse

Irish, meaning 'freedom'. Irish-American actress Saoirse Ronan has been nominated for BAFTAs and an Oscar.

Sapphire
(alt. Saphira)

Hebrew, meaning 'blue gemstone'. Usually associated with the blue gem popular in jewellery.

Sarah
(alt. Sara, Sarai, Sariah)

Hebrew, meaning 'princess'. Also an important character in the Bible. A particularly popular name in the 1960s.

Sasha
(alt. Sacha, Sascha)

Russian, meaning 'defender of mankind'. Used for both girls and boys, and now spreading more widely outside of Russia. Sasha is one of President Obama's daughters.

Saskia
(alt. Saskie)

Dutch, meaning 'the Saxon people'. In Danish the name also means 'valley of light'.

Savannah
(alt. Savanah, Savanna, Savina)

Spanish, meaning 'treeless'. Also one of Queen Elizabeth II's great-grandchildren, Savannah Phillips.

Scarlett
(alt. Scarlet)

English, meaning 'scarlet'. Usually associated with the character of Scarlett O'Hara, from the novel and film Gone with the Wind, or actress Scarlett Johansson.

Scout

French, meaning 'to listen'. The main female character from the classic novel To Kill a Mockingbird, by Harper Lee.

Sedona
(alt. Sedna)

Spanish, from the city of the same name. Also the name of a city in Arizona, USA.

Selah
(alt Sela)

Hebrew, meaning 'cliff'. Also a phrase used in the Hebrew Bible meaning 'stop and listen'.

Selby

English, meaning 'manor village'.

Selena
(alt. Salena, Salima, Salina, Selene, Selina)

Greek, meaning 'moon goddess'. Famous Selenas include singers Selena Gomez and Selena Quintanilla-Perez (known simply as Selena) and actress Selena Royle.

Selma

German, meaning 'Godly helmet'. Versatile actress Selma Blair has starred in a range of film genres as well as Hollywood hits.

Seneca

Native American, meaning 'from the Seneca tribe'. Also the name of a prominent ancient Roman philosopher, Seneca the Younger.

Sephora

Hebrew, meaning 'bird'. In Greek, the name also means 'beauty'.

September

Latin, meaning 'seventh month'.

Seraphina
(alt. Serafina, Seraphia, Seraphine)

Hebrew, meaning 'ardent'. St Serafina was an Italian woman whose illness and suffering contributed to her strong faith.

Serena
(alt. Sarina, Sereana)

Latin, meaning 'tranquil'. Serena Williams dominated women's tennis for long periods.

Serenity

Latin, meaning 'serene'. Also a sci-fi film.

Shania
(alt. Shaina, Shana, Shaniya)

Hebrew, meaning 'beautiful'. Shania Twain is the Canadian country/pop singer-songwriter whose real first name is Eilleen.

Shanice

American, meaning 'from Africa'. Singer Shanice is known for songs including 'I Love Your Smile'.

Shaniqua
(alt. Shanika)

African, meaning 'warrior princess'. More commonly used in the USA.

Shanna

English, meaning 'old'. There is a comic book character *Shanna the She-Devil*. Shanna is a name shared by a number of famous Americans, including Shanna Zolman, the female professional basketball player.

Shannon
(alt. Shannan, Shanon)

Irish Gaelic, meaning 'old and ancient'. The name is believed to be a reference to Sionna, who was a goddess in ancient Irish mythology.

Shantal
(alt. Shantel, Shantell)

French, meaning 'stone'. Often used as a spelling alternative to Chantal.

Shanti
(alt. Shantih)

Hindi, meaning 'peaceful'. Also mentioned in T.S. Eliot's poem *The Waste Land*.

Sharlene

German, meaning 'man'. Often used as a spelling alternative to Charlene.

Sharon
(alt. Sharen, Sharona, Sharron, Sharyn)

Hebrew, meaning 'a plain'. Famous Sharons include swimmer Sharon Davies, presenter Sharon Osbourne and actress Sharon Stone.

Shasta

American, from the mountain of the same name. Also the name of a Native American tribe.

Shauna
(alt. Shawna)

Irish, meaning 'the Lord is gracious'. More commonly used in the USA.

Shayla
(alt. Shaylie, Shayna, Sheyla)

Irish, meaning 'blind'. Shayla Worley is an American gymnast.

Shea
Irish Gaelic, meaning 'from the fairy fort'. Usually associated with the tree and the nut that goes into creating shea butter.

Sheena
Irish, meaning 'the Lord is gracious'. Singer Sheena Easton rocketed to fame when she featured in an early British reality TV show, The Big Time, in the late 1970s.

Sheila
(alt. Shelia)

Irish, meaning 'blind'. Actress Sheila Hancock has had a long and varied career that has taken her from the West End and Broadway, through TV and film to Radio 4 and documentary.

Shelby
(alt. Shelba, Shelbie)

Norse, meaning 'willow'. Can be used as a boys' name and girls' name.

Shelley
(alt. Shelli, Shellie, Shelly)

English, meaning 'meadow on the ledge'. Famous Shelleys include skeleton athlete Shelley Rudman and actress Shelley Winters.

Shenandoah
Native American. In the Iroquoian language it means 'deer'. A river in the state of Virginia, USA.

Sheridan
Irish Gaelic, meaning 'wild man'. Actress Sheridan Smith appeared in Two Pints of Lager and a Packet of Crisps and Gavin and Stacey.

Sherry
(alt. Sheree, Sheri, Sherie, Sherri, Sherrie)

Shortened form of Cheryl or Sheryl, meaning 'man'. Also an alcoholic drink.

Sheryl
(alt. Sherryl)

German, meaning 'man'. Famous Sheryls include singer Sheryl Crow, presenter Sheryl Gascoigne and Sheryl Sandberg, a high-profile businesswoman, currently the Chief Operating Officer at Facebook.

Shiloh
Hebrew, meaning 'his gift'. From the biblical place of the same name, made popular by Angelina Jolie and Brad Pitt's daughter.

Shirley
(alt. Shirlee)

English, meaning 'bright meadow'. Famous Shirleys include singer Dame Shirley Bassey, actress Shirley MacLaine and child star Shirley Temple.

Shivani
Sanskrit, meaning 'wife of Shiva'.

Shola
Arabic, meaning 'energetic'. More commonly a boys' name.

Shona

Irish Gaelic, meaning 'God is gracious'. Also associated with the Shona people of southern Africa.

Shoshana
(alt. Shoshanna)

Hebrew, meaning 'lily'. Made popular by the character of Shoshanna Shapiro in *Girls*.

Shura

Russian, meaning 'man's defender'. In Arabic it also means 'consultation'.

Sian
(alt. Sianna)

Welsh, meaning 'the Lord is gracious'. Famous Sians include presenters Sian Lloyd and Sian Williams, and actress Sian Phillips.

Sibyl
(alt. Sybil)

Greek, meaning 'seer and oracle'. Sibyl was a prophetess in ancient Greek mythology.

Sidney
(alt. Sydney)

English, meaning 'wide meadow'. Used as a boys' name more commonly but also a girls' name.

Sidonie
(alt. Sidonia, Sidony)

Latin, meaning 'from Sidonia'. Also the name of a French-German princess of the fifteenth century.

Sienna
(alt. Siena)

Latin, from the town of the same name. Also the name of a type of yellowy-red earth pigment. Sienna Miller is an English model, BAFTA-nominated actress and fashion designer. She recently became mum to Marlowe.

Sierra

Spanish, meaning 'saw'.

Siffhi

Hindi, meaning 'spiritual powers'.

Signa
(alt. Signe)

Scandinavian, meaning 'victory'. Also the name of a town in the province of Florence, Italy.

Sigrid

Nordic, meaning 'fair victory'. Sigrid the Haughty was said to have been the wife of Eric the Victorious in ancient Norse mythology.

Siksika

First Nation, meaning 'silken foot'. The Siksika Nation is a tribe in Canada whose name comes from 'silk' and 'foot'.

Silja

Scandinavian, meaning 'blind'.

Simcha

Hebrew, meaning 'joy'.

Simone
(alt. Simona)

Hebrew, meaning 'to hear'. Female variant of the name Simon, except in Italy, where Simone is the male form of Simon and the female form is Simona. Famous Simones include philosopher Simone de Beauvoir and first female scuba diver, Simone Melchior.

Sinéad

Irish, meaning 'the Lord is gracious'. Used with and without the accent on the 'e'. Famous Sineads include singer Sinéad O'Connor, actress Sinéad Cusack and ice-dancing skater Sinead Kerr.

Siobhan

Irish, meaning 'the Lord is gracious'. Actress Siobhan McKenna is credited with reviving the name in the twentieth century.

Siren
(alt. Sirena)

Greek, meaning 'entangler'. Sirens were beautiful and deadly creatures who lured men to their deaths at sea in ancient Greek mythology.

Siria

Spanish, meaning 'glowing'. Often used as a spelling alternative to Syria.

Skye
(alt. Sky)

Scottish, from the large island of the same name in Scotland.

Skyler
(alt. Skyla, Skylar)

Dutch, meaning 'giving shelter'. The name Skyler has seen a sudden jump in popularity after the success of the drama series *Breaking Bad*, which featured a main character called Skyler White.

Sloane
(alt. Sloan)

Irish Gaelic, meaning 'man of arms'. Usually associated with Sloane Square in London, after which the Sloane Rangers are named.

Socorro

Spanish, meaning 'to aid'.

Sojourner

English, meaning 'temporary stay'. Nineteenth-century civil rights and women's activist Sojourner Truth is known for her phrase 'And ain't I a woman?'

Solana

Spanish, meaning 'sunlight'. The solana is the Spanish word for the side of a mountain or valley where the sun hits.

Solange

French, meaning 'with dignity'. A Christian saint from the ninth century. American singer and actress Solange Knowles is unusual among famous Solanges in that she's not from a French-speaking country.

Soledad

Spanish, meaning 'solitude'.

Soleil

French, meaning 'sun'. Usually associated with performance artists Cirque du Soleil.

Solveig

Scandinavian, meaning 'woman of the house'.

Sona

Arabic, meaning 'golden one'. Sona MacDonald is an actress of film and theatre.

Sonia

(alt. Sonja, Sonya)

Greek, meaning 'wisdom'. Sonia Rykiel is a French fashion designer. Sonia O'Sullivan was a world-class Irish long-distance runner who won medals at World Championships and Olympics.

Sophia

(alt. Sofia, Sofie, Sophie)

Greek, meaning 'wisdom'. Sophia Loren was actually named Sofia. Italy's most famous actress, she won an Oscar, BAFTA and Golden Globes. Other famous Sophias include film director Sofia Coppola and actresses Sofia Vergara and Sophia Myles.

Sophronia

Greek, meaning 'sensible'. Usually associated with the character of Sophronia from the epic poem Jerusalem Delivered, by Torquato Tasso.

Soraya

Persian, meaning 'princess'. Queen Soraya Tarzi was the wife of King Amanullah of Afghanistan (reigned 1919–1929).

Sorcha

Irish and Scottish Gaelic, meaning 'bright and shining'. Irish actress Sorcha Cusack has appeared in Coronation Street and Casualty.

Sorrel

English, from the edible herb of the same name.

Stacey

(alt. Stacie, Stacy)

Greek, meaning 'resurrection'. Famous Staceys include actresses Stacey Keibler and Stacey Dash and presenter Stacey Dooley.

Star

(alt. Starla, Starr)

English, meaning 'star'.

Stella

Latin, meaning 'star'. Leading fashion designer Stella McCartney is known for her ethics and creativity. She's also a mum of four: Miller, Bailey, Beckett and Reiley.

Stephanie

(alt. Stefanie, Stephani, Stephania, Stephany, Stephenie)

Greek, meaning 'crowned'. Famous Stephanies include actress Stephanie Beacham, tennis pro Stefanie 'Steffi' Graf and author Stephenie Meyer.

Sue
(alt. Susie, Suzy)

Shortened form of Susan, meaning 'lily'. Famous Sues include comedienne Sue Perkins and tennis pro turned TV presenter Sue Barker.

Sukey
(alt. Sukey, Sukie)

Shortened form of Susan, meaning 'lily'. Usually associated with the character of Sukey from the nursery rhyme 'Polly Put the Kettle On'.

Summer

English, from the season of the same name. Famous Summers include opera singer Summer Watson and actress Summer Glau.

Sunday

English, meaning 'the first day'.

Sunny
(alt. Sun)

English, meaning 'of a pleasant temperament'.

Suri

Persian, meaning 'red rose'. Suri Cruise is the daughter of Katie Holmes and Tom Cruise.

Surya

Hindi, from the god of the sun.

Susan
(alt. Susann, Suzan, Suzanne; abbrev. Sue, Susie, Suzy)

Hebrew, meaning 'lily'. Famous Susans include actress Susan Sarandon, singer Susan Boyle and suffragette Susan B. Anthony.

Susannah
(alt. Susana, Susanna, Susanne, Suzanna, Suzanne)

Hebrew, meaning 'lily'. Famous Susannahs include artist Susannah Fiennes and actresses Susannah York and Susannah Doyle.

Svea

Swedish, meaning 'of the motherland'.

Svetlana

Russian, meaning 'star'. A popular name in Slavic countries, now starting to spread West. Svetlana Stalin was the daughter of Soviet dictator Josef Stalin.

Swanhild

Saxon, meaning 'battle swan'.

Sylvia
(alt. Silvia, Sylvie)

Latin, meaning 'from the forest'. Famous Sylvias include poet Sylvia Plath, suffragette Sylvia Pankhurst and singer Sylvia Robinson.

T

Girls' names

Tabitha
(alt. Tabatha, Tabetha)

Aramaic, meaning 'gazelle'. A woman raised from the dead by St Peter in the Bible. A very popular name in the USA in the 1970s and 1980s, after Tabitha the child witch TV character.

Tahira
Arabic, meaning 'virginal'.

Tai
Chinese, meaning 'big'.

Taima
(alt. Taina, Tayma)

Native American, meaning 'peal of thunder'. Also the name of an oasis in Saudi Arabia.

Tajsa
Polish, meaning 'princess'.

Talia
(alt. Tali)

Hebrew, meaning 'heaven's dew'. Famous Talias include actresses Talia Shire and Talia Balsam.

Taliesin
Welsh, meaning 'shining brow'. Usually associated with the Welsh poet Taliesin.

Talise
(alt. Talyse)

Native American, meaning 'lovely water'.

Talitha
Aramaic, meaning 'young girl'. The name is mentioned in the Bible when Jesus raises a child from the dead.

Tallulah
(alt. Taliyah)

Native American, meaning 'leaping water'. Famous Tallulahs include actresses Tallulah Bankhead and Tallulah Riley, and the character of club singer Tallulah in the film Bugsy Malone.

Tamara
(alt. Tamera)

Hebrew, meaning 'palm tree'. Famous Tamaras include socialite Tamara Ecclestone and actresses Tamera Mowry and Tamara Taylor.

Tamatha
(alt. Tametha)

American, meaning 'dear Tammy'. Sometimes used as a spelling alternative to Samantha.

Tamika
(alt. Tameka)

American, meaning 'people'.

Tammy
(alt. Tami, Tammie)

Shortened form of Tamsin, meaning 'twin'. Country singer Tammy Wynette's best-known song is 'Stand by Your Man'.

Tamsin

Hebrew, meaning 'twin'. Sometimes used as a shortened form of Thomasina.

Tanis

Spanish, meaning 'to make famous'.

Tanya
(alt. Tania, Tanya, Tonya)

Shortened form of Tatiana, meaning 'from the Tatius clan'. Dr Tanya Byron is a child psychologist, author and TV presenter on parenting issues.

Tao

Chinese, meaning 'like a peach'. Tao is also the notion of a route or path in Chinese cultures.

Tara
(alt. Tahra, Tarah, Tera)

Irish Gaelic, meaning 'rocky hill'. Famous Taras include socialite Tara Palmer-Tomkinson and actresses Tara Fitzgerald and Tara Reid.

Tasha
(alt. Taisha, Tarsha)

Shortened form of Natasha, meaning 'birthday'. Famous Tashas include athlete Tasha Danvers, singer Tasha Thomas and author and illustrator Tasha Tudor.

Tatiana
(alt. Tatyana)

Russian, meaning 'from the Tatius clan'. Famous Tatianas include actress Tatyana Ali, author Tatiana de Rosna and the character of Tatiana Romanova from the James Bond film *From Russia With Love*.

Tatum

English, meaning 'light hearted'. Tatum O'Neal was the youngest person to win a competitive Oscar, picking up the award for *Paper Moon*, in which she starred with her father, Ryan O'Neal.

Tawny
(alt. Tawanaa, Tawnee, Tawnya)

English, meaning 'golden brown'. Usually associated with the colour tawny, as used for example in the descriptive name of the tawny owl.

Taya

Greek, meaning 'poor one'. In several languages the name also means 'princess' or 'goddess'.

Taylor
(alt. Tayler)

English, meaning 'tailor'. Can be used for boys as well as girls. Famous Taylors include singer Taylor Swift and actress Taylor Schilling.

Tea

Greek, meaning 'goddess'. Actress Tea Leoni is known by her middle name, rather than her first name of Elizabeth.

Teagan
(alt. Teague, Tegan)

Irish Gaelic, meaning 'poet'.

Teal

English, from the bird of the same name. Often associated with the bluish-green colour.

Tecla

Greek, meaning 'fame of God'.

Tehile

Hebrew, meaning 'song of praise'.

Temperance

English, meaning 'virtue'.

Tempest

French, meaning 'storm'. Also the title of a Shakespearean play.

Teresa
(alt. Terese, Tereza, Theresa, Therese; abbrev. Terri, Teri, Terrie, Terry)

Greek, meaning 'harvest'. Famous Teresas include nun Mother Teresa, Home Secretary Theresa May and actress Teresa Graves.

Tessa
(alt. Tess, Tessie)

Shortened form of Teresa, meaning 'harvest'. Tessa Virtue is a Canadian ice dance champion, politician Tessa Jowell has served in the Cabinet and javelin thrower Tessa Sanderson represented Britain at every Olympics from 1976–96.

Thais

Greek, from the mythological ancient Greek concubine of the same name.

Thalia

Greek, meaning 'blooming'. There are half a dozen ancient Greek muses, nymphs and graces who share the name Thalia.

Thandie
(alt. Thana, Thandi)

Arabic, meaning 'thanksgiving'. Thandie Newton is a British film actress.

Thea

Greek, meaning 'goddess'. The name Thea can also be a shortened form of Theodora or Dorothea.

Theda

German, meaning 'people'. Theda Bara was one of the silent era's most prolific and popular actresses, appearing in over 40 films.

Thelma

Greek, meaning 'will'. Famous Thelmas include the actress Thelma Barlow, singer Thelma Houston and the film *Thelma and Louise*.

Theodora
(alt. Theodosia)

Greek, meaning 'gift of God'. There are dozens of ancient Roman empresses and other figures named Theodora.

Thisbe

Greek, from the mythological heroine of the same name in the ancient Roman poem Metamorphoses by Ovid.

Thomasina
(alt. Thomasin, Thomasine, Thomasyn)

Greek, meaning 'twin'. Singer Tammi Terrell, who was known for her Motown duets with singer Marvin Gaye, was born Thomasina Montgomery.

Thora

Scandinavian, meaning 'Thor's struggle'. Famous Thoras include actresses Thora Hird and Thora Birch and the figure of Thora Bogarhjort of ancient Norse mythology.

Tia
(alt. Tiana)

Spanish, meaning 'aunt'. Famous Tias include actress Tia Mowry and the goddess Tia from Native American Haida tribal mythology.

Tiara

Latin, meaning 'jewelled headband'.

Tien

Vietnamese, meaning 'fairy child'.

Tierney

Irish Gaelic, meaning 'Lord'.

Tierra
(alt. Tiera)

Spanish, meaning 'land'. Used most commonly in the USA.

Tiffany
(alt. Tiffani, Tiffanie)

Greek, meaning 'God's appearance'. Famous Tiffanys include the singer Tiffany, socialite Tiffany Trump and the book/film/song Breakfast at Tiffany's.

Tiggy
(alt. Tigris)

Irish Gaelic, meaning 'tiger'. Tiggy Legge-Bourke (whose birth name is Alexandra) is known for being a royal nanny to Princes William and Harry.

Tilda

Shortened form of Matilda, meaning 'battle-mighty'. Oscar-winning actress Tilda Swinton's full name is Katherine Matilda.

Tilly
(alt. Tillie)

Shortened form of Matilda, meaning 'battle-mighty'. Has seen a rise in popularity in recent years.

Timothea

Greek, meaning 'honouring God'.

Tina
(alt. Teena, Tena)

Shortened form of Christina, meaning 'anointed Christian'. Famous Tinas include singer Tina Turner, comedian Tina Fey and actress Tina Louise.

Tirion

Welsh, meaning 'kind and gentle'.

Tirzah

Hebrew, meaning 'pleasantness'. Found in the Bible.

Titania

Greek, meaning 'giant'. Also queen of the fairies in Shakespeare's play *A Midsummer Night's Dream*.

Toby
(alt. Tobi)

Hebrew, meaning 'God is good'. More commonly used as a boys' name.

Tomoko

Japanese, meaning 'intelligent'.

Toni
(alt. Tony)

Latin, meaning 'invaluable'. Also a shortened form of Antoinette. Famous Tonis include author Toni Morrison, singer Toni Braxton and choreographer Toni Basil.

Tonia
(alt. Tonja, Tonya)

Russian, meaning 'praiseworthy'.

Topaz

Latin, meaning 'golden gemstone'.

Tori
(alt. Tora, Toria)

Shortened form of Victoria, meaning 'victory'. Singer Tori Amos was born Myra Ellen Amos.

Tova
(alt. Tovah, Tove)

Hebrew, meaning 'good'.

Tracy
(alt. Tracey, Tracie)

Greek, meaning 'harvest'. Famous Tracys include singer Tracy Chapman, artist Tracey Emin and actress Tracey Ullman.

Treva

Welsh, meaning 'homestead'.

Trilby

English, meaning 'vocal trills'.

Trina
(alt. Trena)

Greek, meaning 'pure'. Also used as a shortened form of Katrina.

Trinity

Latin, meaning 'triad'. Usually associated with the Christian Holy Trinity. Also the impossibly cool lead female character in *The Matrix*.

Trisha
(alt. Tricia)

Shortened form of Patricia, meaning 'noble'. Trisha Goddard is a TV talk show host.

Trista

Latin, meaning 'sad'. More commonly used in the USA.

Trixie

Shortened form of Beatrix, meaning 'blessed' or 'voyager'. Also a name used frequently in children's television and film, such as the characters of Trixie the Triceratops in *Toy Story 3* and Trixie the Troublemaker in *LazyTown*.

Trudie

(alt. Tru, Truye)

Shortened form of Gertrude, meaning 'strength of a spear'. Famous Trudies include actress Trudie Goodwin and producer and actress Trudie Styler.

Tullia

Latin, meaning 'bound for glory'.

Tunder

Hungarian, meaning 'fairy'.

Twyla

(alt. Twila)

American, meaning 'star'.

Tyler

English, meaning 'tiler'. More commonly used as a boys' name.

Tyra

Scandinavian, meaning 'Thor's struggle'. Supermodel Tyra Banks is known for her extensive modelling career and is presenter of *America's Next Top Model*.

Tzipporah

Hebrew, meaning 'bird'. Used as a spelling alternative to Zipporah.

Flower names

Acacia	Lily
Bluebell	Petunia
Daisy	Poppy
Flora	Primrose
Hyacinth	Rose
Lilac	Snowdrop

Girls' names

Udaya
Indian, meaning 'dawn'.

Ula
(alt. Ulla)
Celtic, meaning 'gem of the sea'. Also the name of a Manchu tribe from China.

Ulrika
(alt. Urica)
German, meaning 'power of the wolf'. Swedish Ulrika Jonsson has made her TV career in Britain.

Uma
Sanskrit, meaning 'flax'. Actress Uma Thurman is known for her roles in *Pulp Fiction*, *Gattaca* and the *Kill Bill* series.

Una
Latin, meaning 'one'. Famous Unas include enduring British actress Una Stubbs and Irish singer Una Healy of The Saturdays.

Undine
Latin, meaning 'little wave'. Also the name of a water element in alchemy.

Unice
Greek, meaning 'victorious'. A spelling alternative to Eunice.

Unique
Latin, meaning 'only one'.

Unity
English, meaning 'oneness'.

Uriela
(alt. Uriella)
Hebrew, meaning 'angel of light'. Found particularly in German-speaking communities.

Urja
(alt. Urjitha)
Indian, meaning 'energy'.

Ursula
Latin, meaning 'little female bear'. A character in Disney's film *The Little Mermaid*.

Uta
German, meaning 'prospers in battle'.

V

Girls' names

Vada
German, meaning 'famous ruler'.

Valdis
(alt. Valdiss, Valdys, Valdyss)
Norse, meaning 'goddess of the dead', based on the mythological goddess of the same name.

Valencia
(alt. Valancy, Valarece; abbrev. Vale)
Latin, meaning 'strong and healthy'. Also one of the largest cities in Spain.

Valentina
(alt. Valentine)
Latin, meaning 'strong and healthy'. Valentina Cortese is an Italian actress. Russian Valentina Tereshkova was the first female astronaut, in 1963.

Valerie
(alt. Valarie, Valery, Valorie, Valeria; abbrev. Valia)
Latin, meaning 'to be healthy and strong'. Also a song, most recently recorded by Mark Ronson and Amy Winehouse. Valia Venitshaya was an actress in the silent film era.

Vandana
Sanskrit, meaning 'worship'. Also the name of a genus of moths.

Vanessa
(alt. Vanesa)
English, from the Gulliver's Travels character of the same name. Famous Vanessas include TV presenter Vanessa Feltz and Vanessa-Mae, the Singapore-born British professional violinist, who represented Thailand in downhill skiing at the 2014 Winter Olympics.

Vanetta
(alt. Vanettah, Vaneta, Vanete, Vanity)
Greek, alternative of Vanessa, meaning 'like a butterfly'.

Vanity
Latin, meaning 'self-obsessed'.

Vashti
Persian, meaning 'beauty'. Also the name of a Persian queen in the Hebrew Bible.

Veda

Sanskrit, meaning 'knowledge and wisdom'. The Vedas are an important set of texts from ancient India.

Vega

Arabic, meaning 'falling vulture'. Also the name of a bright star in the night sky.

Velda

German, meaning 'ruler'. Also the name of a common ancestor named in *The Seven Daughters of Eve*.

Vella

American, meaning 'beautiful'. Also the name of a genus of leafy plants.

Velma

English, meaning 'determined protector'. A character in the *Scooby-Doo* series.

Venice

(alt. Venetia, Venita)

Latin, meaning 'city of canals'. From the city of the same name in Italy.

Venus

Latin, from the ancient Roman goddess of sexuality and fertility, also the name of the planet.

Vera

(alt. Verla, Verlie)

Slavic, meaning 'faith'. Famous Veras include actress Vera Farmiga, singer Vera Lynn and fashion designer Vera Wang.

Verda

(alt. Verdie)

Latin, meaning 'spring-like'.

Verena

Latin, meaning 'true'. St Verena was a third-century Roman saint who healed the sick.

Verity

Latin, meaning 'truth'. Presenter Verity Sharp is a trained musician and presenter of *The Culture Show*.

Verna

(alt. Vernie)

Latin, meaning 'spring green'. Actress Verna Felton was a voice actress for Disney films and productions.

Verona

Latin, shortened form of Veronica. From the city of the same name in Italy.

Veronica

(alt. Verica, Veronique)

Latin, meaning 'true image'. Famous Veronicas include actresses Veronica Lake and Veronica Carlson and the protagonist of the *Veronica Mars* series and film.

Veruca

Latin, meaning 'wart'. Usually associated with the character of Veruca Salt from the children's novel *Charlie and the Chocolate Factory*, by Roald Dahl.

Vesta

Latin, from the ancient Roman goddess of the same name, said to be in charge of the hearth, home and family.

Vevina

Scottish, meaning 'pleasant lady'. More commonly used in the USA.

Vicenta

Latin, meaning 'prevailing'. More commonly used in Italian-speaking communities.

Victoria

(abbrev. Vicky, Vicki, Vickie, Vikki, Vix)

Latin, meaning 'victory'. The name became popular during and after the reign of Queen Victoria in the nineteenth century, and has remained pretty steadfastly popular ever since.

Vida

Spanish, meaning 'life'.

Vidya

Sanskrit, meaning 'knowledge'. Often used in the Hindu faith to refer to learning and knowledge.

Vienna

Latin, from the city of the same name in Austria.

Vigdis

Scandinavian, meaning 'war goddess'. Most commonly used in Icelandic communities.

Vina

(alt. Vena)

Spanish, meaning 'vineyard'.

Viola

Latin, meaning 'violet'. Also a musical instrument like a large violin.

Violet

(alt. Violetta)

Latin, meaning 'purple'. Also a small purple flower of the same name.

Virginia

(alt. Virginie; abbrev. Virgie, Ginny)

Latin, meaning 'maiden'. Famous Virginias include author Virginia Woolf and tennis player Virginia Wade.

Visara

Sanskrit, meaning 'celestial'.

Vita

Latin, meaning 'life'. Often used to refer to the life story of a saint, or their biography.

Vittoria

Variation of Victoria, meaning 'victory'. More commonly used in Italian-speaking communities.

Viva

Latin, meaning 'alive'. Actress Viva was one of Andy Warhol's muses during the 1960s.

Viveca

(alt. Vivica)

Scandinavian, meaning 'war fortress'. Actress Vivica A. Fox is known for her roles in Independence Day, Kill Bill and Soul Food.

Vivian

(alt. Vivien, Vivienne)

Latin, meaning 'lively'. Famous Vivians include actress Vivien Leigh and designer Vivienne Westwood.

Vonda

Czech, meaning 'from the tribe of Vandals'. Singer Vonda Shepard was known for her soft-pop songs and appearances on Ally McBeal.

Girls' names

Waleska

Polish, meaning 'beautiful'. Most commonly used in German-speaking communities.

Wallis

English, meaning 'from Wales'. Famous Wallises include Wallis Simpson, the late Duchess of Windsor, singer Wallis Bird and the clothing retailer Wallis.

Walta

African, meaning 'like a shield'. Also feminine version of Walter.

Wanda

(alt. Waneta, Wanita)

Slavic, meaning 'tribe of the vandals'. Princess Wanda was a queen of Poland in the eighth century, and there are various legends about her.

Waneta

(alt. Wanita)

Variation of Wanda, meaning 'tribe of the vandals'. Also the name of an infamous Yanktonai Dakota Native American tribal chief during the eighteenth and nineteenth centuries.

Wava

English, meaning 'way'. More commonly used in the USA.

Waverly

Old English, meaning 'meadow of aspens'. Can be used as a girls' name or, more commonly, a boys' name.

Wendy

English, meaning 'friend'. Famous Wendys include actresses Wendy Richard and Wendy Hiller and the character of Wendy Darling in *Peter Pan*.

Wharton

English, meaning 'from the river'.

Whisper

English, meaning 'whisper'.

Whitley

Old English, meaning 'white meadow'.

Whitney

Old English, meaning 'white island'. Singer Whitney Houston was a pop sensation of the 1980s and appeared in the film *The Bodyguard* with Kevin Costner.

Wilda

German, meaning 'willow tree'. More commonly used in Polish-speaking communities.

Wilfreda

English, meaning 'to will peace'. Feminine form of Wilfred.

Wilhelmina

Old German, meaning 'strong-willed warrior'. There are dozens of members of the German royal family who have been named Wilhelmina.

Willa

(alt. Willene, Willia)

German, meaning 'helmet'. American Willa Cather was a Pulitzer Prize-winning author.

Willow

English, from the tree of the same name. Several celebrity babies have been named Willow over the last few years, including Willow Smith (Will Smith's daughter) and Willow Hart (Pink's daughter).

Wilma

(alt. Wilmer)

German, meaning 'protection'. A character from the cartoon *The Flintstones*.

Winifred

(abbrev. Winnie)

Old English, meaning 'holy and blessed'. Famous Winifreds include Winifred Atwell, prison breaker Winifred Herbert, author Winifred Mary Letts and South African activist Winnie Madikizela-Mandela.

Winona

(alt. Wynona)

Indian, meaning 'first-born daughter'. Actress Winona Ryder is named after the town where she was born, Winona in Missouri, USA.

Winslow

English, meaning 'friend's hill'.

Winter

English, meaning 'winter'.

Wisteria

English, meaning 'flower'.

Wren

Old English, meaning 'tiny bird'. Often associated with the species of small birds found throughout the world.

Wynda

Scottish, meaning 'of the narrow passage'.

Wynne

(alt. Wynn)

Welsh, meaning 'very blessed'.

Girls' names

Xanadu

A city in Mongolia. Xanadu was the summer capital of Kubla Khan's empire and the inspiration of Samuel Taylor Coleridge's poem *Kubla Khan*. Also a 1980 film starring Olivia Newton-John.

Xanthe

Greek, meaning 'blonde'. Also the name of several characters in ancient Greek mythology.

Xanthippe

Greek, meaning 'nagging'. Also the name of an influential figure in ancient Greek mythology.

Xaverie
(alt. Xaviera)

Spanish, meaning 'the new house'. The female equivalent of Xavier.

Xena
(alt. Xenia)

Greek, meaning 'foreigner'. The popularity of this name rose after the success of *Xena: Warrior Princess*.

Ximena

Spanish, meaning 'to hear'. More commonly used in Mexico.

Xiomara

Spanish, meaning 'battle-ready'.

Xiu

Chinese, meaning 'elegant'.

Xochitl

Nahuatl, meaning 'flower'. Queen Xochitl was a legendary queen of the Toltec culture.

Xoey

Variant of Zoe, meaning 'life'. Often used as a spelling variation for Zoe or Zoey.

Xristina

Variation of Christina, meaning 'follower of Christ'. Usually associated with singer Christina Aguilera, who often spells her name Xristina.

Xylia
(alt. Xylina, Xyloma)

Greek, meaning 'from the woods'.

Y

Girls' names

Yadira

Arabic, meaning 'worthy'. More commonly used in Spanish- and Portuguese-speaking communities.

Yael

Hebrew, meaning 'mountain goat'. Also the name of a character in the Bible.

Yaffa

(alt. Yahaira, Yajaira)

Hebrew, meaning 'lovely'.

Yamilet

Arabic, meaning 'beautiful'. More commonly used in Spanish-speaking communities.

Yana

Hebrew, meaning 'the Lord is gracious'. Also the name of a spiritual practice in Buddhism.

Yanha

Arabic, meaning 'dove-like'.

Yanira

Hawaiian, meaning 'pretty'. Also the name of a character in ancient Greek mythology.

Yareli

Latin, meaning 'golden'. More commonly used in Spanish-speaking communities.

Yaretzi

(alt. Yaritza)

Aztec, meaning 'forever beloved'. More commonly used in the USA.

Yasmin

(alt. Yasmeen, Yasmina)

Persian, meaning 'jasmine flower'. Famous Yasmins include actress Yasmin Paige, model Yasmin le Bon and DJ Yasmin.

Yelena

Greek, meaning 'bright and chosen'. Extremely popular name in Russia and Ukraine.

Yeraldina

Spanish, meaning 'ruled with a spear'.

Yesenia

Arabic, meaning 'flower'. The name was invented in the 1970s for a Spanish-language television production.

Yetta

English, from Henrietta, meaning 'ruler of the house'. Also used in Yiddish-speaking communities.

Yeva

Hebrew variant of Eve, meaning 'life'.

Ylva

Old Norse, meaning 'she wolf'. The name originated in Sweden in the thirteenth century.

Yoki

(alt. Yoko)

Native American, meaning 'rain'. In Japanese the name also means 'happiness' and 'life force'.

Yolanda

(alt. Yolonda)

Spanish, meaning 'violet flower'. There have been several monarchs of Europe known as Yolanda.

Yoselin

English, meaning 'lovely'. Can also be used as a spelling alternative to Jocelyn.

Yoshiko

Japanese, meaning 'good child'. Princess Yoshiko was the Empress of Japan during the eighteenth and nineteenth centuries.

Yovela

Hebrew, meaning 'jubilee'.

Ysabel

English, meaning 'God's promise'. Often used as a spelling alternative to Isabel.

Ysanne

Contraction of Isabel and Anne, meaning 'pledged to God' and 'grace'.

Yuki

Japanese, meaning 'lucky'. Also the name of a popular Japanese singer and songwriter.

Yuliana

Latin, meaning 'youthful'. Often used as a spelling alternative to Giuliana.

Yuridia

Russian, meaning 'farmer'. Singer Yuridia is one of the most popular pop stars in Mexico.

Yusia

Arabic, meaning 'success'.

Yvette

(alt. Yvonne)

French, meaning 'yew'. Famous Yvettes include presenter Yvette Fielding, actress Yvette Nicole Brown and politician Yvette Cooper.

Z Girls' names

Zafira
Arabic, meaning 'successful'.

Zahara
(alt. Zahava, Zahra, Zayah)
Arabic, meaning 'flowering and shining'. The most famous Zahara is the daughter of Angelina Jolie and Brad Pitt.

Zaida
(alt. Zaide)
Arabic, meaning 'prosperous'. Also a familiar term for grandfather in Yiddish.

Zalika
Swahili, meaning 'well born'. More commonly used in Egypt.

Zaltana
Arabic, meaning 'high mountain'.

Zamia
Greek, meaning 'pine cone'. Also the name of a plant.

Zaneta
(alt. Zanceta, Zanetah, Zanett, Zanetta)
Hebrew, meaning 'a gracious present from God'. More commonly used in Polish and Latvian communities.

Zaniyah
Arabic, meaning 'lily'. Most commonly used in the USA, especially over the last five years.

Zara
(alt. Zaria, Zariah, Zora)
Arabic, meaning 'radiance'. Famous Zaras include Queen Elizabeth II's granddaughter Zara Tindall, actress Zara Cully and fashion brand Zara.

Zelda
German, meaning 'dark battle'. Usually associated with the Nintendo video game series Legend of Zelda or American novelist Zelda Fitzgerald.

Zelia
(alt. Zella)
Scandinavian, meaning 'sunshine'.

Zelma
German, meaning 'helmet'. Sometimes used as a spelling alternative to Thelma.

Zemira
(alt. Zemirah)
Hebrew, meaning 'joyous melody'. An opera by Francesco Bianchi.

Zena
(alt. Zenia, Zina)
Greek, meaning 'hospitable'. Usually used as a spelling alternative to Xena.

Zenaida
Greek, meaning 'the life of Zeus'. St Zenaida is recognised as one of the first Christian physicians, during the second century.

Zenobia
Latin, meaning 'the life of Zeus'. Queen Zenobia was the leader of the Palmyrene empire in Syria during the third century.

Zephyr
Greek, meaning 'the west wind'.

Zetta
Latin, meaning 'seven'. In modern maths, zetta means 10^{21} (that's number 1 followed by 21 zeros).

Zia
Arabic, meaning 'light and splendour'. Musician Zia McCabe is known for being a founding member of the band the Dandy Warhols.

Zinaida
Greek, meaning 'belonging to Zeus'. More commonly used in Russian-speaking communities.

Zinnia
Latin, meaning 'flower'. Also the name of a flowering perennial plant.

Zipporah
Hebrew, meaning 'bird'. Zipporah was one of the wives of Moses in the Bible.

Zita
(alt. Ziva)
Spanish, meaning 'little girl'. St Zita is an Italian patron saint of maids and domestic servants.

Zoë
(alt. Zoe, Zoi, Zoie, Zoey, Zoeya, Zoila)
Greek, meaning 'life'. Famous Zoes include TV and radio presenter Zoë Ball and actresses including Zoë Wanamaker, Zoe Saldana and Zooey Deschanel.

Zoraida
Spanish, meaning 'captivating woman'.

Zorina
Slavic, meaning 'golden'.

Zosia
(alt. Zosima)
Greek, meaning 'wisdom'. Actress Zosia Mamet is known for her roles in Mad Men, Parenthood and Girls.

Zoya
Greek, meaning 'life'. Zoya Kosmodemyanskaya is one of the former Soviet Union's most revered heroines, after fighting for the Russian rebellion during World War II.

Zula
African, meaning 'brilliant'.

Zuleika
Arabic, meaning 'fair and intelligent'. Also the name of Potiphar's wife in the Bible.

Zulma
Arabic, meaning 'peace'.

Zuzana
Hebrew, meaning 'lily'. More commonly used in the Czech and Slovak republics.

Zuzu
Czech, meaning 'flower'. The nickname for one of George Bailey's children in the film It's A Wonderful Life.

Names with positive meanings

Allegra – cheerful

Augusta – magnificent

Felicia – lucky

Hilary – cheerful

Lucy – light

Phoebe – radiant

Thalia – flourishing

Yoko – positive